2004
AMERICAN GUIDE
TO U.S. COINS

Charles F. French

EDITED BY Scott Mitchell

A FIRESIDE BOOK
Published by Simon & Schuster
NEW YORK   LONDON   TORONTO   SYDNEY   SINGAPORE

13743448

FIRESIDE
Rockefeller Center
1230 Avenue of the Americas
New York, NY 10020

For information regarding special discounts for bulk purchases,
please contact Simon & Schuster Special Sales at
1-800-456-6798 or business@simonandschuster.com

Manufactured in the United States of America

10   9   8   7   6   5   4   3   2   1

ISBN 0-7432-1500-1

Photos courtesy of Stack's Rare Coins.
Photos of the new State Quarters and the Sacagawea Golden Dollar courtesy of the United States Mint.

Contents

Part Three: Coin Values

Introduction
A BRIEF HISTORY OF AMERICAN NUMISMATICS

The discovery in 1843 of the celebrated 1804 silver dollar is one of the earliest indications we have of interest in American numismatics. While there is a great deal of discussion regarding this coin's origin, it is generally agreed that the earliest were struck with the revision of mint operations during the 1830s. From 1858 on, the United States Mint struck proofs for collectors and, although not many of these were issued, this shows that there was numismatic interest at that time.

The middle of the nineteenth century saw great interest in revising our coinages. It was the policy of the mint to strike "trial" or experimental coins. Such unusual denominations as two-cent, three-cent, and twenty-cent pieces appeared, none of which met with much popularity in circulation. They therefore were ultimately discontinued. Trial pieces became very popular with collectors in the 1860s and 1870s, and it is possible that a good many of these were struck purely for the delight of the collector. Usually only a dozen or so patterns (coins struck from designs that were being considered for general circulation) were needed, but quantities of up to five hundred of some were struck.

The latter part of the nineteenth century saw the start of the American Numismatic Association and the publishing of America's first monthly magazine devoted exclusively to numismatics. Students of numismatics pursued their field ardently, and as a result many valuable books were published toward the end of the century. The majority of these books were about cents and half cents; other topics included Colonial coins, half dimes, quarters, halves, and dollars. The continuing popularity of large cents explains why there were so many publications about these interesting coins.

The following authors were pioneers in their subjects and paved the way for the many publications that have since appeared: Ebenezer Gilbert, Ed Frossard, Sylvester Crosby, W. W. Hays, Thomas Elder, F. W. Doughty, George H. Clapp, H. R. Newcomb, H. P. Newlin, D. W. Valentine, A. W. Browning, J. W. Haseltine, M. L. Beistle, Dr. M. W. Dickeson,

Dr. Edward Maris, Philip Nelson, Sydney P. Noe, Carl Wurzbach, and Miller-Ryder. (For further information on these early reference works, please refer to Part Four at the end of this book.)

There is no accurate record of the number of collectors in those days, but I would estimate that they must have numbered between three and five hundred. There were no "coin boards" or plastic holders. Collectors had to improvise. The wealthier had wooden cabinets built, fitted with velvet-lined trays; others lined cigar boxes with velvet and placed their coins in these. Collectors spent a great deal of time going over coin collections, pointing out prized pieces to friends. Trading and exchanging coins with fellow numismatists became the thing to do.

Probably the first coin holders to become popular were the small, round cardboard "pill" boxes manufactured by T. James Clarke of Jamestown, New York. These boxes were just the right size for holding large cents. Collectors would put cotton in the bottom of the box, place the coin in it, and write its description on the cover.

At the beginning of the twentieth century, coin collecting was a hobby only for those who were serious students of the subject. There were perhaps several thousand collectors at this time. They formed a national "clique" deeply interested in coin research and finding new rarities and varieties. Many of these collectors had discovered the hobby as a direct result of the issue of several million Columbian half dollars during the World's Fair in Chicago in 1892. This was the first coin struck in America commemorating an event and offered for sale to all. It opened the eyes of the public to the possibilities of coin collecting and showed how it could be both an interesting and profitable hobby. The success of this first commemorative encouraged the issue of many more from 1915 on. While these commemoratives helped keep the hobby active, they did not, however, materially increase the number of collectors.

In the middle of the 1920s, the largest coin dealer was B. Max Mehl, who used radio and national newspaper advertising to foster the sale of his new and excellent coin book, the *Star Rare Coin Encyclopedia*. This book gave collectors buying prices for all United States coins and also included many articles on coins from all parts of the world. The book was a truly educational volume. It cost him thousands of dollars to advertise, but since he sold hundreds of thousands of books at a dollar each, we suspect he didn't lose any money. Mehl's coin book helped give the public a new awareness of numismatics, an awareness that was tremendously far-reaching. Even today we occasionally hear his great slogan: "I'll give fifty dollars for a 1913 Liberty Head nickel." In fact, it was B. Max Mehl who made the 1913 Liberty Head nickel such a popular and desirable coin.

During the Depression years of 1929–33, coin values gradually increased, as did the number of new coin collectors. I would estimate that in 1930 there were probably ten thousand coin collectors in the United States—many of them hard-pressed for money due to the Depression. During those years, collectors' coins could be purchased very reasonably. With the return of prosperity, a new stimulus came to numismatics. The many new issues of commemorative coins in 1935 and 1936 encouraged coin speculation on a large scale for the first time. Easy profits brought the speculator into the field. Commemorative prices skyrocketed, and the value of all United States coins rose substantially. Not surprisingly, when commemoratives crashed in 1937–38, many of these "fast-buck boys" lost interest in the hobby.

The first auction sales took place very early in the nineteenth century. There were only one or two well-known coin auctioneers at that time. Toward the latter part of the 1930s, many new auctioneers went into the business. I still have a letter from a well-known dealer and auctioneer, Thomas Elder, bemoaning the fact that with all the auctions being conducted and coins being offered, prices would surely crash and coins would become worthless. If only he had lived to see how greatly the hobby has grown! Of all the American auction firms that have their roots in the 1930s, only Stack's of New York has maintained its preeminence and survived to this day, having celebrated its sixty-fifth anniversary as an auctioneer in October 2000.

In the beginning of the 1940s, many coin collectors were confident of the future of numismatics. They reasoned that if the number of collectors continued to increase and there were no more coins to be had, then prices would surely rise. They began accumulating uncirculated rolls of current coins against future demands. These investors would secure the rolls at their banks, or order them from dealers who specialized in this kind of business. Uncirculated rolls were viewed as excellent investments. At worst, the coins could be deposited in their bank at face value. Those who held these rolls long enough made small fortunes.

During the Depression, the Whitman Publishing Company released an attractive, reasonably priced series of coin boards designed to encourage new collectors. They showed novices what and how to collect (mostly from their pocket change), and were offered throughout the United States in many kinds of stores. These coin boards helped to increase the number of coin collectors and, though Whitman has since been acquired by St. Martin's Press, they are still a major factor in encouraging newcomers to the hobby.

Numismatics experienced another revival in 1936, when the United States Mint in Philadelphia resumed the manufacture of proof sets. Not many proofs were sold from 1936 through 1942 and none were made during the war and postwar years of 1943–49. The number of proof sets coined from 1950 onward clearly indicates their increasing popularity. When one considers that there were 51,386 sets coined in 1950 and that the U.S. Mint today routinely produces approximately two million sets each year, it is quite apparent that the hobby has expanded exponentially.

Probably one of the greatest boons to numismatics over the past several decades has been the introduction of coin newspapers, magazines, and newsletters—published weekly, biweekly, and monthly. Thousands upon thousands of coin collectors, dealers, and even people who are only slightly interested in coins subscribe to these publications. (Please consult Part Four of this book for the reference section where there is a listing of current publications.)

Years ago, coin clubs began springing up throughout our country. Today there are very few cities that do not have their own clubs. Usually once a month, they meet to conduct their business meetings, discuss numismatics, and perhaps hold a small auction among the members. Occasionally a club may sponsor a coin show, where collectors and dealers can buy and sell and exhibit material. These clubs are always interested in gaining new members. More recently, the Internet has become a hugely popular meeting place for coin collectors, whether they are discussing coins or conducting transactions. As a result, nearly every major dealer has established a website, wherein the dealer can further promote business and provide numismatic information to collectors.

The large number of collectors and clubs has encouraged the development of regional associations—you will find that these associations exist all over the country. Joined by clubs and collectors in their regional territory, these associations hold one or two conventions every year. Many have auction sales at their conventions, as well as a bourse where dealers from all over the United States congregate to offer their coins for sale. Collectors are encouraged to display their collections and win prizes for their efforts on a competitive basis. (Please refer to Part Four for a listing of the major national and regional coin clubs and associations.)

Numismatics has become a very well-organized and firmly entrenched hobby and discipline throughout the country. Since its start in 1891, the American Numismatic Association has greatly expanded its membership and influence. Based in Colorado Springs, the ANA holds an annual national convention, sponsored by a different city every August. There is also the American Numismatic Society in New York City, which maintains an outstanding museum of rare coins and devotes much of its efforts to research. The ANS has a remarkable library and issues many new publications for collectors and dealers.

PART ONE

The Evolution of United States Coinage

1
EARLY AMERICAN COINS

Were we to transport ourselves back three and a half centuries to the early days of Colonial America, we would find that industry was very small and that business, for the most part, was conducted by barter and trade. While there was a need for coins, the shortage was not as problematic as it proved to be later, when Colonial America became more industrialized and began acquiring wealth. Even so, attempts to issue coins were made.

The first New England coins—crude silver pieces with a simple "NE" design on the obverse, and the denomination indicated as "XII," "VI," or "III" on the reverse—were the first coins struck in the Colonies. Shortage of change and the inability to get relief from England prompted the Massachusetts Colony to embark upon this coining venture.

Following quickly came the Willow, Oak, and Pine Tree series. Some found use in circulation, for in those days a coin was a coin regardless of who issued it, and the amount of metal it contained determined its value. The famous Pine Tree coinage, a shilling of which is depicted on page 85, was the last type in this four design series struck by coiner John Hull.

After several years, when the coining operations were brought to the attention of King Charles II of England, action was taken to prohibit any further issues. While the majority were dated 1652, it is generally acknowledged that the production of the four design types collectively spanned thirty years, despite the King's disapproval. These crude and early pieces are actively sought by collectors and bring good prices today. They were coined in shillings, sixpence, threepence, and twopence pieces.

There were other very early experiments in coinage in other Colonies. The Mark Newby farthing and halfpenny, struck in Dublin in the 1670s, were originally coined for Ireland but found their way to New Jersey. There were also the Lord Baltimore pieces for Maryland, which were coined in England and brought over for circulation here. Other seventeenth-century coins which circulated in the Colonies include the American Plantations token and the Elephant tokens.

After these early attempts, we find little coining activity until the first part of the eighteenth century, when a small flurry again occurred. The Gloucester tokens of 1714, the Woods Hibernia series and Rosa Americana coins of 1722 through 1724 are among the issues of this period. There were also the early French Colony copper and billon coinages. With the exception of the Gloucester tokens, of which little is known, the rest were struck in foreign lands and shipped here for use, due to the dire need. The Higley, or Granby, coppers of 1737–39 saw considerable circulation, even though they were unauthorized and coined on this continent.

A gap of just over twenty years without any significant additional colonial coinage production ended in 1760 with the Voce Populi coinage. The 1766 Pitt tokens and 1767 French Colony pieces followed shortly thereafter.

The next and most important era commenced around the time of the beginning of the American Revolution. From this time until the opening of the first United States Mint, in 1792–93, we find innumerable varieties and experiments—in fact, all types of coins. Some received recognition and actually circulated. Others should be classified as pattern or experimental pieces.

State Coinage

As early as 1776, New Hampshire struck coppers. The paltry number of survivors from this issue are all very well worn and, therefore, these pieces must have seen considerable circulation. Vermont issued many varieties of coppers from 1785 through 1788, and they were actively used in circulation. Although New York apparently did not officially authorize the production of coinage, a number of copper coins are attributed to this colony. Some of these coins could be considered experimental pieces while others actually circulated. The state of Connecticut probably had the most active coinage system from 1785 through 1788. Massachusetts went into regular coinage production during 1787 and 1788. New Jersey issued a wide variety of coppers from 1786 through 1788. An issue of copper halfpennies was authorized for Virginia in 1773 while still an English colony.

EXPERIMENTAL PIECES AND TOKENS

During the time of the American Revolution, a wide variety of experimental coins or tokens appeared. In this group, we find the so-called Continental dollars of 1776 struck in pewter, brass, and silver. The Immune Columbia pieces, the Confederatio coppers, and Brasher's experimental pieces are also among such issues. Belonging here, too, are the U.S.A. Bar cents, Mott tokens, Talbot, Allum, and Lee tokens, Auctori Plebis tokens, Kentucky tokens, Myddleton tokens, North American tokens, Pitt tokens, Rhode Island Ship tokens, and Franklin Press tokens.

WASHINGTON PIECES

Now we come to what may be the forerunners of our first regular coinage, the Washington pieces. George Washington's great popularity at the end of the American Revolution made it natural to want to copy the practice of foreign nations and place the head of the ruler on the obverse of the coin. Since there was no "ruler" of the United States, the president was the logical equivalent. If this practice had been accepted and carried out to the present day, we would have had a change in coin design with each president. The bust or head of each president would have appeared on our coins while he was in office. This would have been an interesting series for coin collectors, but the many changes might very possibly have confused our coinage. (This frequent changing of coin designs did not occur in kingdoms, for the rulers generally reigned for life.)

Therefore, the practice of using Washington's head was discarded and the Liberty Head designs were adopted. Many of the designs from the Washington pieces, however, were later utilized at least in part. The reverse of the Unity cents coinage of 1783 is almost identical to the reverse design that appears on the wreath-type cents of 1793 and the following years. The eagle on the reverse of the various Washington cents and half dollars is very similar to the eagle adopted for the reverse of our silver coins. Similarly, the designs of the half disme, disme, Birch cent, and silver-center cents are almost identical to the designs adopted on our coins of 1793.

You will notice that all of the above were coinages designed to fill the need for minor coins as these were the sizes that were needed most. Business requirements in larger transactions were carried on in gold Spanish-American doubloons and their fractions, English guineas, and even French louis d'or. Silver requirements were largely met by the masses of one-, two-, four-, and eight-real coins of Spanish America.

2
PIRATE AND REVOLUTIONARY MONEY

Our coasts were infested with pirates and privateers during the early days of our colonial history. British, French, and particularly Spanish ships were liable to be boarded, stripped of their cargo, and then sunk. With the exception of the Spaniards shipping gold and silver treasure back to Spain (usually in bullion form, as it was easier to handle than coins), other cargoes usually consisted of articles needed by settlers in the New World: guns, ammunitions, and luxuries desired by the rich. The Spaniards lost many treasure ships at this time, either through pirate raids or to devastating hurricanes.

During the American Revolution, the need for hard money was so great in the United States that it encouraged private ship owners to turn "pirate." Known as privateers, these sleek, fast ships roved our coast and captured any ship they could as a prize of war, placing their American crews on them and sending them to the colonies. For the ship captains and owners, this was a very lucrative business and many of the wealthy clipper ship owners of the next fifty years started out in this manner. The wealth of unobtainable material these privateers brought to the revolting Colonies was of terrific aid to the American war effort. Not only were goods brought to our shores, but also a sorely needed quantity of hard money. Many English gold guineas were confiscated as they were being shipped over to the continent to pay English armies.

We must try to visualize the situation of that day in order to realize the need for this money. The early Americans had always considered hard coins the only money of real value; gold coins were used for business transactions of merit. It made no difference from what country the coins came as long as they were coins; this also applied to silver and copper. The dire needs of the war caused the individual colonies to issue paper currency, which was not looked upon with much favor. When the Continental Congress began issuing paper currency to pay bills, their money was looked down upon and inflation swept the country to a degree that almost wrecked the war efforts. The expression "not worth a Continental" comes to us from those days when everyone shied away from these bills. They never were redeemed and finally became of no value. For the most part, however, the earlier notes issued by the individual colonies were redeemed, but in varying percentages of their face value. To aggravate the situation further, the British resorted to counterfeiting our paper money and attempting to circulate it.

3
HISTORY OF THE DOLLAR

From the time of the Roman Empire and through the Dark Ages, the predominant size of silver coins was copied after the Ancient Roman Denarius, about the size of our present-day dime. Much later, in the year 1516, a rich silver mine was discovered in Joachim's Dale, a mining district in Bohemia. The Count of Schlitz, who appropriated the mine, struck a great number of large silver coins. The first had the date 1518 and the effigy of St. Joachim upon it. These were to be of the same value in silver as the many gold gulden then used in trade. This Joachimsthaler has the distinction of being known as the first "thaler" or silver coin, of approximately one ounce in weight and around the size of our silver dollars.

From that time on, the thaler became one of the most popular coins in Europe. Most countries and German states issued hundreds of varieties of these. The French issued coins of similar size called "ecus," the English their "crowns," the Spanish their "pieces of 8" (eight-reales).

The name of such coins in other countries were changed to "daler," "dalar," "daalder," or "tallero."

In the Western Hemisphere the Spanish "pieces of 8" circulated widely during colonial days. The British kept as much English specie as possible from the American colonies, creating serious shortages here. They also prohibited the minting of coins. It is therefore not surprising the Spanish "pieces of 8" became the principal medium to circulate and soon became known as the "Spanish milled dollar." It is said that the dollar George Washington threw across the Rapahannock River was one of these and indeed it must have been, for our country did not coin any silver dollars until 1794.

People sometimes wonder why we did not adopt the English denominations when we first started coining. Pounds, shillings, and pence were used in all transactions with England, the parent country, during the colonial days. We find that early colonial paper money was issued in English denominations. During and after the Revolution one finds the gradual change to dollars and cents, some of the earlier notes even being redeemable in "Spanish milled dollars." No doubt antagonism over the war with England and the use of the Spanish coins influenced our country to adopt the dollar and cents denominations.

Our silver dollar has had a stormy path. From 1794 through 1803 they were coined in varying quantities. From 1804 through 1840 we have a gap of thirty-six years during which there are no silver dollars of these dates coined for circulation. Those dollars struck in 1804 were actually dated 1803. It seems the amount of silver contained in the early dollars was too great. In 1837 Congress passed a law providing that 3½ grains of the alloy be extracted from the authorized weight of the dollar, which at that time weighed 416 grains. This made the new dollar weight 412½ grains. The only dollars struck from 1805 through 1839 were those dated 1804, and the rare Gobrecht pattern or experimental pieces of 1836, 1838, and 1839, forerunners of the regular issued Liberty Seated dollars of 1840. The excessively rare 1804 dollars, considered by many to be the "king" of American coins, were actually struck in the 1830s.

Standard silver dollars were again suspended with the issue of Trade dollars in 1873, designed to capture trade in the Orient. As these were not successful, their coining for circulation was terminated in 1878 and standard silver dollars were again coined from then on until 1904. The few Trade dollars that were issued between 1879 and 1885 were struck for collectors only. In 1904, all dollars were discontinued due to a lack of silver bullion.

The Peace dollar first made its appearance in 1921, seventeen years later, and was coined continuously from then until 1935, the last year that silver dollars were struck for circulation.

In 1971, the Eisenhower dollar appeared. It had a seven-year run and was then supplanted by the Susan B. Anthony dollar, which was wildly unpopular. Susan B. Anthony dollars were struck for general circulation in 1979 and 1980. The coins of this type dated 1981 were struck for inclusion in proof and mint sets only. When stockpiles of the Anthony dollar were depleted, the design had a brief respite in 1999 before finally being replaced by the golden Sacagawea dollar.

4

GOLD COINS

In 1787, the year before Washington was elected to the presidency, a jeweler named Ephraim Brasher, whose place of business was on Queens Street in New York City, appealed to the state legislature for permission to strike copper coins to circulate in that state. Permission was refused, but that did not stop Brasher from using the dies he had made. He struck his coins in gold, his "doubloon" having an intrinsic value of approximately $16, similar to that of the current Spanish doubloons. The unique specimen, with "EB" on the breast of the eagle, is one of the highest-priced coins in the world. Additionally, a unique half doubloon is in the collection of the Smithsonian Institution. As history has it, these coins proved to be the predecessors of the private gold coins struck during the mid-1800s.

By 1830, there were laws that forbade the individual states from striking gold coins. There were none, however, forbidding private persons or private companies from doing so. A treaty with Great Britain opened the ports of the West Indies and South America to American commerce. Likewise, a treaty with Turkey opened the Black Sea. Around the same time, Templeton Reid, an assayer, jeweler, and gunsmith (just to name a few of his many trades), moved his Milledgeville office to Gainesville. This placed him in the center of the gold-mining district in Lumpkin County, Georgia. It is here where Reid issued the first of his private gold coins. It is not definitely known how long his business existed or when it started, but the first coins to bear his stamp were dated 1830. The coins issued from his Georgia establishment contained gold of a higher standard and fineness than any other ever issued by either private persons or the government. It is likely that many of his coins were melted, which is why they are so scarce today.

Christopher Bechtler's mint was located in Rutherford County, North Carolina. The first of his gold coins, although undated, are attributed to either 1830 or the early part of 1831. About 1842, he passed his business on to his son August, who continued until about 1852. The gold for these pieces came from North Carolina and Georgia.

Civilization had already pushed its way westward when the cry of "gold" came from California and resounded from coast to coast. There was a great exodus from the East; people poured into the West in droves. The discovery of gold in California was a boon to a world suffering from a gold shortage. It changed the whole outlook of industry and commerce. Prices skyrocketed to unbelievable heights. For a while gold dust was used as a medium of exchange, but this was soon found to be cumbersome and impractical. The demand for gold coins was great but there were no mints in the West. To ship gold dust to the East to be minted into coins was out of the question. An attempt was made by the provincial government in the Oregon Territory to establish a mint, but this failed. A private organization, the Oregon Exchange Company, started operations in Oregon City in 1849. They employed a blacksmith to make the apparatus and an engraver, who happened to be one of the company's members, to make the dies.

The Mormons, who for years had been migrating westward, having been expelled from New York, Illinois, and Nebraska, finally settled on the shores of the Great Salt Lake in Utah, while it was still Mexican territory. They started their mint in 1849, striking coins from the gold dust received from California. Their twenty-dollar gold piece was the first to be struck in this country, but the intrinsic value was found to be only between $16 and $18.

There were about fifteen private mints operating in California between 1849 and 1855, striking millions of dollars' worth of gold coins. Norris, Gregg & Norris coined the first, a five-dollar coin of 1849; Moffat & Company struck the first ten-dollar coin; Baldwin & Company, the first twenty; Moffat & Company, the first fifty. The fifty-dollar coin was octagonal, bearing the stamp of the United States Assayer Augustus Humbert. F. D. Kohler & Company and Moffat & Company, among others, issued ingots stamped from gold bars. The last private-issue coins from California came from the mints of Wass, Molitor & Company and Kellogg & Company, dated 1855, just one year after the San Francisco Mint was opened.

In 1857, a panic overtook the country due to overcapitalization, overbuilding of railroads, rise of prices, speculation, bad crops, bad state banking, and diminishing gold output. While there was agitation between the states over the question of states' rights and the Dred Scott decision, the first Atlantic cable was being laid. Silver was discovered in Nevada and a new gold district was discovered in the West. The forty-niner rush was repeated but not in the same proportions as the rush a decade before.

There were three private minting firms in Colorado at this time. The first coins to be produced were struck by Clark, Gruber & Company in 1860. Coins of all United States gold denominations, with the exception of ones and threes, were issued. In 1862, the government purchased the Clark, Gruber establishment, which was thereafter conducted as a United States Assay Office. The original bill called for a government mint at Denver, but this did not materialize until 1906.

John Parsons & Company, located at Tarryall Mines, and J. J. Conway & Company in Georgia Gulch, operated their private mints during this time for a limited period. Parsons issued quarter eagles ($2.50) and half eagles ($5.00); Conway, quarter eagles, half eagles, and eagles ($10.00).

None of the coins bear dates, but they were most likely struck in 1861. All are quite rare, Conway's exceedingly so.

The designs on these privately issued gold coins are varied. Some are very plain with only the name of the mint or minter, date, and denomination or weight. Others have very attractive original designs, and still others are so very much like the regular government coinage that to the ordinary layman they are easily mistaken.

5
GOLD DOLLARS AND GOLDEN EAGLES

Prior to the establishment of our United States Mint, a proposal was made in 1785 to coin five-dollar pieces. However, the actual approval of our first gold pieces did not come until Congress passed the Coining Act of April 1792, authorizing the coinage of eagles ($10.00), half eagles ($5.00), and quarter eagles ($2.50). The half eagle, or five-dollar gold piece, was the first gold coin struck by our mint in accordance with this act. Dated 1795, it had Liberty's head facing right with a turbanlike headdress. The reverse shows an eagle with spread wings, holding a wreath of laurel in its beak and standing on a palm branch. This design was thought to have been copied from a Roman first century B.C. onyx cameo. In addition to half eagles, limited quantities of quarter eagles and eagles were coined, but only on demand. Half eagles were our mint's major output. Even so, these were issued in very limited quantities. The eagles were to be 247½ grains pure, 270 grains standard. Half eagles were to be 123½ pure, 135 grains standard; quarter eagles were to be 61⅞ pure and 67½ grains standard. The standard weight included an alloy to make the coins wear better.

These gold coins were pegged to silver on a 15 to 1 ratio, namely fifteen ounces of silver to one ounce of gold, and while this ratio was adequate at the time the bill was passed, by 1799 the ratio in Europe had reached 15¾ to 1. The overvalued gold coins began to flow out of the country or were melted down to get the extra value they contained. For each one hundred dollars' worth of old-type coins, one could get at least $106. Gold therefore disappeared from circulation, as did silver dollars.

It wasn't until June 28, 1834, that a new law reduced the weight of gold coins. From that time on, our gold pieces appeared in the new smaller size, returned to circulation, and created a new interest in and demand for gold. Gold mines profitably increased their production. Our mint first struck twenty-dollar double eagles in 1849. We also find our first gold dollars appearing, closely followed by three-dollar gold pieces. The three-dollar gold piece, first coined in 1854, was never a popular coin and was frequently linked with bad luck by the superstitious.

The quantities of gold and shortages of gold coins in the West prompted the coinage of pioneer pieces in many denominations. Privately issued and not under rigid regulations, many of these were not up to standard fineness; as late as the latter part of the 1920s, these pioneer pieces were looked down upon as low-grade, undervalued coins and were redeemed by financial institutions at less than face value. Today, these low-grade coins are rare and worth high premiums, not for their gold value but for their numismatic value.

From the time shortly after the Civil War until the banking holiday in 1933, numismatic interest in collecting gold coins was not high, perhaps because of the coins' face value. Anyone who wanted to collect them could easily have secured the majority of all denominations for very little over face value, even back to 1834, when the new smaller size was adopted. A great many of the first gold pieces prior to 1808 could have been purchased for much less than their rarity should have dictated.

Proof gold coins were not popular with collectors. With the exception of the last nine years of the denomination, no more than fifty gold proof dollars had been struck of most dates minted in that series. There simply were not enough collectors to warrant higher mintages at that point. Similar small quantities were coined in proofs for quarter eagles, threes, half eagles, eagles, and double eagles. The largest quantity of gold proof dollars of any year was struck in 1889, and this only amounted to 1,779 pieces. The majority of proofs struck in all denominations per year usually ran on the order of twenty to forty specimens. Over ten times that amount or more were struck for coins in silver and copper. It is no wonder that perfect gold pieces bring very high prices today.

Due to the Depression of 1929–33 and the uncertainty of the country's financial position, hoarding of gold coins by individuals became so common that it seriously endangered our financial structure. This was one of the major reasons that the government ordered the recovery of gold coins. The purpose of this order was to end hoarding and stimulate economic activity. The first announcement of the government order was widely publicized and stressed the penalties for failure to comply, which at the time were drastic and included stiff jail sentences. The order accomplished what it intended and millions of dollars in gold coin were deposited in banks and Federal Reserves.

Because of the hysteria of the time, many very rare gold coins were forever lost to collectors. The government, however, was not interested in the coins themselves, but only in hoards. Within a few weeks, the original order exempting gold coins in quantities of a hundred dollars was amended to exempt gold coins that were considered rare and held in coin collections. Over a period of years, subsequent amendments gradually continued to ease the stringency of the original order. At first, limits were lifted with the exception of two-and-one-half-dollar pieces. Restrictions on the two-and-one-half-dollar pieces limited ownership to not more than two of any date or mint mark. This restriction was lifted next and the offense was changed from a criminal to a civil one with a fine.

Since the Hoarding Act of 1933, interest in gold coin collecting has been growing by leaps and bounds. As soon as the government discontinued making gold coins, collectors began taking great interest in them.

There are no restrictions regarding the export or import, purchase, sale, or collecting of gold coins of any date officially released by the U.S. Mint for circulation or for collectors in the United States.

6
CHRISTIAN GOBRECHT'S FLYING EAGLE DOLLAR

In the year 1836, interest was revived in the coining of silver dollars, as none had been coined since 1804—in fact, silver dollars struck in 1804 were actually dated 1803. With the proposed passage of a law reducing their weight, permission was granted to resume minting this denomination.

Famed engraver Christian Gobrecht executed the dies for these beautiful coins. The Philadelphia artist Thomas Scully submitted the Liberty Seated design, and the Flying Eagle on the reverse was designed by Titian Peale, son of the painter Charles Willson Peale. In 1836, 1838, and 1839 limited quantities of these dollars were struck with minor varieties on a more or less experimental basis. All are rare, some extremely so. Additionally, some proof restrikes are known, generally believed to have been struck between 1858 and 1860.

It was not until 1840 that the silver dollar regained prominence among coins issued for circulation. Robert Ball Hughes, an Anglo-American sculptor, was the designer of this newly issued coin. He closely copied the Liberty Seated design of the Gobrecht dollar on the obverse, but changed the Flying Eagle to a standing position on the reverse. This famous Liberty Seated design was used on silver dollars through 1873 and on other smaller denomination silver coins as late as 1891.

7
THE COINS OF THE MORMONS

"During the year 1846, the beginning of the great exodus from Nauvoo, Illinois, to Salt Lake Valley, Utah, there appeared a strange little brass token that has created and attracted the attention of church members and collectors from all over the country" (*Numismatist,* July 1911, p. 241). The date and the emblem—the beehive, meaning "Let everyone do his duty," and clasped hands, signifying friendship—indicate that the coin is associated with Brigham Young and the Mormons. However, some believe that it is in no way connected with the Mormons, because the emblem of the beehive was conceived after their arrival in the valley. We do not know whether this token was used as an exchange medium or as a commemorative issue, nor do we know what its value was. Its size was about that of a dime.

When the Mormons went west, they took very little money with them. Droughts, insects, and other adverse conditions drained what money they had. Hard work ultimately conquered all their handicaps and eventually Indians were no longer a threat. Trade and barter were their mediums of exchange. In 1847, a Mormon battalion from the Mexican War brought home a certain amount of money, which began to circulate. It is recorded that Captain James Brown left the valley in 1847 to collect his men's back pay, returning with $5,000 in Spanish gold doubloons valued at $16 each. Many other instances of small quantities of coin coming into the hands of the Mormons are on record, but the discovery of gold in the ground was the start of a desire to issue coins.

A very interesting and integral character in Mormon history was Thomas Rhoads, more commonly referred to as Father Rhoads. Rhoads and his family left Missouri in the spring of 1846 for Sutter's Fort on the Sacramento River. When gold was discovered in the channel of the mill race at Sutter's Sawmill, Rhoads and his sons joined the other adventurers in their quest for gold, which later proved very rewarding. After accumulating a small fortune, Rhoads and his family left California for the Great Salt Lake in the latter part of 1848. News of the Rhoads fortune leaked out and while they were making their way through the California mountains, they were attacked by bandits. Had it not been for the intervention of some passing travelers, the ambush might have been successful. With the help of the travelers, the Rhoads family was able to repel the attack.

According to Colonel Lock, Father Rhoads brought with him several sacks of gold, among which there was a sixty-pound sack. This sack was the largest amount that had been brought into the valley. Father Rhoads turned all the gold over to Brigham Young, who in return had a home built for Rhoads and allowed him to withdraw from the tithing office all the food supplies that he deemed necessary. Rhoads also received a herd of cattle in consideration for the gold dust.

William T. Fullett, a battalion member, was credited with having made the first deposit of gold dust in the valley on December 10, 1848. He deposited fourteen and one-half ounces of gold dust, which was then worth $232, equal to $16 per ounce. Within four months, close to $8,000 in dust and a little coin was deposited in the "bank." Since the city was fairly well supplied with gold dust, the council unanimously agreed that it was time to convert the dust into coins. In order to accomplish this, President Young solicited the aid of John Kay and John Taylor in planning the first mint ever to be established in the Great Salt Lake Valley.

John Kay, skilled in pattern making, and John Taylor were persuaded to work on suitable designs for the coins. After some time and difficulty, the preparations were finally completed and Kay began to melt the gold and roll it into sheets. A punching press was then used in punching out the gold planchets, while a coining press stamped the designs on the planchets.

Kay turned out ten-dollar pieces that were paid out at a premium of fifty cents on the piece. Whether the coins were at a premium because of the novelty value or because of them being overweight is not known. Twenty of them were charged out to Brigham Young and five to John Kay. A week later, twenty-one pieces were coined and charged out at par to Brigham Young. No more were coined until September 1849, because the crucibles were broken in the preliminary runs and melting could not be continued until others were obtained.

Since the coining could not be continued, the punching press was dismantled and shipped by ox team to Parowan, where it could be put to use while the crucibles were being made. During the short time the press was in Parowan, it was used for cutting nails. The sheet iron was cut into strips and then headed in a vise. In October 1848, the press was returned to the valley where it was used in connection with the coinage of the 1849–50 gold coins and later, the 1860 gold coins.

Finally, Kay completed his work on preparing the new crucibles, and at last the mint was ready for operation. In order to test the crucibles,

Kay struck a few pattern pieces bearing a design on only one side. This time the crucibles did not break. Apparently the workers were satisfied with the results, because the mint went into full production and remained so for the rest of the year.

It is generally believed that during the early coinage, no effort was made to assay or refine the gold since there was no one connected with the mint capable of determining such standards. This fact has been substantiated by Captain H. Stansbury in his report on his exploration and survey of the Great Salt Lake. The coinage was done in good faith, however, because of the then-prevailing theory of "relative fineness"; in other words, the Mormons based the worth of all gold upon the purity of California gold. Little did they realize that the coins minted from native gold were very low in assay due to the fineness of the gold, although it was full weight. According to Colonel Lock, the 1849 five-dollar gold piece was actually worth $4.51. This mistake was later brought to light but not before losses had been sustained by many who had purchased gold on the relative-fineness theory. Given the limited facilities, the designs on the pieces were not too elaborate, but original and praiseworthy nonetheless. On the obverse of the gold coins minted in Salt Lake City, there are clasped hands in the center with the date 1849 below. The legend reads "G.S.L.C.P.G." (Great Salt Lake City Pure Gold), "Two and half Do." On the reverse is a crown over the all-seeing eye, around the edge of which are the words "HOLINESS TO THE LORD." The designs on the 1849 and 1850 coins were all the same, with the exception of the 1850 five-dollar piece. This had nine stars around the edge and a slightly different crown. The 1860 five-dollar gold piece, often referred to as the "beehive," displays an eagle behind a straw beehive on the reverse. The reverse legend reads "DESERET ASSAY OFFICE PURE GOLD 5.D." The obverse exhibits the Lion of Judah at the center with the words "HOLINESS TO THE LORD" phonetically written in the Deseret alphabet at the periphery. The Mormons used this alphabet during the period from 1852 to 1869.

8
HARD TIMES TOKENS

President Andrew Jackson disapproved of a fiscal system under which public funds were deposited in a single, privately controlled institution—the Bank of the United States. In 1832, Jackson vetoed the bill to continue the Bank's existence after the expiration of its charter in 1836. This was in opposition to Clay and what many regarded as the financial interests of the country. The result was an upheaval in both political parties.

Jackson's party split into two opposed groups while Clay's supporters fought to restore the bank. Jackson and his successor, Martin Van Buren, succeeded in warding off the attacks and successfully established their reforms. They discontinued depositing funds in the Bank of the United States and established a subtreasury system. Metallic currency was the only medium of payment for public lands.

At the time, the country was undergoing a severe depression. That, plus the uncertainty of the banking system, led to hoarding hard money. Paper money was considered to be so unreliable that nobody wanted to accept it. The demand on the large cent, and the disappearance of small change, led to the manufacture of the Hard Times tokens. Those with political slogans were the first campaign tokens. Following are some of the legends from political tokens:

- "Andrew Jackson President Elected 1828 re-elected 1832—We commemorate the glorious victories of our hero in war and in peace."
- "Gulian C. Verplanck Our Next Govnr A Faithful friend of our Country."
- Small bust of Jackson with "My Substitute for the U.S. Bank. My Experiment, My Currency, My Glory."
- Running Jackass: "I follow in the steps of my illustrious predecessor."
- Jackson sitting in a strongbox with a sword and a bag of money: "I take the responsibility."
- Ship *Constitution* under full sail: "Webster credit Currency."

- Ship named *Experiment* wrecked on the rocks: "Van Buren Metallic Currency."
- Slave tokens: "Am I Not a Man and Brother" and "Am I Not a Woman and Sister."

There are many varieties of Liberty Head Hard Times tokens, similar to the large United States cents. Some are very ugly. In addition to some of the reverses already mentioned, Liberty Head tokens are also found with "Millions for Defense, Not One Cent for Tribute," "Mint Drop Bentonian Currency," and "Mint Drop Benton Experiment." You will also find ones with an Ugly Head obverse that reads "Loco Foco" instead of "Liberty" on the headband.

Many enterprising merchants of the day issued tokens advertising their wares to be used as small change. Some of these tokens have the same obverses as the political tokens. Others have the type of business on them—a clockmaker has a clock; a bootmaker, a boot; a barber, a comb and scissors, and so forth. A gold beater has an arm and sledge, an anvil represents hardware and cutlery. A circus rider on two horses stands for the Hippodrome, and a railroad coach represents the New York and Harlem Railroad. A liquor store might have an inebriate with a glass, while an umbrella maker has an open umbrella, and a chair maker, an upright chair. Tokens representing public baths feature a nude.

Lyman H. Low listed 183 types of Hard Times Tokens dated from the period between 1832 to 1844. Russell Rulau's more recent reference lists nearly five hundred different Hard Times token types. While many are easily available, there are others which are quite rare. Made in bronze, brass, and white metal, the bronze tokens are generally the most common. The majority are the size of large cents.

9
CIVIL WAR MONEY

Patriotism ran high in the newly formed Confederacy, and the cry went out to everyone to help in the war effort by turning in their gold, silver, and other precious metals in exchange for both state and Confederate notes. Southern bonds were issued to finance the war—all with promises to pay within a certain number of years after the ratification of peace between the North and South. There was no question about who would win. This temporary paper money was just as good as having the gold coins it represented—or so the Confederates thought.

Financing the war was no easy task. The South, not having much heavy industry of its own, had to rely on foreign aid for supplies—which they had to pay for with hard cash. An issue of bonds backed by cotton and sold in Europe proved to be a failure. Coins soon went out of circulation. There was an attempt to continue operation of the New Orleans Mint, but due to lack of metal this failed, and the only coins that were struck there for the Confederacy were the cent and half dollar—both are experimental pieces, and very rare. The Dahlonega and Charlotte mints were closed for good.

As the war progressed and things began to look bleak, public confidence waned. There was a scramble for gold, and some state bank notes (formerly considered "as good as gold") were redeemed for gold at a small fraction of their face value. As more money was needed, more and more Confederate paper was printed. Huge quantities were printed in 1864—the last year this paper money was issued. Printing presses were turning out denominations valued at anywhere from fifty cents up to five hundred dollars. (The only one thousand dollar bill printed by the Confederacy was issued at the very start of their banknote production in 1861.) The collapse of the Southern effort put an end to this, and rendered all Confederate money valueless; the land was left destitute as a result. While much of the money was destroyed, some found its way into attics, in cartons and trunks, where it lay for decades—a useless reminder of the great war effort. Many stories have been told since of old Southern families with trunks full of Confederate money stored in their attics.

The vastly increased interest in the Confederate series over the past several decades has brought much of this currency out of its storage places. There are a few rarities in existence, such as the Montgomery, Alabama, one thousand-, five hundred-, one hundred-, and fifty-dollar notes, plus a few others, which sell for considerable amounts of money. The majority of these paper bills, however, are generally available. At present they garner significant demand.

Whereas the war effort in the South was plagued with difficulties, the capabilities of the North were quite different. Heavily industrialized, the North was far better equipped to cope with the problems presented by the war. There, too, small change soon went out of circulation. The loss of the New Orleans Mint cut coin output in half, throwing the burden of coin manufacture on the shoulders of the Philadelphia and San Francisco mints. Although these mints were also hampered by the shortage of metal, they were not hit nearly as hard as the South.

Contributing to the great shortage of hard cash was the desire of many to hoard and the greatly increased need for small change in day-to-day business transactions. Housewives going to market were constantly plagued by a lack of change. Merchants, therefore, were compelled to improvise methods of providing change, resulting with the use of postage stamps as currency. While a necessity, the use of stamps for this purpose proved to be a nuisance, since the stamps often stuck together, lost their gum (one reason why so many of our early issues are found in mint condition without gum), and also were very fragile.

A year after the war began, a Mr. J. Gault patented the first encased postage stamps. An encased postage stamp consisted of a round brassy metal frame in which stamps of various denominations were inserted and subsequently covered with a transparent piece of mica. This encasement protected the stamp, served the purpose of a coin and could be used much longer because of its cover. Encased postage was issued in denominations of one, two, three, five, ten, twelve, twenty-four, thirty, and ninety cents.

The enterprising Mr. Gault arranged to have advertising placed on the back cover, and while many have his name on them, dozens of northern firms paid to use this convenient method of providing change. Outstanding among these are such companies as Ayers Pills, Drakes Plantation

Bitters, Burnetts Cooking Extracts, Lord and Taylor, and North American Life Insurance Co. All of these encased postage stamps are quite rare, with many of the most prized examples in this series being among the higher denominations.

Another answer to the coin shortage was the series known as Civil War tokens. They first appeared in the latter part of 1861 and were coined in great quantities until 1864, when laws—still in effect today—abolished all private money coining. It is estimated that about fifty million of these tokens were coined during this period. There were two main varieties: patriotic, with novel political legend, such as "Our flag, should anyone tear it down, shoot him on the spot" and "Millions for contractors, not one cent for widows" and storecard tokens, which appeared with legends advertising wares. Although these were not legitimate money, they were used as cents.

In 1862, Congress passed a bill authorizing postage currency. Notes in denominations of five, ten, twenty-five, and fifty cents, had facsimiles of the current five- and ten-cent postage stamps printed on them. This was brought about by the wide use of postage stamps as small change.

In 1863, a new act was passed authorizing the first issue of fractional currency (i.e., small denomination banknotes). This currency circulated until as late as 1876, when an act authorized its redemption in silver coin.

During 1866 and 1867, the Treasury Department made up special fractional currency shields. These were an ornate arrangement of specimen notes, printed on one side and framed. They included notes of all issues, both obverse and reverse, for the first three series. The fifteen-cent Grant and Sherman notes were included, even though these never appeared in circulation. Shields were distributed to banks to assist them in detecting counterfeits. These shields are quite rare and difficult to find in good condition. Many were taken apart in the hope that the notes could be sold or spent.

Before the Civil War, state bank charters were easy to obtain. The rapid expansion of our economy had created the need for more money and state banks were authorized to issue paper money against their deposits. This system was satisfactory as long as there was prosperity. In recession, however, deposits were withdrawn, banks closed their doors, and money became valueless.

While paper money was looked upon with suspicion during the Civil War, the government was compelled to issue currency. These included the demand notes of 1861 and the legal tender notes of 1862 and 1863. Issued in denominations of one dollar to one thousand dollars, they were called "greenbacks" from the color on the reverse side.

The one-dollar and two-dollar denominations were often sent to the "boys in blue" at the front. It became the practice to pin these notes to a heavy piece of paper so they could not be detected in the mail and stolen. Many of the notes in this series found today have these same pinholes in them.

In the South, the mint in New Orleans was not permitted to resume operations until 1879, and for over a decade it only issued silver dollars. In the West, a new mint was opened in 1870 at Carson City. The San Francisco Mint continued to operate, turning out gold and silver coins. The Philadelphia Mint bore the brunt of our nation's small-change needs. As the economy gradually got back on a normal footing, change eventually became more plentiful.

10
TEDDY ROOSEVELT'S TWENTY-DOLLAR GOLD PIECE

At the request of President Theodore Roosevelt, Cornelius Van Schaak Roosevelt donated to the Smithsonian an experimental ultrahigh-relief double eagle (or twenty-dollar gold piece), dated 1907 in Roman numerals and designed by Augustus St. Gaudens. This remarkable coin is one of the greatest rarities of the United States coin series, and also has an unusual historical background. Theodore Roosevelt, who devoted considerable efforts toward its design and production, owned it originally.

In fact, in the winter of 1905, Theodore Roosevelt met with Augustus St. Gaudens, whose sculptures the president admired greatly, at a dinner in Washington. The conversation drifted to the beauty of ancient Greek coins, described by St. Gaudens as the only coins of real artistic merit. Why couldn't the United States have coins as beautiful as those of the ancient Greeks, the president wished to know. If St. Gaudens would model new coinage designs, the president assured St. Gaudens that he would have them minted.

Thus started a unique venture in modern monetary history. Manifesting his versatility and extraordinary energy, Theodore Roosevelt found the time personally to conduct the campaign for a more artistic series of United States coinage designs. On November 6, 1905, in a letter to St. Gaudens regarding these designs, the president said:

> I want to make a suggestion. It seems to me worthwhile to try for a really good coinage; though I suppose there will be a revolt about it! I was looking at some gold coins of Alexander the Great today, and I was struck by their high relief. Would it not be well to have our coins in high relief, and also to have the rims raised? The point of having the rims raised would be, of course, to protect the figure on the coin; and if we have the figures in high relief, like the figures on the old Greek coins, they will surely last longer. What do you think of this?

For two years, president and sculptor gave much time and energy to the task of producing the new coin designs. The models finally adopted for the double eagle were unusually artistic. The obverse showed a standing figure of Liberty, holding aloft in her right hand the torch of enlightenment and in her left, the olive branch of peace. On the reverse side was a rendering of a flying eagle above a rising sun.

A very small number of these experimental ultrahigh-relief specimens were struck at the president's order. These exceedingly rare pieces can be easily distinguished from those issued later for general circulation, which also have a high relief. The field of the rare experimental pieces is excessively concave and connects directly with the edge without any border, giving it a sharp knifelike appearance. Liberty's skirt shows two folds on the side of the right leg; the Capitol building in the background at the left is very small; and the date, 1907, is in Roman numerals. The sun, on the reverse side, has fourteen rays.

In addition to these experimental pieces, 11,250 high-relief twenty-dollar gold pieces were struck on a medal press for general distribution and, though rare, are found today in some collections. Their relief is somewhat lower than that of the experimental pieces. They have a border around the edge, Liberty's skirt has three folds on the side of the right leg, and the Capitol is considerably larger. As on the ultrahigh-relief pieces, the 1907 date is indicated in Roman numerals. On the reverse, there are only thirteen rays extending from the sun.

For practical reasons and especially since these high-relief coins could not be struck on a regular coin press and would not stack, it was decided soon to modify the relief, giving the coin a flatter appearance. A large number of modified-relief double eagles were issued in 1907 (these pieces show the date in Arabic numerals) and in later years up to 1933, when the issuance of gold coins was discontinued.

Theodore Roosevelt's twenty-dollar gold piece is on permanent display in the Smithsonian's hall of monetary history. It should remind us of Roosevelt's words about this piece: "Certain things were done, of which the economic bearing was more remote but which bore directly upon our welfare, because they add to the beauty of living and therefore to the joy of life." In addition to this change in the design of twenty-dollar gold pieces, the ten-, five-, and two-and-a-half-dollar gold pieces also underwent design changes. St. Gaudens also created the Indian Head design adopted on the ten-dollar gold pieces first struck in 1907.

11
COMMEMORATIVE COINS

The opening of the Chicago World's Fair in 1892 was the occasion for the issue of our first commemorative coins, the Columbian half dollars. Designed to help defray expenses, they did not at first meet with great enthusiasm. A good many were coined in 1892 and still more in 1893. It was hoped that nearly two million five hundred thousand of both dates could be sold at one dollar each.

Many were sold, brought home by visitors, and kept for years as souvenirs of the exposition. A great many, however, did not sell and ultimately were placed in circulation at face value. For many years it was not unusual to receive one of these Columbian half dollars, particularly one dated 1893, in one's pocket change. The Isabella quarters, struck in 1893, were issued in much smaller quantities and therefore were more easily absorbed than the Columbian halves. Even though these commemoratives did not meet with great enthusiasm, the series was started, and the idea of selling special coins at premiums to raise money for special events took hold.

In 1900 we had our first commemorative dollar, the Lafayette dollar. Until this time, no special denomination had been adopted for commemorative coins and they began to appear in all kinds. With the advent of the 1903 Louisiana Purchase commemorative gold dollars, we have the first in a series of gold coins. The Panama-Pacific fifty-dollar slugs, which appeared in 1915, became very rare. Coined in very limited numbers, they were issued more as historical souvenirs than as coins. Even so, at the time of issue, it was difficult to dispose of them at over face value.

People resented having to pay a premium for a coin, no matter how interesting it was or how small an issue. Little did those buyers know how greatly they would increase in value. Even in the late 1920s, dealers were more than pleased to get their capital investment out of the Panama-Pacific fifty-dollar piece plus a small premium for their efforts. While approximately a thousand of these Panama-Pacific fifty-dollar pieces were struck of each type, nearly half of them were turned in to the mint to be melted. This leaves a little over a thousand of both in existence today.

The Panama-Pacific set—two fifty-dollar gold pieces, a gold quarter eagle, a gold dollar, and a fifty-cent piece—was the first of its kind. Since both the price and the size of the half dollar were the most popular, future commemorative coins were struck in this denomination. In 1918 the Lincoln-Illinois Centennial half dollar was issued, and from 1920 on, one or more different commemoratives were coined every year.

It was difficult to sell all the commemoratives that were authorized, for while the series had enlisted many ardent followers, there were not as many as there were coins. In 1921, the idea of making varieties that would be rarer than the regular series was first put into effect. We find the Alabama Centennial with and without 2x2, the Grant Memorial with and without star, and the two Missouri Centennial varieties. This was the first step toward trying to sell more coins to a limited number of buyers. As time went by, many commemorative halves were issued, some by associations that only wanted to dispose of enough coins to fill their need for funds. More enterprising interest groups had the halves made for many years, from many mints, and with all kinds of minor varieties to create rarities.

The quantity of commemorative coins issued hit a peak around 1935–36. Interest at that time also hit a peak. Speculators and collectors were getting on the band wagon, buying commemoratives in large quantities, making up sets, and carrying around graphs showing the fluctuations of price trends. It was not unusual to deal in hundreds and thousands of one issue. The speculation was similar to that of the stock market. Some rare issues skyrocketed from $5 to $75 within a week. Such rapid profits were unheard of in the numismatic world until this time.

As might have been expected, it could not last. The crash came. Overnight, no one wanted to buy commemoratives and everyone was loaded with hundreds of one kind. It took many years to get over this debacle and for holders of commemoratives to dispose of their hoards. When this finally occurred, most issues were widely distributed, and a gradual and more secure rise in values began. The sale of new issues after 1936 was very difficult, and the government approved few. For many years the only new commemoratives struck were those under authorization from previous years, such as the Boone, Oregon Trail, Texas, and Arkansas. Very few coins were struck each year because of the sharply reduced demand and the repetition of designs. Collectors were disgusted with the "rackets," as they called them. Some hope was raised with the issue of the 1946 Iowa Centennial, for this was a new, single, and interesting coin. However, it was quickly followed by the mass of varieties of the Booker T. Washington and Washington-Carver series, the last of which, with twelve different varieties, ended in 1954.

There followed a lapse of over twenty years in the production of commemoratives. The administration, on the advice of the U.S. Mint, frowned upon commemorative issues. The exploitation of many issues of the series had caused a good deal of discontent. The feeling was that the U.S. Mint was too busy to issue these special coins and that commemoratives tended to confuse the coinage of the country, creating too many designs. It was also felt that commemoratives should be issued in the form of medals. Medals, however, had never reached the popularity among collectors that coins enjoyed; the collector likes to feel his collection is of basic intrinsic value, no matter how small. The number of medals versus proof sets issued by the U.S. Mint is evidence of this.

The U.S. Mint did produce Bicentennial commemorative dollars, half dollars, and quarters in both 1975 and 1976 with the coinage of each denomination bearing the dates "1776-1976." In 1982, the administration resumed what has proved to be a long line of commemoratives, the first issue of which was the 250th Anniversary George Washington half dollar. Today, commemoratives are thriving, as indicated by the production of coins ranging from half dollars to ten-dollar gold pieces. The range of subjects for these issues include many important Americans, significant historic places and landmarks, as well as noteworthy anniversaries of key events in history. (For a complete listing of these issues, please refer to Part Three.)

12
PROOF COINS

Proof coins are generally described by most publications as coins specially struck with mirrorlike surface for collectors. Additional proof finishes include sandblast (matte) and Roman finish (satin) proofs. While this description is accurate, there is more which must be clarified above and beyond what this simple definition suggests.

The term "proof" refers to the manner in which a coin was struck. Proof coins are generally minted using a different quality striking technique than that used for coins intended for circulation. Proofs are coined by using specially prepared planchets and dies. The planchets are struck more than once in order to give the coin a very bold strike. Most proofs encountered in the U.S. series are brilliant proofs, exhibiting mirrorlike fields. In addition to these, there are matte proofs and satin or Roman finish proofs. As with business strike coins (i.e., coins intended for circulation), proof coins will be seen in different states of preservation. As would be expected, proof coins that are of the highest quality will carry much greater premiums than those which are hairlined or display other impairments.

Today, proofs are very carefully struck in an effort to insure perfection. Most U.S. proof coins are currently struck at the San Francisco Mint, and bear the "S" mint mark on the obverse. In the manufacture of proofs, the dies used are polished, as are the planchets. This gives the coins their mirrorlike finish.

Modern proof coins are generally perfect when first struck. The field, including the tiny spaces between letters and designs, must have this mirrorlike finish. The highlights of the coin are sharp and have a "frosted" or cameo contrast, causing the designs to stand out from their mirrorlike background. The edges are usually sharp and the coin is perfectly centered.

Proofs are truly beautiful coins, whether they are made of gold, silver, or copper. Sandblast or matte proofs have all the above qualifications, with the exception of the mirrorlike finish. They will instead have a dull, velvetlike surface.

While the first regularly recognized issue of proofs for collectors commenced in 1858, proofs were coined before that time. The first early proofs were trial or experimental pieces to test designs and dies. Very few were struck and consequently they are very rare. These were usually not offered for sale to collectors. More often, they were used as presentation pieces and samples of coinage.

In 1858, proofs were first offered for sale to collectors. Records of how many proofs were coined prior to 1877 are spotty, but from what information we have, we can tell that the quantities were very small. By examining the records, one can see how the interest in proof coins steadily increased as the years went by. Lower denominations were the most popular proof coins.

During the nineteenth century, proof sets were offered as minor sets, complete sets, and those with gold. The minor sets were by far the most popular, with the complete sets following second in popularity. Proof gold coins were not as well received, even though their premium cost was very little over the face value. This lack of interest was in large part due to the initial face-value investment involved. The coinage of proof double eagles ranged from only 20 to 158 proofs per year during the period from 1865 to 1907.

Proofs were almost entirely discontinued in 1915; production did not resume again until 1936. The maximum number of proofs struck in 1915 for any denomination was 1,150 pieces. In comparison, the number of proof sets struck in 1936 totaled 3,837. While this was quite an increase, it pales in significance when compared to later mintage increases of proof sets. The number of sets produced in 1957, for example, reached 1,247,952. Interestingly enough, before 1950 proof coins were sold either in sets or individually, giving collectors the opportunity to create their own sets if they wished to.

Many early strikes of regular issue coins have an appearance similar to that of proofs, as the new dies frequently give the coins a mirrorlike surface. This is often true with branch mint coins, although it must be remembered that hardly any proofs were struck at the branch mints during the early years. While it is sometimes very difficult to determine whether a particular coin is a proof or a "first strike" uncirculated coin, there are a number of characteristics that stand out. For example, business strikes usually do not have the sharp, well-struck edges of a genuine proof. Furthermore, the devices are not usually as sharp as those seen on proofs.

One frequently comes across attempts to simulate a proof surface. Buffing will give an uncirculated coin a mirrorlike finish, but this usually can be detected by a trained eye. Careful examination of the tiny surfaces between the letters and design features will often fail to exhibit any simulated reflectivity on coins which have been "doctored" to resemble proofs. Of course, the sharp edges of a genuine proof are normally lacking also on such coins.

There are many uncirculated coins that are frequently mistaken for proof coins. They include: silver dollars (1878 and forward) from all mints; late date Liberty Seated halves; late date Liberty Seated quarters; a few dimes in the 1870s; late date three-cent silver pieces; many dates in the three-cent nickel series; Type III gold dollars (particularly in the 1880s); and some of the later three-dollar gold pieces. With regard to the gold two-and-one-half-, five-, ten-, and twenty-dollar pieces, these sometimes are found with prooflike luster, but are usually somewhat scratched, indicating contact with other coins.

Several of the scarcer, shorter issues (such as the four-dollar Stellas, the three-dollar coins of 1875 and 1876, the twenty-cent pieces of 1877 and 1878, the nickel three-cent pieces of 1877 and 1878, and the two-cent pieces of 1873) were only struck as proofs, even though used specimens or "impaired" proofs occasionally appear. Pieces such as these were minted purely for collectors to maintain a consecutive run of dates. The 1873 two-cent pieces and the 1877 and 1878 twenty-cent pieces struck for this reason turned out to be the last of their respective series. The four-dollar Stellas were really trial or experimental pieces and were never coined for actual use. Some denominations during the 1880s became unpopular for regular use but were coined for a decade or so in small quantities, most likely to satisfy the collectors' demand for a complete run of dates.

PART TWO

Practical Advice for Collectors

13
HOW COINS ARE MADE

Although an entire reference in and of itself could be written with regard to the topic of coin production, it is certainly important to at least outline the process by which modern coins are made.

Coin production naturally begins with the metal or alloy in question being melted and cast into the form of very large ingots. These ingots are subsequently rolled into very large, long coils. After the coils are annealed (heated and cooled to strengthen the metal and make it less brittle), they are then cleaned, rinsed, and wire brushed. In the case of clad coins, the clad strip is then applied to either side of the coil and the coils are rolled into the proper thickness for the coin in question. The coils are now run through a blanking press, which punches the blank planchets from the coil strip. The blank planchets are fed through a riddling machine designed to remove planchets that are clipped or otherwise too small. The riddled blanks are again annealed and cleaned prior to being run through the upsetting mill. Upsetting is a process by which the rims are slightly raised in preparation for striking. The upset planchets are placed into a press wherein they are struck. They are then inspected, weighed, counted, and bagged prior to shipment. Any rejects made during this process are sent back to the furnace for remelting into ingots.

All coins are struck from dies. A coin design normally begins with the artist preparing drawings that he/she feels are suitable and which are subsequently approved. In many cases, there are competing designs that are submitted and from which the U.S. Treasury chooses a final design. Progressing from the drawing stage, plaster models are fashioned. Later, the designs are reduced into galvanos and transferred to hubs. Hubs are a steel punch from which the working coin dies are made. Modern coinage presses are designed to strike many coins at a time, thus there are several sets of dies in use simultaneously in any one press.

14
MINT ERRORS

With the U.S. Mint producing billions upon billions of coins each year, it is inevitable that various types of minting errors escape detection by mint inspectors and find their way into circulation. In reading this chapter, bear in mind the minting process outlined earlier. Unfortunately, there are unscrupulous dealers that will attempt to deceive unsuspecting collectors by offering them coins that have been altered or otherwise treated in such a way as to resemble genuine error coins. A proper understanding of what can and cannot happen during the minting process will help avoid the possibility of being fooled.

The following mint errors are listed in descending order of importance to collectors. Please be reminded that the order of importance listed here is intended to be general in nature for the entire U.S. series. There are certain designs and denominations where the rarity and level of interest for a particular error type will not follow these general guidelines, thereby warranting assessment on a more individual basis. Furthermore, this listing, though including the vast majority of major error types, is not intended to be exhaustive.

MULES

Simply stated, a mule is a coin struck using an obverse and reverse die not intended for use on coins of the same denomination (i.e., a coin struck using a twenty-five-cent obverse die and a one-dollar reverse die). This excessively rare error type was first uncovered on a U.S. coin during the year 2000 with the reporting of coins struck on Sacagawea dollar planchets and bearing a Statehood twenty-five-cent obverse and Sacagawea dollar reverse. Mules are the numismatic equivalent of double denomination banknotes and are of the utmost importance to error collectors.

DOUBLED DIE ERRORS

Doubled die errors owe their origin to faulty quality control during the production of the dies. On very rare occasion, an error in transferring the image of a given design from the hub to a die can result in a doubling of all or part of the legends and/or design elements on the die in question. As a result, all coins struck from this doubled die will bear the same doubling on that side of the coin.

Perhaps the most famous U.S. error coin of this type is the rare 1955 Doubled Die cent. This particular doubled die bears very bold obverse doubling at the legends and date.

OFF-METAL ERRORS/WRONG PLANCHET ERRORS

Coins struck on planchets intended for use on a different denomination are referred to as off-metal errors. An example of such an error would be a five-cent piece struck on a planchet intended for use on a cent. Errors of this type are virtually always (there are a very isolated number of unexplained exceptions) struck on planchets with a smaller diameter than the planchet intended. This is to be expected as the planchet must fit into the collar in order for the coin to be properly struck.

Additionally, the U.S. Mint has on occasion struck coins for other countries. It is possible to obtain U.S. coins struck on planchets intended for foreign countries.

MULTIPLE STRIKES

As the name of this error type suggests, coins that bear more than one striking image on each side of the coin are referred to as multiple strikes. This can include double strikes, triple strikes, or more. Flip-over multiple strikes bearing images from both dies on either side of the coin occasionally occur. Another very rare variation of this error type includes coins struck twice with each striking being from a different denomination die (i.e., a dime planchet struck both from cent dies and dime dies).

Brockage, Capped Die, and Counter-Brockage Errors

A coin becomes stuck in the die after striking. This coin subsequently strikes another planchet. The newly struck planchet has become what is known as a brockage.

Brockage errors will display a mirror image of the opposite side of the coin on the misstruck side. The coin that became stuck in the die is known as a cap. Caps can become very dramatic errors if the cap remains in the die for a long period of time, resulting in a large amount of metal distortion. A counter-brockage is a rare variation of this error. It occurs when a brockage coin in turn becomes a cap and begins to strike additional coins.

Improper Stock Errors

On rare occasion, planchets are punched from improper planchet stock. The result will be a coin of the proper diameter, but improper thickness. An example of such a coin would be a quarter struck from stock intended for use on dimes.

Off-Center Errors

Coins that have been struck out of the collar and improperly centered fall into this category. Such errors will be missing at least part of the intended design of the coin.

Broadstrike Errors

Similar to an off-center coin, a broadstruck coin is also struck out of the collar. In this case, however, the strike is properly centered, thereby causing an abnormally spread planchet about the entire coin design.

BLANK PLANCHETS

A blank of metal intended for minting, but which escaped the mint without being struck is called a blank planchet. There are two types of blank planchets; both with and without upset rims.

CLIPPED PLANCHETS

The machinery that punches the blanks from the metal strip can sometimes in error punch holes that overlap. The malformed blanks are known as clipped planchets. Although these planchet clips are normally curved, straight clips, elliptical clips, ragged clips, and partial clips are also encountered. Additionally, coins can sometimes exhibit multiple clips.

DEFECTIVE DIE ERRORS

Any number of errors involving problems with a die or dies would fall into this category. These include but are not limited to die cracks, die breaks, clogged dies (i.e., grease in the die), and clashed dies (dies that have struck each other due to the lack of a planchet being fed into the press).

DEFECTIVE PLANCHETS

Various errors that reflect defects in the planchet used to strike a coin include: planchet cracks, laminations, slagmarks/planchet streaks (normally the result of an improper alloy mix), and struck-through errors (the result of foreign matter, such as lint, iron filings, thread, etc., on the die or planchet).

15
COUNTERFEITS AND ALTERED COINS

The rapid price rise of nearly all United States coins has created a flood of counterfeits, altered dates, and other kinds of forgeries, many of which are so clever that the best experts are sometimes fooled. Further reading as well as exposure to thousands and thousands of coins is necessary before any numismatist can claim proficiency in authentication.

AUTHENTICATION 101

Counterfeits can vary widely in quality and deceptiveness. In determining the authenticity of a U.S. coin, it is important to consider several characteristics of the coin in question.

Color. Many lesser-quality counterfeit coins simply do not look "right" for a number of reasons. The first of these reasons is the initial coloration of the coin. For example, counterfeit gold coins are often not made of the proper fineness of gold, thus the coloration of the coin is very suspect.

Lustre. Counterfeit coins are often detected due to their unnatural lustre. By looking at hundreds and hundreds of coins of a given type, an informed numismatist will eventually acquire a "feel" for what type of lustre is seen on products of the U.S. Mint and what types simply are not. Unnatural lustre is inevitably related to the means by which a coin was produced.

Strike. Certain dates and mint marks within a given series tend to exhibit a particular type of strike. If the coin in question is struck either too sharply or too weakly for the given date of the coin, then that particular coin warrants a certain amount of suspicion. Furthermore, many inferior quality counterfeit coins will exhibit a very unnatural "mushy" degree of detail.

Surfaces. In many instances, examination of the fields, devices, rims, or edge of a counterfeit coin will reveal telltale signs of inauthenticity. A good magnifying glass, keen eyesight and, in many cases, years of experience in authenticating coins are important tools in this type of study.

Weight. Perhaps the simplest procedure in helping to determine whether a suspect coin has a chance of being authentic is performed simply by using an accurate scale. If a coin is not within the proper weight tolerance for the type in question, it cannot possibly be genuine. Bear in mind, however, that a coin that does have the proper weight is not necessarily genuine.

ALTERED COINS

For many decades, unscrupulous dealers have attempted to fool novice collectors by adding mint marks, removing mint marks, altering dates, or in some other way changing the detail of a coin for their own illicit personal gain. Regardless of the series, if a coin is a key date or variety, someone has attempted to fool the unsuspecting buyer. Whether the coin in question is a 1914 "D" cent with an added mint mark or a 1937 "D" three-legged nickel with a planed-off leg on the buffalo—you name it, and someone has tried it. It is essential to be informed to avoid being deceived in a sale. (Please refer to Part Four for a list of further reading on this very important topic.)

16
HOW COIN VALUES ARE DETERMINED

New collectors take up the hobby of coin collecting every day. Older coins disappear from circulation very quickly and the supply coming into the market from the breakup of collections usually cannot keep pace with the demand that comes from ever greater numbers of collectors in American coins. Thus, the demand for these coins tends to grow while, at best, the supply remains constant. The result has tended to be a somewhat predictable rise in the value of American coins, at least in the long term.

Besides rarity, however, there is another factor that affects a coin's value—namely, its state of preservation or condition. Collectors will often pay many times more for a coin in superior condition than they would for a specimen of the same coin that is just of average quality.

The prices listed in this book are indicated generally for various grade levels of the date, mint mark, and denomination in question. The grading scale used in establishing the quality level of a given coin encompasses a broad range of classifications. From lowest to highest, the terms used in coin grading are:

- Poor (P)
- Fair (F)
- About Good (AG)
- Good (G)
- Very Good (V. Good)
- Fine (F)
- Very Fine (V. Fine)
- Extremely Fine (Ex. Fine)
- About Uncirculated (A Unc.)
- Uncirculated (Unc.)
- Choice Uncirculated (Ch Unc.)
- Gem Uncirculated (Gem Unc.)

A *fine* coin is one that shows a reasonable amount of wear but is still not without some level of desirability. The basic outline is still clear although much of the more intricate detail is worn away. All lettering should be easily legible.

The next grade below this, *very good,* is reserved for a worn but not altogether unattractive coin. A coin in this condition should be free of serious gouges or other mutilations but it may be somewhat tired from rather excessive use.

A coin that is rated only *good* generally represents a coin at the lowest point within the "collectible" grade range. The date and mint mark would be legible and the major portions of the design distinguishable.

Grades of *about good, fair,* and *poor* encompass badly worn coins that are usually not acceptable to a collector. Coins of these grades are generally used as space fillers, only until such time as a better coin can be acquired.

The *very fine* grade indicates a coin on which the design is still quite clean, and which over all shows light to moderate amounts of wear.

An *extremely fine* coin shows light wear or rubbing only on the high points of the design.

Uncirculated indicates a coin absolutely without wear.

The price lists in Part Three of this book should give you an approximate idea of how to calculate the value of your coins. The values shown are the prices that dealers can be expected to charge when they sell coins in the grade level indicated. Values indicated for proof coins generally represent proofs that are in the *choice* grade range.

17
HOW TO DETERMINE IF A COIN IS UNCIRCULATED

I cannot stress enough how important it is to classify accurately the condition of coins. To become a smart coin collector, this exacting work is one of the first skills to master. You can lose a lot of money by paying high prices for coins or coin collections that have been grossly overrated. If, when buying coins, there is any doubt in your mind as to whether a certain piece is in good condition, take it to an expert or another experienced collector. He will gladly give you an opinion free of charge. When purchasing a large collection, don't hesitate to have a dealer appraise it for you and give you his written expert opinion. It may cost you a fee for an expert appraisal, but this sum may save you many hundreds in the long run. Experienced dealers are trained at grading coins and know what to look for.

Another option is to purchase coins that have been graded by third-party grading services. These "slabbed" coins, which have been professionally graded and encapsulated in plastic, can provide buyers with a higher degree of confidence in their purchases. The price of such coins, however, often reflects the added value of professional grading.

With the high premiums attached to many uncirculated coins, it is essential that the serious collector know how to determine whether or not a coin is really uncirculated. Because of some of the cleaning processes used today, very careful scrutiny is necessary. Often times, a cleaned coin can give the appearance of a wholesome mint-state example at first glance. Closer scrutiny, however, may show that the coin has been cleaned in an effort to camouflage some wear on the high points of the design. Too frequently, we look at a coin and, because it appears bright and new, consider it uncirculated, when the actual wear upon such a piece should be the determining factor.

Initial Points of Wear for Selected Designs

I shall try to describe what I have found to be the first spots to wear on particular coins (i.e., the first places to look for wear on what appears to be an uncirculated coin).

Lincoln cents show their first wear on the cheekbone of Lincoln's bust. In the 1920s, for a few years, Lincoln cents were struck very poorly so the coinage appears indistinct. Such softly struck coins would be considered uncirculated.

Indian Heads first show wear on the obverse at the lock of hair at the lower right part of the bust. The ribbon hanging down is next to show wear. On the reverse, the highlights of the bow at the bottom of the wreath wear first.

The tip of the headdress above the word "Liberty" first shows wear on *large cents dated 1840 and later.* Prior to that date, the hairlock below the headdress, the eyebrow, and the cheek give telltale evidence of wear. On the reverse, the highlighted leaves in the wreaths must be watched for wear. Color plays a vitally important part in the valuation of large cents. Coins which retain an abundance of original mint color are most desirable, particularly when free of any significant spotting. Medium brown, evenly toned examples are also in demand. Dark, corroded, or otherwise unevenly toned or speckled pieces will trade at a discount. You can also look at these same spots in the *half-cent series* to determine whether a coin has been circulated.

Earlier large cents must be examined on a case-by-case basis as striking characteristics can often be misleading to the novice.

The *Flying Eagle cents* of 1856 through 1858 first show signs of wear upon the eagle's breast directly below the wing. The wing tip and eyebrow should also be examined. Some cents of this type exist with very smooth tailfeathers. This does not indicate wear, however, for many were lightly struck there.

Two-cent pieces are easy to detect, since the "we" of the motto is the first item to go. Blurred horizontal lines in the shield are frequent, but these are not necessarily signs of wear, for many were coined in this manner.

The lock of hair above the ear first shows signs of wear on the *three-cent nickel piece.* These should also be closely examined for color—soiled or discolored pieces are not desirable. Mint bloom should be evident upon these.

The *Jefferson nickel* wears first on Jefferson's cheekbone. On the reverse, just below the dome of Monticello, first signs of wear can be detected by a slight dulling or discoloration.

Buffalo nickels are about the most difficult to identify in uncirculated condition. First, examine them for their original glossy mint bloom or color. If this is satisfactory, then examine the sharp edges of the coins for slight telltale hints of wear. After this, closely examine the shoulder of the buffalo, the hip, tail tip, and horn. Attempt to determine the difference between wear and weakness of strike in these areas. Next examine the cheek and just above the braid on the Indian's head for the same traces of friction.

The *Liberty nickel* first shows wear on the lock of hair over the temple and on the reverse highlights of the leaves in the wreath. The majority of Liberty nickels were sharply struck, but blurred coinage is known for many dates. Slight dulling of the original mint bloom on the highlights is the first sign of wear, as was the case with the Jefferson nickel.

The tiny crosslike emblem atop the shield of the *Shield nickel* shows evidence of wear first. On the reverse, examine the "5" for minute signs of wear.

Many of the *three-cent silver pieces* were not struck very sharply. These should have mint bloom, and they lack light high point friction as well.

The first signs of wear on *Liberty-Seated coins,* whether they are *half dimes, dimes, quarters, halves,* or *silver dollars,* appear on the head and on the thigh of Liberty. The ribbon below the wreath, on the reverse of the dime and half dime, wears first. Quarters and halves first show wear on the eyebrow and upper beak of the eagle, then on the upper wing tips.

Bust-type quarters and halves wear first on the lock of hair near the ear, next on the clasp on the ribbon at the lower part of the bust. On the reverse, the eagle's upper bill and the top edges of the wings wear first. Some of these coins have been lightly struck, so the general appearance of the rest of the coin must be taken into consideration.

Telltale signs of wear first show up on the eagle's wing in the center of *Peace dollars.* On *Morgan dollars,* wear appears first on the eagle's breast and head. With both of these coins, the reverse seems to show wear much faster than the obverse.

Barber quarters, halves, and dimes wear first on the obverse on the lock of hair over the forehead and temple directly below the word "Liberty." The cheek next shows discoloration and dulling. The reverse of the quarters and halves wears first directly above the eye of the eagle and the claws in his left talon.

The *Liberty Walking half dollar coins* first show wear on the breast of the eagle on the reverse. The head, breasts, and left leg of Miss Liberty are the next telltale signs.

Franklin half dollars show their first sign of wear right in the center of the bell and on the cheek of Franklin. A slight dullness is the very first sign of wear.

Liberty Standing quarters first show signs of wear on the knee of Miss Liberty. A slight flattening appears as the first sign of wear. A number of these quarters were coined with flat heads, which appear worn, but this does not necessarily mean the coin is not uncirculated. Watch the knee for the first real signs of wear. On the reverse, the eagle's breast wears first, but not nearly as soon as the knee on the obverse. I have seen many beautiful Liberty Standing quarters with full heads, but almost always with that sign of wear on the knee. Don't be fooled by this one! *Washington quarters* first wear on the eagle's breast.

On *Trade dollars,* the knee, left breast, and head on the obverse show the first signs of wear. The reverse first reveals wear on the eagle's left leg and upper tips of the wings.

Commemorative coins should be examined carefully as many show wear, particularly in the early series. The first spots to wear on selected commemorative silver coins are listed below:

Columbian Half Dollars
Obverse: cheek and center lock of hair
Reverse: center sail of ship; next, center of globes
New Rochelle, New York, 300th Anniversary
Obverse: the calf's hip
Reverse: highlights of the fleur-de-lis
Iowa Centennial
Obverse: the eagle's breast
Reverse: center columns, building, and the tower
Booker T. Washington Memorial
Obverse: cheek and nose
Reverse: highlights of center letters
Washington-Carver
Obverse: the prominent cheek
Reverse: the whole map of the United States
Isabella Quarter
Obverse: cheek
Reverse: head and left forearm
Lafayette Dollar
Obverse: cheek of Washington
Reverse: leg of equestrian; next, head
Panama-Pacific Exposition (1915)
Obverse: head and left arm
Reverse: eagle's breast
Lincoln, Illinois, Centennial
Obverse: cheekbone
Reverse: eagle's breast directly below forward part of left wing
Maine Centennial
Obverse: fingers of left figure on scythe
Reverse: ribbon holding wreath at bottom
Pilgrim Tercentenary
Obverse: cheek, hat brim, and book tip
Reverse: high side of ship

Missouri Centennial
Obverse: cheek and side of hat
Reverse: pioneer's arm, both heads

Alabama Centennial
Obverse: Kilby's cheek and forehead
Reverse: eagle's breast directly above left leg

Grant Memorial
Obverse: hair at temple
Reverse: leaves of trees

Monroe Centennial
Obverse: cheek and hair over temple
Reverse: the faint figures in the maps of North and South America (This is a lightly struck coin, hard to tell when slightly used.)

Huguenot-Walloon Tercentenary
Obverse: outstanding rim and top of hat; also cape
Reverse: hull of ship and shrouds

Lexington-Concord Sesquicentennial
Obverse: fingers holding the gun
Reverse: point of block house at center

18
HOW TO COLLECT, WHAT TO COLLECT

Although there are many foreign and ancient coins that truly are wonderful and make for countless hours of collecting enjoyment, the same can be said for coins within the U.S. series.

DIVERSIFICATION VS. SPECIALIZATION

There are two schools of thought with regard to strategy in assembling a collection. The first school is most often encountered and supported by those that have an "investor's" mentality.

Typically, in assembling a portfolio of stocks and bonds, a key word used by financial consultants is "diversification." The concept of limiting risk through the purchase of a variety of securities has always held great credence among Wall Street investors. After all, it can be extremely risky to "put all of your eggs in one basket." Mutual funds, for example, are an ideal way to limit risk and own a very impressive, diversified portfolio of securities. Likewise, a coin buyer can use a very similar "investor's" style in assembling his/her coin holdings. This type of buyer would attempt to purchase a variety of different coins, normally in the highest grade that he/she can afford. A risk of this buying style is the possibility of ending up with a hodgepodge "accumulation" of coins rather than a collection.

Should one care to follow this collecting philosophy, I would recommend the possibility of assembling a type set (i.e., buying one coin of each denomination and design). A type set, in and of itself, accomplishes the goal of diversification simply because each coin will differ in some way from its companions. Though some type collectors are content to simply fill each hole in their album, others want to do so only within a particular grade range. Type collecting, therefore, requires the individual to have the ability to accurately grade coins across the entire spectrum of U.S. numismatics. Errors in the grading and evaluation of a coin, particularly at the very high end of the grading scale, can become quite costly. Competence in grading, as well as in evaluating visual appeal, is essential for assembling a high-grade type set. Furthermore, I would recommend that those who opt for this kind of collection find some way to differentiate your type collection from the countless others who have the same strategy. Ways to differentiate include, but are not limited to, buying only first year of type, buying only last year of type, buying only coins with a certain attractive toning pattern, or perhaps buying only a scarce or rare date of each type.

The second method of building a collection is much more to my own liking, particularly if the collector is new to the hobby. In a nutshell, this method espouses the concept of "specialization." By concentrating one's buying interest to perhaps one, two, or at most three areas, the items being purchased will naturally acquire the context of a "collection" rather than simply an accumulation. Furthermore, by setting limits upon the scope of the collection, it reduces the probability of making a mistake in buying an improperly graded coin. The collector is able to learn the idiosyncrasies of grading within his/her specialty and is not spreading thinly throughout the entire cross-section of U.S. numismatics. Furthermore, it is important to acquire coins that will be challenging for those with similar collecting interests to duplicate. Inevitably, mediocre, easy-to-acquire coins garner uninspiring prices when they are sold.

In my many years of numismatic experience, it is those who have painstakingly assembled collections of premium quality coins in popular, specialized collecting areas who have generally realized the best results. After all, a collector or dealer is more inclined to travel to an auction if the auction contains an entire offering of coins within his/her specialty, rather than simply a smattering of readily obtainable pieces.

Within this collecting context, the area or areas of concentration that a collector may choose are highly contingent upon their historical and/or aesthetic tastes and preferences, as well as their pocketbook. Generally speaking, there are no "right" or "wrong" areas in which to collect. Every area is simply "different," and will appeal to a different group of collectors. Those who love U.S. history may opt for a series such as Commemorative half dollars, Colonials, or Territorial gold. Art lovers may find themselves attracted to Patterns, Type coins, or simply St. Gaudens double eagles. Whatever you choose to collect, be absolutely certain that you have fun and that you not get in over your head!

19
CLEANING COINS

When it comes to the subject of cleaning coins, I have one resounding rule that should always be remembered: <u>DO NOT CLEAN COINS.</u> Knowledgeable collectors prefer coins to be in their wholesome, natural state. Those who have learned to detect unnatural color or lustre heavily discount coins that have been changed by cleaning agents. That being said, there are a few exceptions to this general rule that you should keep in mind as you build your collection.

DARK OR "UGLY" COINS

In my opinion, if a coin is so black or otherwise totally unappealing that it can only be helped, then it is acceptable to attempt to rejuvenate such a coin through judicious cleaning. It is important, however, for the collector who is evaluating the visual appeal to be able to determine the appropriate agents for such cleaning. What appears to be ugly "tarnish" to the novice may be gorgeous, deep iridescent toning to an experienced numismatist. Furthermore, it is important to note that most third-party grading services will not encapsulate coins that have been cleaned or have otherwise altered surfaces. Those grading services that do encapsulate such coins will do so only with the proviso of mentioning such detractions. (For further information on third-party independent grading services, please refer to Chapter 20.)

"DIPPING" VS. ABRASIVE CLEANING

Using tarnish removing solutions to clean toning and tarnish spots is a generally accepted means to enhance the visual appeal of gold, silver, and sometimes nickel coins. (Tarnish removers should never be used on copper coins as they will irreparably alter the original patina.) If done properly, such cleaning will not alter or otherwise impair the lustre of a coin, and will make the coin more desirable to collectors. The repeated use of tarnish removing solutions or the improper rinsing of coins after being "dipped" will eventually impair or otherwise mute the lustre of the treated coins. For this reason, a collector should perform such actions sparingly and also become suspicious of lackluster coins that might otherwise seem to benefit from "dipping."

Having mentioned the practice of dipping gold and silver coins, I feel compelled to express my own tastes as a numismatist. I much prefer attractive, original material over items that have been otherwise enhanced in any way. There is something about the personality of a wholesome coin that appeals to me, particularly if the toning exhibits visually enticing hues of violet, blue, lavender, and/or other shades of pastel iridescence. It takes many decades for a coin to acquire such beauty yet it can take less than a minute to destroy it. Think twice before removing the toning on a coin. Of course, the practice of artificially toning coins by the use of heat and/or chemicals is an abomination of numismatics and should always be avoided. Skilled numismatists can detect these practices very easily.

Whereas "dipping" has established a legitimate place in numismatics, the abrasive cleaning of coins certainly has not. Bicarbonate of soda, cyanide, silver polish, wire brushes, scouring pads, buffing wheels, and the like have permanently destroyed the value of many coins over the years and should *never* be used. Telltale signs of such cleaning are an unnatural color or lustre and the appearance of faint hairlines over the surfaces of affected coins.

PVC AND ITS REMOVAL FROM COINS

A modern-day problem for some coin collectors is the removal of polyvinyl chloride (PVC) from coins that have been improperly stored in vinyl holders for an extended period of time. These vinyl holders have a tendency to decompose as they age, thereby leeching filmy deposits of PVC on all the coins they contain. For this reason, it is very advisable to store coins in inert holders made from materials like Mylar or Lucite. If you're using vinyl holders, they should *always* be changed at least once per year. For those who prefer to have third-party grading services encapsulate their coins, it is important to note that these services will not grade coins that display any PVC.

Luckily, PVC is removable through the use of certain degreasing solvents. If properly used, these solvents will not affect the original color of the coin and effectively solve this problem. (There's one exception: mint red copper coins will sometimes turn a lavender color when such solvents are used.)

Effective solvents include, but are not necessarily limited to, acetone, trichloroethane, trichlorotrifluoroethane, trichloroethylene, PKP, and unisolvent. These chemicals should always be used in a well-ventilated room and may not be available for public sale in every state.

The application of these solvents is best accomplished using a cotton swab. Improperly rubbing a proof coin with a cotton swab—whether or not it contains solvents—may produce hairlines on the surface. Always handle proof coins, or any coin for that matter, with *extreme care.*

20
GRADING SERVICE PROS AND CONS

Since the early days of numismatics, collectors have often sought confirmation of the quality and value of the items that they add to their collections. This long-suffering anxiety has, in part, been satiated by the advent of modern third-party grading services some two to three decades ago. Likewise, dealers seeking to legitimatize the levels at which they price their coins also use many of these same services. Some of the earliest grading services to pioneer this area of the hobby include the American Numismatic Association Certification Service (ANACS), the Numismatic Certification Institute (NCI), Accugrade, and the International Numismatic Society (INS). Knowledgeable collectors prefer those grading services that tend to have the strictest standards, whereas certain dealers who choose to prey on novice "investors" often submit their inventory to the grading services that would provide them with the most favorable grades.

The roller-coaster coin market of the late 1970s and early 1980s saw fortunes both made and lost by collector and dealer alike. Many of the collectors who were left holding the proverbial "bag" were those who had purchased allegedly high-quality coins in 1979 and early 1980 at historically astounding price levels. By 1981 and 1982, these same collectors often came to the realization that the market had not only dropped precipitously, but also that the "portfolio" (which they had assembled through their dealer) impressively certified as MS67 by a grading service actually contained an entire set of coins which was no better than MS63.

By the mid-1980s, the need for greater uniformity in grading standards had become a much more prominent issue. The Federal Trade Commission managed to put an end to many of the dealers and telemarketers who were the worst abusers of their clientele, thus largely causing the demise of unethical grading services. With the elimination of these dealers and graders, there was an opportunity to galvanize more effectively the image of numismatics. In an effort to entice the billion-dollar potential of Wall Street and its financial service companies, numismatic entrepreneurs brainstormed the idea of the "sight unseen" bid/ask market, similar to the stock market, for the trade of rare coins. In order for this "stock market for rare coins" to be successful, it would be necessary for the independent grading service supplying this market to attain a very high level of precision and consistency. By 1986, the first such grading service to develop a network of dealers providing sight unseen bid/ask levels for rare coins had been successfully launched. This service, the Professional Coin Grading Service (PCGS), was followed shortly thereafter by the Numismatic Guaranty Corporation (NGC). Additionally, ANACS, no longer associated with the American Numismatic Association, maintained a share of this new market.

As the years went by, it became evident that grading consistency remained an issue. Dealers increasingly discovered the potential of "cracking out" premium coins from their sealed grading service encapsulations and resubmitting them for a possible upgrade. This practice still flourishes today and, when successfully accomplished by those able to differentiate which coins have such potential, can result in increasing the perceived value of the coin by a factor of two, three, or even ten! The innate subjectivity of grading eventually brought about the realization that Wall Street could not trade a PCGS MS65 1881 "S" Morgan dollar in the same fashion in which it would trade a share of IBM. Indeed, though every share of IBM is exactly alike, every 1881 "S" Morgan dollar is not. Inevitably, coins of the same numerical grade were found to differ in terms of lustre, strike, color, surface quality, and overall visual appeal.

The issue of grading subjectivity and precision notwithstanding, a vain attempt was made to eliminate this problem through the use of computers. An interesting footnote to numismatic grading history of the late 1980s is a grading service by the name of Compugrade. Compugrade used computers to scan coins that were placed onto a moving platform. Compugrade billed itself as offering nearly unbending grading precision. After all, computers cannot be subjective in any way, thus allowing the computer to assign a numerical grade to a coin down to the precision of a tenth of a grade point. Collectors, however, were not prepared to turn their grading over to a computer and receive in exchange coins graded MS63.7 and the like; thus, Compugrade is no more.

PCGS, NGC, and ANACS, however, have received competition from additional services, some of which are no longer active, including Hallmark, PCI, ICG, and SEGS, to name a few.

It is most important to remember both the advantages and limitations of third-party independent grading. Grading services are not numismatic demigods; thus, they can and do make mistakes. First and foremost, therefore, collectors must always buy the coin and not simply the number indicated on the grading service encapsulation. Whether a coin is raw (i.e., not graded by a third party) or slabbed (i.e., graded by a third party), only purchase coins with which you are completely satisfied.

21
HOW TO SELL A COIN COLLECTION

For some time I have wanted to write about how to conduct a coin sale and how to ensure you are selling your coins for their true worth. A reader of mine wanted to know what a widow should do to sell a coin collection. This can be a very difficult problem for an inexperienced person.

How to go about selling a collection depends upon the value of the collection. If it is a matter of a few hundred dollars, an outright sale is the best. If it is a collection with a value on the order of ten thousand dollars or more, the story is entirely different. Collectors should make arrangements for the sale of their collection while they are still able to do so. This could mean selling the collection themselves or giving explicit instructions to their heirs. Since they have dealt with many large dealers, they are in a good position to form an opinion as to who should be trusted with the liquidation of the collection. This information should be passed on to the heirs. The sale of a collection of size, in many cases, has to depend upon absolute trust in the dealer purchasing it or handling its sale. There are many honest dealers in this country, but there are a few others who will use all kinds of chicanery to get the most for the least amount of money.

HANDLING AN ESTATE

When a collector passes away, the executor will normally arrange for the appraisal of the collection for both state and federal inheritance taxes. Appraised values in this case are normally calculated at the date of death and can be done on both a low wholesale or a high retail basis. Expert appraisers can supply both wholesale and retail valuations. For inheritance tax purposes, particularly if the collection is to be sold, a competitive liquidation value is normally the value of choice.

It is advisable not to keep the appraisal valuations too low, especially if liquidation is imminent. If the date of death appraisal is overly conservative, the estate would be subject to capital gains taxes on the difference between the appraised value and the actual value realized for the collection. These capital gains taxes are normally more costly to the estate than paying a higher inheritance tax.

The choice of an appraiser is very important. Attempt to get the best and to your knowledge the most honest. Be willing to pay their fee, if there is one, and do not necessarily feel obligated to sell the collection through this appraiser if you do not care to do so. Avoid appraisers who attempt to keep values down low with an eye to purchasing the collection based on these values. Although many prefer that the appraiser be a disinterested third party and not the prospective purchaser of the collection or his agent, it is possible that many dealers will choose not to perform such an appraisal. As an alternative, some dealers will charge an appraisal fee and rebate all or part of that fee if the collection is sold either to them or through them at auction.

It is always advisable that collectors keep some appropriate form of inventory for their collections. Although many collectors choose to generate and update this inventory by hand, many others choose to utilize computer software for such purposes. As there are constantly new programs manufactured for this purpose, it is my suggestion that all interested parties read any of the number of advertisements for such software that can be found in current periodicals.

AUCTION VS. OUTRIGHT SALE

Next we come to the manner of selling, whether it is outright for cash or at auction. If sold outright, one should expect to receive between 50 and 85 percent of the retail sales value. As a rule of thumb, the higher the value of the coin, the lower the margin of profit between wholesale and retail. Additionally, many high-volume coins tend to carry lower profit margins as their values tend to be more straightforward. It is worth noting that important coins and key rarities can retail for more than full guidebook prices, and in many instances for considerably above these valuations. Extreme rarities in great demand can go at two, three, and even ten times catalog value. Circulated coins of the more common variety, even ordinary uncirculated coins, often garner more mundane prices.

The discount paid from retail values of 50 to 85 percent depends upon the type of material the collection contains and the amount of work involved in selling the material. In fact, very low-priced coins may wholesale for a small fraction of their catalog value. One must always remember that a dealer is in business to earn his living and is entitled to profits for his/her efforts.

Now we come to selling at auction. This is the manner in which most of the more extensive, advanced collections are sold. It has advantages and disadvantages. While cash advances on a consignment can usually be obtained, the final settlement is usually slower than a cash sale because of the length of time it takes to handle the sale. The auctioneer is very anxious to realize as much as possible for the collection. The more he can realize, the more his commission will be. He will catalog the coins to their best advantage, and hidden or unknown rarities that otherwise might not be mentioned in an outright sale will be featured in order to get the most for the collection.

Surprises also occur that even conscientious dealers might not expect when purchasing outright. A small incremental difference in grade at the high end of the grading scale can sometimes mean a very large incremental difference in value. In such cases, grading subjectivity can result in significantly different evaluations of a coin, even among experts.

Other advantages of the auction method include a published and printed record in the catalog of the collection, complete with a prices realized list (what the collection brought for every lot). Lastly, when desired, the name of the collector is published in conjunction with the sale of the collection, crediting him/her for their efforts in compiling it.

The auction method does take time. It can take the auction house a month or more to prepare the catalog. Another month should be allowed to print and mail the catalog. Then three to five weeks should be allowed for the collectors and dealers to send in their bids. At the termination of the sale, another month should be allowed for payments to arrive for the lots sold. So one can expect to have settlement in full approximately forty-five days after the termination of the auction sale. In total, it can be five to six months between the time a consignor signs a contract with the auction house and the time the consignor is paid the proceeds.

The fee an auction house receives for their service ranges between 10 and 25 percent of the prices realized and should include all costs, insurance, advertising, printing, etc. This fee is generally split between the buyer and the seller.

Inexperienced people sometimes fear the auction method, being afraid the coins will go for a price way below value. This is not the case. Auctioneers who run large, nationwide sales cover the market so completely, as do dealers and collectors, that there is little opportunity for any lot to go for a ridiculous price. However, there are peaks and valleys in any given auction sale. Though generally coins realize within their fair market range, some coins bring surprisingly impressive results while others are realized at a lower price than expected.

The best auctions are those run by dealers who have specialized in this selling method for many years, for in so doing they have built up a clientele and a reputation that encourages good bidding. The best sales are a combination of mail bids and a public sale commenced with the high mail bid. This system brings the best prices, encourages competition, and the prices realized are publicly announced. The Internet has added an additional wrinkle to the sale of coins at auction and is also a facet to modern auction sales that any potential consignor should take into consideration.

ARE YOU QUALIFIED TO SELL YOUR COINS OUTRIGHT?

Selling a coin collection on an outright basis can be a very traumatic experience for the novice or underinformed seller. If you do not have a good handle on the value of the collection that you are selling, or you do not have a relationship with a dealer that you can trust, you are treading on treacherous ground in selling coins on an outright basis. Many sellers who find themselves unable to make a proper evaluation of the material which they are liquidating should seek out the services of an auction house. There is a high degree of safety in selling a collection at auction through the proper house. Furthermore, the level of anxiety will be greatly reduced, thereby allowing the seller considerable peace of mind.

ARE COMMISSIONS THE ONLY FACTOR TO CONSIDER WHEN SELECTING AN AUCTION HOUSE?

Although it is certainly important to consider the commission rate that an auction house is charging to both the buyer *and* the seller, there are a number of other factors which must also be studied. These factors include but are not necessarily limited to the following:

1. The strength of the mailing list (i.e., how large is the mailing list and how many of these customers receive the catalog by mail).
2. The dates of the sale and the quality of other material consigned to the sale.

3. The quality of the catalog, knowledge of the cataloging staff, and reputation of the auction house.
4. The terms given to potential buyers and how willing these buyers will be to bid under such terms.
5. The terms of any cash advance given to the consigner.
6. The timing and location of the auction sale.
7. The additional exposure the auction will receive (i.e., advertising, Internet, press releases, etc.).
8. Referrals from other consigners who have been satisfied with their experience. (The reference section in the back of this book includes a listing of many of the major auction houses and dealers in the United States. Please be reminded that we are neither endorsing nor condemning any dealer or auctioneer. This list is intended to be a tool by which potential buyers or sellers can begin to make their own judgments.)

Local club auctions. These are honest sales but they do not have the number of bidders necessary to bring the strongest prices. They are usually started with a minimum bid, which causes a good percentage of the items to be returned unsold, as no one will take up the bidding. On the other hand, a majority of those that are sold go for the minimum, which may be very low.

Part-time auctioneers. They do not have the clientele or experience to do a good job on your collection. It takes many years of experience to catalog correctly, build a reputation, and get lots of active bidding from both dealers and collectors. Despite the potential shortcomings of local and part-time auction houses, certain consigners may find such auctioneers to be a viable choice. The possibility of reduced commission rates and/or the willingness to handle smaller consignments may make such houses enticing to the right consigner.

22

THE COIN MARKET IN REVIEW

THE PULSE OF THE MARKET BASED UPON U.S. AUCTION SALES AND
MAJOR CONVENTIONS

Having seen the early part of 2001 show tremendous promise for the coin market, and the tragic events of September 11 bring uncertainty to all aspects of our life, the market direction for early 2002 was yet to be seen.

The first major auctions of the year, held in conjunction with the Florida United Numismatists Convention in Orlando, were conducted by Bowers and Merena Galleries and Heritage Rare Coin Auctions. The January 8 Bowers and Merena Rarities Sale realized an impressive $3.1 million. Heritage, in auctions that spanned the length of most of the convention, sold $10 million in numismatic properties. If dealers and collectors were harboring any doubts as to the strength of the market, their fears had been quickly alleviated.

Stack's Americana Sale, held January 15 through 17, was a landmark event for collectors of colonial coinage. This marvelous auction, featuring the Hain Family Collection of Massachusetts Silver Coinage, was a huge success. Containing over 140 lots of Massachusetts silver, as well as a multitude of other important colonial and regular issue U.S. coins and banknotes, the total prices realized exceeded $7.3 million. Highlights of the Hain sale included a record-breaking price of $207,000.00 for a very rare Willow Tree Shilling graded Extremely Fine. An excessively rare Brilliant Uncirculated 1792 Silver Centered Cent sold for $414,000.00, also a record for this issue.

The month of February confirmed that the overall market was quite strong, though there was some indication of selectivity. In particular, the price levels of both scarcer date and/or earlier type coins showed impressive strength. This strength was most noticeable among higher grade, problem-free examples. Such coins were becoming increasingly easier for dealers to sell and harder for them to replace at current levels. Two major February auctions were indicative of this market strength.

Superior Rare Coin Galleries' sale of the C. Douglas Smith and Dr.

Robert A. Shuman Collections held prior to the February Long Beach Coin & Collectibles Expo realized $1.3 million, including $115,000.00 for a PCGS MS67 1807 Capped Bust, Reverse of 1808 Half Eagle.

The Benson II Collection sold by Ira and Larry Goldberg, also just prior to the Long Beach Convention, brought $6.1 million, the highlights of which included a PCGS MS67 1893-S Morgan Dollar ($161,000.00) and an NGC PR65 1853 Arrows and Rays Half Dollar ($126,500.00).

In March, demand continued to be powerful and covered areas ranging from colonial coins to Brilliant Uncirculated rolls. Due to huge demand for premium quality coins, the auction market had become even more competitive. Average, generic coins, however, continued to languish with price levels remaining flat. Low interest rates and a weak stock market only served to fuel the market for any rare coin that was genuinely scarce, and attractive for the grade.

Stack's March 7 through 8 sale realized over $2 million, including a then record price of $126,500.00 for a proof 1884 Trade Dollar, $115,000.00 for a Choice Brilliant Uncirculated 1876-CC 20 cent piece, and $80,500.00 for a proof 1875 $3.00 gold piece.

The Bowers and Merena sale of the Wayne S. Rich Collection (March 21–23) typified the strength of the market, realizing $5.3 million; a strong $1 million over the auction house presale estimate.

It should also be noted that a market for ultrahigh-grade low population modern coins was trying to be developed by a number of dealers. Certain issues were beginning to bring exorbitant premiums. Caution is recommended to all those choosing to enter this highly speculative area of the coin market.

During April and May, the predicament of the average dealer continued to be buying, not selling coins as turbulence in the financial markets meant strong prices for tangibles such as coins. The Heritage Rare Coin Auctions May Central States Numismatic Society Sale was illustrative of this trend, realizing just over $9.8 million including $138,000.00 for an 1884 proof Trade Dollar (ex Norweb Collection) and $155,250.00 for a Gem Brilliant Uncirculated 1918/7-D nickel. The realized price for the 1884 Trade Dollar was another new record, eclipsing the Stack's coin sold just two months earlier.

By midyear, it was quite evident that this market was "for real." Prices had continued to be stable at the least, and upwardly mobile at the best, depending upon the series in question. As a result, the confidence level in the coin market in particular, and tangibles market in general, was very strong relative to the equities market. A greater and greater share of potential buyers were becoming more willing to put money in coins rather than stocks. The supply of better quality collector coins was, consequently, being greatly outstripped by demand. Numismatic website hits, new inquiries, and auction participation were all on the upswing as above-average and premium-quality coins continued to command strong prices. By June, gold prices had improved to over $325 per troy ounce and silver prices had surpassed $5.00 per troy ounce.

Two major auctions took place in June. The first sale, Superior Galleries' Robinson Brown/ Bill Weber Collections Auction, brought $1.3 million and $931,000.00, respectively. Shortly thereafter, Bowers and Merena Galleries conducted their sale of the Isaac Edmunds Collection, held in conjunction with the Mid-America Coin Expo in Rosemont, Illinois. A total of more than $2.55 million was realized, including $115,000.00 for a 1794 Silver Dollar graded PCGS EF40.

The American Numismatic Association annual summer convention (July 31–August 4), held this year in New York, proved to be the most significant event of the year. After much publicity and anticipation, the celebrated sale of the 1933 Double Eagle (ex Farouk Collection and the only example legally in collectors' hands) finally took place. The auction, a joint venture by both Sotheby's and Stack's, was held at Sotheby's York Avenue offices. After much legal wrangling—at one point it seemed that Stephen Fenton, the then owner of the coin, was headed for prison—a settlement was reached with the U.S. Mint. The settlement called for the proceeds of the sale to be split between Fenton and the U.S. Mint Enterprise Fund. For more information regarding this fascinating, highly important coin in particular, and the history of the 1933 Double Eagle in general, the interested reader is directed to obtain a copy of the auction catalog, currently available through Stack's of New York.

Years of legal proceedings, publicity, and nationwide exhibition of the coin culminated in a world record result. The winning bid of $7,590,020.00, paid by an anonymous telephone bidder, is a world record for any single American coin. This realized price decisively shattered the prior record of $4.14 million, paid for the Childs Specimen of the excessively rare 1804 Silver Dollar in 1999.

Other important auctions (a total of six were held either directly before or during the period of the ANA Convention) included sales by Superior Rare Coin Galleries, Bowers and Merena Galleries, Heritage Rare Coin Auctions, and R. M. Smythe & Company. In all, a total of more than $33.6 million was realized at these auctions. This is above and beyond the millions and millions sold on the floor of the convention itself. Other important highlights from these sales include a 1795 Draped Bust Silver Dollar NGC MS67 (Bowers and Merena) at $345,000.00, an 1870-CC Double Eagle PCGS EF40 (Bowers and Merena) at $149,500.00, an 1876-CC Half Eagle PCGS MS65 (Bowers and Merena) at $138,000.00, an 1856-O Double Eagle NGC AU55 (Heritage) at $132,250.00, an 1833 Quarter Eagle NGC MS67 (Superior) at $124,998, and an 1839 No Drapery Half Dollar PCGS PR63 (Superior) at $115,000.00. After all was said and done, the ANA Convention reaffirmed that the market was quite strong and resilient, albeit to some extent selective.

Stack's Western Reserve Historical Society Sale was the first major auction held after the "feeding frenzy" of the ANA Convention. This sale realized a solid $1.28 million and was highlighted by a price of $63,250.00 paid for a proof 1879 Flowing Hair $4.00 Stella.

The spotlight in late September focused on Bowers and Merena Galleries and their Rarities Sale. This auction, held in Beverly Hills prior to the popular Long Beach Coin & Collectibles Expo, realized over $3 million, including $109,250.00 for an MS64 1918/7-D Buffalo Nickel. Immediately following the Rarities Sale, Superior Galleries held its pre-Long Beach Fall Sale 2002. This sale garnered a total of $1.4 million, including $80,500.00 for a PCGS PR67 1895 Morgan Silver Dollar.

The month of October proved to be yet another memorable period in a year that was filled with important numismatic events. October, highlighted by both the strength of the St. Louis Silver Dollar Show and the sale of the Queller Family Collection of U.S Half Dollars by Stack's, proved to be highly important to specialists in both these areas. The Queller Sale realized $4.5 million and featured many coins that brought prices in excess of $100.000.00. Perhaps the two most important highlights were a Choice Brilliant Uncirculated 1794 Half Dollar and a Proof

1838-O Half Dollar that garnered $195,000.00 and $184,000.00, respectively.

Although the weather outside may have been chilly during the month of November, the coin market certainly remained quite hot. This continuing market strength was readily apparent at the Bowers and Merena Galleries auction sale of the Russell J. Logan & Gilbert G. Steinberg Collections. Held from November 6 through November 9, this auction garnered $7.4 million; the highlights of which included a $10.00 1850 Baldwin & Company "Cowboy" territorial gold piece PCGS MS64 ($155,250.00), an 1879 Flowing Hair $4.00 Stella PCGS PR63 Deep Cameo ($86,250.00), and a 1797 Small Eagle $10.00 gold piece PCGS AU55 ($73,600.00).

With most auction houses traditionally avoiding the distractions of the holiday season, December once again turned out to be a rather uneventful month. The only December auction of any magnitude proved to be the Stack's December 4 to 5 sale of the Vanberg Collection. Despite some negative economic news preceding the dates of the auction, this sale proved to be quite strong, garnering total pieces realized in excess of $1 million.

In summary, the 2002 coin market enjoyed impressive strength in part due to strong auction content, Internet exposure, and plenty of television publicity. Low interest rates, downward volatility on Wall Street, and greater public awareness also contributed to a banner year for numismatics. Dealers and collectors alike look forward to 2003 with great expectations!

MARKET EMPHASIS

It has been said that the three most important factors in buying real estate are location, location, and location. Likewise, for many years, during the late 1970s, and through the 1980s, the three most important factors in buying coins were condition, condition, and condition. By the end of the 1980s, however, the perceived rarity of many high-grade "generic" coins started to change in a way that forever transformed much of the coin-buying public.

Major grading services publish population reports listing the denomination, date, mint mark, and grade of every coin they encapsulate, which greatly influenced this change in perception. Although condition is still tremendously important, the current breed of collectors increasingly seeks coins that also offer an established degree of rarity. Ideally for them, a coin should be rare *and* within a grade range that will be challenging for their collecting comrades to duplicate. Rather than the average collector focusing only on coins which grade MS65 or better, today's collector may be more than happy to acquire a coin grading extremely fine, particularly if the coin in question is largely unavailable in any higher grade.

Condition has been rightfully forced to share its numismatic throne with rarity. The astute collector will be best served by keeping this fact in mind when making decisions regarding the acquisition of material.

23
THE UNITED STATES MINT 50 STATE QUARTERS™ PROGRAM

The fourth year of the U.S. Mint 50 State Quarters™ Program witnessed the issuance of coin designs featuring the states of Tennessee, Ohio, Louisiana, Indiana, and Mississippi. The circulation of these issues, along with those of 1999 (Delaware, Pennsylvania, New Jersey, Georgia, Connecticut), 2000 (Massachusetts, Maryland, South Carolina, New Hampshire, Virginia), and 2001 (New York, North Carolina, Rhode Island, Vermont, Kentucky) has resulted in a tremendous amount of exposure and newly discovered interest in numismatics amongst noncollectors. An entirely new cadre of budding numismatists, comprised largely of children in the seven- to thirteen-year-old age group, has steadfastly been searching through their parents' pocket change in an effort to obtain an example of each issue. It is the hope of many hobby leaders that this new generation of young collectors will some day be prepared to carry the numismatic torch well into the new century.

24
THE SACAGAWEA GOLDEN DOLLAR

In an effort to improve on the very limited performance and public acceptance of the Susan B. Anthony dollar, the U.S. Mint began the striking of a new one-dollar coin released in the year 2000. This new dollar, in many respects, bears similarity to its highly successful Canadian counterpart.

Similar to the Canadian "Loon" dollar and unlike the Anthony dollar, the coloration of this issue is quite different from any other U.S. coin currently in circulation. The new "golden" dollar actually is composed of a pure copper core covered by outer layers of a manganese-brass alloy (.770 copper, .120 zinc, .070 manganese, .040 nickel). Although the weight, diameter, and thickness all are identical to the Anthony dollar (this standard being maintained primarily for compatibility in dollar-coin-accepting vending machines), the edge is plain, as opposed to the reeded edge seen on the Anthony dollar.

With one of the primary criticisms of the Anthony dollar being its similarity in size, feel, and coloration to the U.S. quarter, this edge device and new coloration effectively remedies this problem. Additionally, the new design is very pleasing. The obverse bears a symbolic likeness of a young Sacagawea carrying her baby son. Sacagawea was a Shoshone woman who acted as a guide to explorers Lewis and Clark during their westward expedition. The reverse depicts a bald eagle in flight amidst a ring of stars and suitable legends.

PART THREE

Coin Values

ABBREVIATIONS USED IN THE COIN VALUE LISTS

Unc.	Uncirculated
Ex. Fine	Extremely Fine
V. Fine	Very Fine
V. Good	Very Good

25

COLONIAL COINS BEFORE THE DECLARATION OF INDEPENDENCE: 1652–1776

MASSACHUSETTS
NEW ENGLAND PIECES
Shilling

	Good	Fine
NE Shilling	20,000.00	42,500.00
NE Sixpence (8 known, very rare)	—	—
NE Threepence (Unique)	—	—
WILLOW TREE PIECES (1652)		
Willow Tree Shilling	12,500.00	35,000.00
Willow Tree Sixpence	—	37,500.00
Willow Tree Threepence (3 known, very rare)	—	—

OAK TREE SHILLING   **OAK TREE THREEPENCE**

OAK TREE PIECES (1652)

Oak Tree Shilling	1,150.00	2,850.00
Oak Tree Sixpence	1500.00	3,850.00
Oak Three Threepence	1200.00	3,150.00
Oak Tree Twopence (1662)	850.00	2,300.00

PINE TREE SHILLING   **PINE TREE THREEPENCE**

PINE TREE PIECES (1652)

Pine Tree Shilling, Large Planchet	1,100.00	2,700.00
Pine Tree Shilling, Small Planchet	1,000.00	2,500.00
Pine Tree Sixpence	700.00	2,150.00
Pine Tree Threepence	650.00	1,950.00

MARYLAND (1658)
LORD BALTIMORE COINAGE

Shilling	1,450.00	5,250.00
Sixpence	1,200.00	3,800.00
Fourpence	1,300.00	4,750.00

NEW JERSEY
MARK NEWBY COINAGE

	Good	Fine
St. Patrick Halfpenny	375.00	900.00
St. Patrick Farthing with Brass Plug on Obverse	225.00	650.00
St. Patrick Farthing without Brass Plug	225.00	650.00
St. Patrick Farthing, Silver	1,250.00	2,750.00

AMERICAN PLANTATIONS TOKEN

	Good	Fine	Unc.
(1688) James II Plantation Token, 1/24 part real—Tin	200.00	500.00	2,150.00

LONDON ELEPHANT TOKENS

	Good	Fine	Ex. Fine
(1664) Halfpenny GOD PRESERVE LONDON (Thick Planchet)	200.00	450.00	1,300.00
(1664) Halfpenny GOD PRESERVE LONDON (Thin Planchet)	250.00	675.00	2,250.00
(1664) Halfpenny GOD PRESERVE LONDON (Diagonals in center of shield)	300.00	725.00	2,850.00
(1664) Halfpenny, similar. Variety with sword in second quarter of shield instead of first (Rare)	—	—	—
(1664) Halfpenny LON DON	500.00	2,250.00	4,500.00

CAROLINA ELEPHANT TOKENS

	Good	Fine	Ex. Fine
1694 PROPRIETERS	—	7,500.00	—
1694 PROPRIETORS	2,750.00	5,750.00	12,500.00

NEW ENGLAND ELEPHANT TOKENS

	Good	Fine
1694 NEW ENGLAND (Very rare)	15,000.00	26,000.00

FRENCH COLONIES

	V. Good	V. Fine	Ex. Fine
1721 Mint Mark B, Sou	175.00	600.00	825.00
1721 Mint Mark H, Sou	100.00	300.00	500.00
1722 Sou	100.00	300.00	500.00
1722 Sou, 2 over 1	175.00	375.00	575.00
1767 Sou	75.00	225.00	525.00
1767 Sou Counterstamp "R.F."	65.00	140.00	350.00

1722 ROSA AMERICANA PENNY

WILLIAM WOOD'S COINAGE
ROSA AMERICANA

	Good	Fine	V. Fine
Twopence (no date)	100.00	275.00	550.00
1722 Twopence, Period after REX	150.00	265.00	500.00
1722 Twopence, No Period after REX	150.00	265.00	500.00
1722 Penny UTILE DULCI	85.00	225.00	350.00
1722 Penny VTILE DVLCI	85.00	225.00	375.00
1722 Halfpenny D.G.			
REX ROSA AMERI. UTILE DULCI	80.00	225.00	425.00
1722 Halfpenny DEL GRATIA			
REX UTILE DULCI	80.00	200.00	350.00
1722 Halfpenny VTILE DVLCI	500.00	1,850.00	—
1723 Twopence	100.00	250.00	425.00
1723 Penny..............................	75.00	125.00	300.00
1723 Halfpenny	85.00	150.00	325.00
1723 Halfpenny Uncrowned Rose (Rare)	725.00	1,300.00	2,500.00
1724 Penny (Rare)	—	—	5,000.00
1724 Penny (Undated)			
ROSA:SINE: SPINA (3 known)	—	—	7,500.00

1722 HIBERNIA HALFPENNY

HIBERNIA

	V. Good	V. Fine	Ex. Fine
1722 Halfpenny, First Type, Harp at Left	75.00	250.00	500.00
1722 Halfpenny, Second Type, Harp at Right	60.00	175.00	300.00
1722 Farthing	135.00	450.00	775.00
1723 Halfpenny	50.00	100.00	200.00
1723 Over 22 Halfpenny	75.00	275.00	500.00
1723 Farthing	60.00	125.00	235.00

	Good	Fine	Ex. Fine
1724 Halfpenny	50.00	100.00	450.00
1724 Farthing	75.00	175.00	625.00

HIGLEY COPPERS

	Fair	Good	Fine
1737 THE•VALVE•OF•THREE•PENCE—			
3 Hammers CONNECTICVT	—	6,500.00	18,500.00
1737 THE•VALVE•OF•THREE•PENCE—			
3 Hammers—I•AM•GOOD•COPPER	—	7,000.00	19,000.00

	Fair	Good	Fine
1737 VALUE•ME•AS•YOU•PLEASE— 3 Hammers—I•AM•GOOD•COPPER	—	6,000.00	17,000.00
1737 VALVE•ME•AS•YOU•PLEASE— 3 Hammers—I•AM•GOOD•COPPER (rare) . .	—	—	—
(1737) VALUE•ME•AS•YOU•PLEASE— Broad Axe—J•CUT•MY•WAY•THROUGH . .	—	7,000.00	19,000.00
(1737) Similar. Wheel Design (Unique)	—	—	—
1739 VALUE•ME•AS•YOU•PLEASE— Broad Axe—J•CUT•MY•WAY•THROUGH . .	—	8,500.00	21,500.00

1760 VOCE POPULI HALFPENNY

VOCE POPULI

	V. Good	V. Fine	Ex. Fine
1760 Halfpenny	85.00	240.00	500.00
1760 Halfpenny VOCE POPULI	100.00	300.00	550.00

1760 VOCE POPULI FARTHING

1760 Farthing, Large Letters	275.00	1,000.00	1,850.00
1760 Farthing, Small Letters (Rare)	600.00	4,250.00	7,750.00

1766 PITT TOKEN HALFPENNY

PITT TOKEN

1766 Halfpenny	300.00	1,050.00	1,850.00
1766 Farthing (Rare)	—	5,000.00	8,500.00

VIRGINIA HALFPENNY

VIRGINIA

	V. Good	Fine	Unc.
1773 Halfpenny, Period after GEORGIUS	65.00	100.00	800.00
1773 Halfpenny, No period after GEORGIUS ...	75.00	125.00	975.00

26
STATE COINAGE

1787 CONNECTICUT COPPER

CONNECTICUT COPPERS

	Good	Fine	V. Fine
1785 Bust Right	75.00	250.00	600.00
1785 Bust Left	200.00	600.00	1,150.00
1786 Bust Right	85.00	325.00	725.00
1786 Mailed Bust Left	65.00	225.00	500.00
1786 Draped Bust	85.00	375.00	875.00
1787 Mailed Bust Right	110.00	450.00	1,650.00
1787 Mailed Bust Left	60.00	175.00	450.00
1787 Draped Bust Left	50.00	125.00	375.00
1788 Mailed Bust Right	50.00	175.00	500.00
1788 Mailed Bust Left	50.00	150.00	450.00
1788 Draped Bust Left	50.00	200.00	500.00

(Note: There are many minor varieties of Connecticut coppers.)

1788 MASSACHUSETTS CENT

MASSACHUSETTS

	Good	Fine	Ex. Fine
1787 Cent. Arrows in Eagle's Right Talon (Ex. rare)	3,750.00	9,000.00	—
1787 Cent. Arrows in Eagle's Left Talon	75.00	200.00	1,000.00
1787 Cent. Horn (Die Break) from Eagle's Head	75.00	200.00	1,000.00
1787 Half Cent	85.00	225.00	1,000.00
1788 Cent	85.00	225.00	1,050.00
1788 Half Cent	100.00	250.00	1,050.00

NEW HAMPSHIRE

	Good	Fine	Ex. Fine
1776 New Hampshire Penny (Very rare)	20,000.00	—	—

1787 NEW JERSEY COPPER

NEW JERSEY COPPERS

	Good	Fine	V. Fine
1786 IMMUNIS COLUMBIA (Very rare)	—	—	30,000.00
1786 Date under Plow Handle (Very rare)	—	25,000.00	45,000.00
1786 No Coulter	750.00	2,500.00	4,500.00
1786 Narrow or Wide Shield	75.00	275.00	500.00
1787 Small or Large Planchet	60.00	200.00	450.00
1787 Outlined Shield	75.00	225.00	475.00
1787 Pluribs instead of Pluribus	100.00	450.00	1,100.00
1788 Horse Head Right	75.00	225.00	525.00
1788 Horse Head Left	300.00	1,100.00	2,750.00
1788 Running Fox before Legend	150.00	500.00	1,500.00

(Note: There are many minor varieties of New Jersey coppers.)

NEW YORK COPPERS

	Good	Fine	V. Fine
1786 NON VI VIRTUTE VICI	4,000.00	7,750.00	16,000.00
1786 IMMUNIS COLUMBIA	—	—	30,000.00
1787 Excelsior Eagle Right	1,750.00	4,500.00	10,000.00
1787 Excelsior Eagle Left	1,650.00	4,250.00	9,500.00
1787 Excelsior Large Eagle (Very rare)	—	—	45,000.00
1787 Excelsior. Indian	4,500.00	9,000.00	16,000.00
1787 Excelsior. George Clinton	6,750.00	15,000.00	24,000.00
1787 Indian. Eagle on Globe	8,000.00	17,000.00	28,000.00
1787 NOVA-EBORAC, Figure Right	125.00	375.00	1,000.00
1787 NOVA-EBORAC, Figure Left	110.00	350.00	850.00
1787 NOVA-EBORAC, Small Head	2,250.00	6,500.00	—
1787 NOVA-EBORAC, Large Head	500.00	1,500.00	4,000.00
1787 IMMUNIS COLUMBIA	450.00	1,200.00	2,600.00

1788 VERMONT COPPER   **1786** VERMONT LANDSCAPE COPPER

VERMONT COPPERS

	Good	Fine	V. Fine
1785 IMMUNE COLUMBIA	3,250.00	6,000.00	—
1785 Landscape, VERMONTS	200.00	950.00	2,250.00
1785 Landscape, VERMONTIS	200.00	900.00	2,100.00
1786 Landscape, VERMONTENSIUM	175.00	800.00	1,900.00
1786 Baby Head. Bust Right	300.00	1,000.00	3,350.00
1786 Bust Left	150.00	750.00	2,000.00
1787 Bust Left (Rare)	3,250.00	11,500.00	—
1787 Bust Right	125.00	450.00	1,000.00
1787 BRITANNIA on Reverse	100.00	250.00	525.00
1788	100.00	350.00	850.00
1788 GEORGIUS III REX	275.00	1,250.00	3,000.00

27

ADDITIONAL COLONIAL COINS AND TOKENS

CONTINENTAL DOLLAR

CONTINENTAL DOLLAR

	Good	Fine	Ex. Fine
1776 CURENCY, Pewter	2,850.00	5,750.00	9,750.00
1776 CURENCY, Brass (Very rare)	12,000.00	22,500.00	40,000.00
1776 CURENCY, Silver (Very rare)	—	—	—
1776 CURENCY, Pewter	3,000.00	7,250.00	12,000.00
1776 CURENCY, Pewter, E.G. Fecit	2,900.00	7,000.00	11,000.00
1776 CURENCY, Silver. E.G. Fecit (Very rare) .	—	—	—
1776 CURRENCEY, Pewter (Very rare)	—	—	—

NOVA CONSTELLATIO (SILVER)

	V. Good	Fine	Ex. Fine
1783 MARK (1000), Silver (Rare)	—	—	—
1783 QUINT (500), Silver—Type 1 (Rare)	—	—	—
1783 QUINT (500), Silver—Type 2 (Rare)	—	—	—
1783 BIT (100), Silver (Rare)	—	—	—
1783 FIVE (5) (Unique)	—	—	—

1785 NOVA CONSTELLATIO

NOVA CONSTELLATIO COPPERS

	Good	Fine	Ex. Fine
1783 CONSTELLATIO, Small U.S.	90.00	200.00	800.00
1783 CONSTELLATIO, Large U.S.	100.00	225.00	950.00
1783 CONSTELATIO, Blunt Rays	90.00	200.00	900.00

	V. Good	Fine	Ex. Fine
1785 CONSTELATIO, Blunt Rays	100.00	225.00	1,000.00
1785 CONSTELLATIO, Pointed Rays	95.00	200.00	875.00
1786 CONSTELLATIO (Very rare)	—	—	—

IMMUNE COLUMBIA COPPERS

	Good	Fine	V. Fine
1785 CONSTELLATIO (Very rare)	—	—	12,500.00
1785 CONSTELATIO (Very rare)			
Known in Copper and Gold	—	35,000.00	—
1785 George III Obverse	3,000.00	5,500.00	—
1785 VERMON AUCTORI Obverse	3,250.00	6,000.00	—

CONFEDERATIO CENTS
1785 Stars in Large or Small Circle

(All very rare)	—	—	17,500.00

FUGIO CENT

THE FUGIO CENTS

	V. Good	Fine	Ex. Fine
1787 Club Rays	350.00	675.00	3,000.00

POINTED RAYS FUGIO CENTS

1787 UNITED above STATES below (Rare)	—	—	—
1787 UNITED STATES at sides of circle	200.00	360.00	1,200.00
1787 STATES UNITED at sides of circle	200.00	340.00	1,100.00

(Note: There are several minor varieties of the Fugio cents.)

MISCELLANEOUS TOKENS
RHODE ISLAND SHIP TOKEN

	Good	Fine	Ex. Fine
1778 Wreath below Ship	250.00	600.00	1,500.00
1778 No wreath	225.00	550.00	1,250.00

NORTH AMERICAN TOKEN

	Good	Fine	V. Fine
1781	50.00	125.00	240.00

J. CHALMERS
ANNAPOLIS, MARYLAND

1783 Shilling—Birds, Long or Short Worm	850.00	2,250.00	5,000.00
1783 Shilling—Rings (Ex. rare)	—	—	—
1783 Sixpence, Small Date	1,250.00	3,000.00	7,000.00

	Good	Fine	V. Fine
1783 Sixpence, Large Date	1,100.00	2,750.00	6,500.00
1783 Threepence	1,000.00	2,400.00	5,500.00

THE BAR CENT

	Good	Fine	Ex. Fine
Undated (1785) Bar Cent	750.00	1,650.00	3,750.00

AUCTORI PLEBIS TOKEN

	Good	Fine	V. Fine
1787	100.00	275.00	575.00

BRASHER'S DOUBLOONS

1787 "E.B." on Breast or Wing (All very rare) ...	—	—	—

THE MOTT TOKEN

	Good	Fine	Ex. Fine
1789 Mott Token, Thick Planchet	150.00	300.00	1,000.00
1789 Mott Token, Thin Planchet	200.00	375.00	1,350.00

STANDISH BARRY BALTIMORE, MARYLAND

1790 Threepence (Very rare)	6,500.00	12,500.00	—

ALBANY CHURCH PENNY

(1790)	—	8,500.00	—

1792–94 KENTUCKY TOKEN

KENTUCKY TOKEN

	V. Good	V. Fine	Unc.
Cent (1792–94), Plain Edge	100.00	200.00	1,000.00
Cent, Engrailed Edge	—	525.00	2,500.00
Cent, Lettered Edge	100.00	225.00	1,100.00

FRANKLIN PRESS TOKEN

	V. Good	V. Fine	Unc.
1794	125.00	275.00	900.00

1795 TALBOT, ALLUM, AND LEE

TALBOT, ALLUM, AND LEE CENTS

	V. Good	V. Fine	Unc.
1794 With NEW YORK	85.00	260.00	1,300.00
1794 Without NEW YORK	450.00	1,300.00	5,250.00
1795	85.00	225.00	1,000.00

MYDDLETON TOKENS

	Good	Fine	Proof
1796 Copper, Proof only	—	—	8,000.00
1796 Silver, Proof only	—	—	7,250.00

WASHINGTON PIECES

	Good	Fine	Ex. Fine
1783 GEORGIUS TRIUMPHO	75.00	225.00	950.00
1783 WASHINGTON & INDEPENDENCE Small Military Bust	50.00	100.00	400.00
1783 Same, Engrailed Edge	65.00	125.00	525.00
1783 Large Military Bust	45.00	100.00	350.00
1783 Draped Bust	50.00	100.00	400.00
1783 Draped Bust with button	75.00	150.00	525.00
1783 Restrike in Copper, Proof only, Plain Edge .	—	Proof	750.00
1783 Restrike in Copper, Proof only, Engrailed Edge	—	Proof	550.00
1783 Restrike in Silver, Proof only, Engrailed Edge	—	Proof	1,250.00
1783 UNITY STATES	65.00	200.00	450.00
(1783) Double Head Cent	65.00	125.00	425.00
1784 Ugly Head (Very rare)	—	35,000	—

1791 GEORGE WASHINGTON SMALL EAGLE CENT

1791 Cent, Small Eagle	150.00	400.00	800.00

1791 GEORGE WASHINGTON LARGE EAGLE CENT

	Good	V. Fine	Ex. Fine
1791 Large Eagle	125.00	500.00	725.00
1792 WASHINGTON PRESIDENT	1,650.00	6,500.00	—
(1792) WASHINGTON BORN VIRGINIA	1,500.00	4,850.00	—

	Good	Fine	Unc.
1792 Roman Head Cent (Rare)	—	Proof	22,500.00
1795 Grate Token, Lettered Edge	100.00	250.00	1,650.00
1795 Grate Token, Reeded Edge	75.00	135.00	850.00

WASHINGTON PENNIES AND HALFPENNIES

1791 LIVERPOOL HALFPENNY	400.00	1,000.00	5,500.00

1793 GEORGE WASHINGTON SHIP HALFPENNY

	Fine	V. Fine	Ex. Fine
1793 Ship Halfpenny	225.00	375.00	700.00
(1795) Liberty & Security Penny, Lettered Edge .	225.00	400.00	850.00
1795 Liberty & Security Penny, Edge "AN ASYLUM FOR THE OPPRESSED OF ALL NATIONS"	—	—	—

1795 LIBERTY & SECURITY HALFPENNY

	Fine	V. Fine	Ex. Fine
1795 Liberty & Security Halfpenny, Plain Edge ...	140.00	275.00	550.00
1795 Liberty & Security Halfpenny, Lettered Edge	130.00	225.00	500.00
1795 Liberty & Security Halfpenny, Edge "AN ASYLUM FOR THE OPPRESSED OF ALL NATIONS"	250.00	500.00	1,150.00
1795 NORTH WALES Halfpenny	250.00	500.00	775.00

GEORGE WASHINGTON SUCCESS TOKEN, LARGE PLANCHET

SUCCESS Token Large, Plain & Reeded Edge ..	225.00	475.00	850.00

GEORGE WASHINGTON SUCCESS TOKEN, SMALL PLANCHET

SUCCESS Token Small, Plain & Reeded Edge ..	275.00	550.00	1,000.00

WASHINGTON PATTERNS BY PETER GETZ

1792 Silver (Very rare)	—	—	—
1792 Silver, Ornamental Edge (Very rare)	—	—	—
1792 Copper	4,500.00	7,250.00	10,750.00
1792 Copper, Ornamental Edge	—	—	—

28
FIRST MINT ISSUES

	Good	Fine	Unc.
1792 DISME known in Silver and Copper (Very rare)	—	30,000.00	100,000.00

	Good	Fine	Ex. Fine
1792 HALF DISME, Silver	7,500.00	17,500.00	35,000.00
1792 HALF DISME, Copper (Very rare)	—	—	—
1792 Silver Center Cent (Very rare)	—	—	130,000.00
1792 BIRCH CENT (Very rare)	—	—	210,000.00

29
HALF-CENT PIECES: 1793–1857

Note: All half cents in *fair* to about *good* condition (i.e., unmutilated but very heavily worn) are valued at about one-third of the good column.

1793 Liberty Cap half cent

LIBERTY CAP TYPE

	Mintage (in thousands)	Good	Fine	V. Fine
1793	35	1,600.00	3,450.00	5,500.00

1794 Liberty Cap half cent

1794	82	285.00	650.00	1,500.00

Liberty Cap half cent

	Mintage	Good	Fine	V. Fine
1795 Lettered Edge, Pole to Cap	140	250.00	650.00	1,450.00
1795 Lettered Edge, Punctuated Date	(included above)	260.00	750.00	1,400.00
1795 Plain Edge, Punctuated Date	(included above)	245.00	650.00	1,200.00
1795 Plain Edge, No Pole	(included above)	250.00	675.00	1,400.00
1796 Plain Edge, Pole	1	8,500.00	15,000.00	19,000.00
1796 Plain Edge, No Pole (Very rare)	(included above)	16,000.00	40,000.00	55,000.00
1797 Plain Edge, All Kinds	128	265.00	875.00	1,650.00
1797 Lettered Edge	—	1,000.00	3,750.00	8,500.00

DRAPED BUST TYPE

	Mintage (in thousands)	Good	Fine	V. Fine
1800	203	50.00	85.00	185.00
1802 2 over 0, Rev. of 1800	200	15,000.00	30,000.00	45,000.00
1802 2 over 0, New Rev.	(included above)	600.00	3,500.00	8,500.00
1803	92	50.00	100.00	275.00
1804 Stemless Wreath, All Kinds	1,055	45.00	75.00	135.00
1804 Stems to Wreath, Crosslet 4	—	45.00	75.00	120.00
1804 Stems to Wreath, Plain 4	—	50.00	165.00	275.00
1805 Stemless Wreath, All Kinds	814	50.00	80.00	140.00
1805 Small 5, Stems	—	700.00	2,250.00	4,250.00
1805 Stems to Wreath, Large 5	—	50.00	75.00	135.00
1806 Stemless, All Kinds	356	45.00	75.00	120.00
1806 Stems, Small 6	—	225.00	625.00	1,250.00
1806 Stems, Large 6	—	45.00	80.00	120.00
1807	476	45.00	75.00	150.00
1808, All Kinds	400	45.00	75.00	140.00
1808 over 7	—	135.00	575.00	1,350.00

CLASSIC HEAD TYPE

1809 over 6, All Kinds	1,155	40.00	90.00	110.00
1809	—	35.00	60.00	75.00
1810	215	35.00	95.00	200.00
1811	63	135.00	575.00	1,675.00

	Mintage (in thousands)	Good	Fine	V. Fine	Unc.
1825	63	35.00	55.00	80.00	950.00
1826	234	35.00	55.00	75.00	625.00
1828 13 Stars, All Kinds	606	35.00	55.00	65.00	350.00
1828 12 Stars	—	35.00	60.00	95.00	1,150.00
1829	487	35.00	55.00	75.00	400.00

	Mintage (in thousands)	Good	Fine	V. Fine	Unc.	Proof
1831	2	3,850.00	4,500.00	5,500.00	—	6,500.00
1832	154	35.00	55.00	65.00	375.00	5,500.00
1833	120	35.00	55.00	65.00	350.00	5,600.00
1834	141	35.00	55.00	65.00	350.00	4,500.00
1835	398	35.00	55.00	65.00	350.00	5,500.00
1836 Original	—	—	—	—	—	5,150.00
1836 Restrike	—	—	—	—	—	5,150.00

BRAIDED HAIR HALF CENT

BRAIDED HAIR TYPE

	Mintage (in thousands)	Good	Fine	Ex. Fine	Unc.	Proof
(1840–1849 Small Date, Proof only, each 4,000.00)						
1849 Large Date	40	40.00	55.00	95.00	700.00	—
1850	40	35.00	55.00	110.00	750.00	4,000.00
1851	148	30.00	50.00	75.00	325.00	4,850.00
1852 Proof only	—	—	—	—	—	4,650.00
1853	130	30.00	50.00	75.00	325.00	4,500.00
1854	55	30.00	50.00	75.00	325.00	4,500.00
1855	57	30.00	50.00	75.00	325.00	4,500.00
1856	40	30.00	55.00	85.00	335.00	4,000.00
1857	35	50.00	75.00	120.00	400.00	3,850.00

Note: In this book the value for *Unc.* is for M.S.-60 (i.e., "Mint State-60") to M.S.-63 condition. This grade range shows absolutely no wear, but may be toned, have bag or keg marks, or have an uneven strike.

30

ONE-CENT PIECES: 1793 AND FORWARD

Note: All large cents in *fair* to about *good* condition (i.e., unmutilated but very heavily worn) are valued at about one-third of the good column.

1793 CHAIN CENT

CHAIN TYPE

	Mintage (in thousands)	Good	Fine	V. Fine
1793 Chain type, AMERI	36	4,000.00	8,250.00	13,500.00
1793 Chain type, AMERICA	—	3,350.00	6,850.00	12,000.00

1793 WREATH CENT

WREATH TYPE

	Mintage (in thousands)	Good	Fine	V. Fine
1793 Wreath type, Vine and Bars on Edge, All Kinds	63	1,150.00	3,100.00	4,350.00
1793 Wreath type, Lettered Edge	—	1,200.00	3,250.00	4,600.00

LIBERTY CAP CENT

LIBERTY CAP TYPE

	Mintage (in thousands)	Good	Fine	V. Fine
1793 Liberty Cap type	11	2,850.00	8,250.00	22,500.00
1794, All Kinds	919	240.00	550.00	1,250.00
1794 Starred Rev	—	9,000.00	24,500.00	37,500.00
1795 Lettered Edge	37	250.00	575.00	1,275.00
1795 Plain Edge	502	225.00	450.00	1,100.00
1796 Liberty Cap type	110	240.00	775.00	1,600.00

1798 DRAPED BUST CENT

DRAPED BUST TYPE

	Mintage (in thousands)	Good	Fine	V. Fine
1796 Draped Bust type	363	120.00	550.00	1,275.00
1797 Stems on Wreath, All Kinds	898	85.00	250.00	500.00
1797 Stemless Wreath	—	120.00	425.00	1,450.00
1798, All Kinds	1,841	50.00	160.00	385.00
1798 over 97	—	125.00	375.00	1,650.00
1799 over 98, All Kinds	—	1,600.00	7,250.00	22,500.00
1799	42	1,500.00	7,000.00	18,500.00
1800, All Kinds	2,822	55.00	180.00	450.00
1800 over 1798	—	50.00	250.00	725.00
1800 over 1799	—	60.00	185.00	525.00
1801, All Kinds	1,363	50.00	165.00	385.00
1801 3 errors—1/000, one stem and IINITED	—	100.00	650.00	1,500.00
1801 Fraction 1/000	—	55.00	200.00	500.00

	Mintage (in thousands)	Good	Fine	V. Fine
1801 Fraction 1/100 over 1/000	—	60.00	250.00	650.00
1802, All Kinds	3,435	50.00	145.00	300.00
1802 Stemless Wreath	—	50.00	145.00	300.00
1802 Fraction 1/000	—	55.00	250.00	575.00
1803, All Kinds	3,131	45.00	145.00	325.00
1803 Large Date	—	55.00	300.00	600.00
1803 Stemless Wreath	—	45.00	165.00	375.00
1803 1/100 over 1/000	—	50.00	225.00	450.00
1804	97	700.00	2,000.00	3,350.00
1805	941	45.00	165.00	375.00
1806	348	55.00	185.00	425.00
1807, All Kinds	829	45.00	135.00	325.00
1807 over 6, Large Date	—	50.00	135.00	325.00
1807 over 6, Small Date	—	2,250.00	7,500.00	13,500.00

CLASSIC HEAD CENT

CLASSIC HEAD TYPE

1808	1,007	60.00	275.00	600.00
1809	223	115.00	425.00	1,250.00
1810, All Kinds	1,459	55.00	325.00	625.00
1810 over 9	—	50.00	325.00	625.00
1811, All Kinds	218	75.00	425.00	900.00
1811 over 10	—	70.00	525.00	1,450.00
1812	1,076	55.00	275.00	575.00
1813	418	50.00	285.00	625.00
1814 Plain 4	358	55.00	300.00	550.00
1814 Crosslet 4	(included above)	50.00	275.00	575.00

CORONET CENT

CORONET TYPE

	Mintage (in thousands)	Good	Fine	V. Fine	Unc.
1816	2,821	15.00	35.00	100.00	475.00
1817 13 Stars	3,948	15.00	27.00	70.00	400.00
1817 15 Stars	(included above)	16.00	30.00	140.00	3,250.00
1818	3,167	15.00	32.00	70.00	350.00
1819, All Kinds	2,671	15.00	30.00	70.00	400.00
1819 over 18	—	15.00	37.00	125.00	850.00
1820, All Kinds	4,408	15.00	30.00	75.00	350.00
1820 over 19	—	16.00	30.00	125.00	1,000.00
1821	389	27.00	140.00	450.00	10,000.00
1822	2,072	15.00	45.00	100.00	1,000.00
1823, All Kinds	1,262	75.00	325.00	700.00	12,750.00
1823 over 22	(included above)	65.00	275.00	575.00	12,500.00
1824, All Kinds	(included above)	17.00	40.00	200.00	1,200.00
1824 over 22	(included above)	20.00	75.00	350.00	5,250.00
1825	1,461	16.00	40.00	135.00	1,650.00
1826	1,517	15.00	30.00	95.00	950.00
1827	2,358	15.00	30.00	80.00	725.00
1828	2,261	15.00	30.00	95.00	650.00
1829	1,415	15.00	30.00	100.00	750.00
1830	1,712	15.00	25.00	75.00	650.00
1831	3,359	15.00	25.00	65.00	375.00
1832	2,362	15.00	25.00	75.00	375.00
1833	2,739	15.00	25.00	65.00	450.00
1834	1,855	17.00	30.00	75.00	375.00
1835 Type of '34, All Kinds	3,878	15.00	25.00	65.00	325.00
1835 Type of '36	—	15.00	25.00	60.00	325.00
1836	2,111	15.00	25.00	60.00	375.00
1837 Plain Hair Cord, All Kinds	5,558	15.00	25.00	55.00	350.00
1837 Beaded Hair Cord	—	15.00	25.00	55.00	325.00
1838	6,370	15.00	25,00	55.00	325.00
1839, 9 over 6	3,129	225.00	875.00	1,850.00	—

	Mintage (in thousands)	Good	Fine	V. Fine	Unc.
1839 Type of '38	(included above)	15.00	25.00	60.00	375.00
1839 Silly Head	(included above)	15.00	30.00	70.00	1,300.00
1839 Booby Head	(included above)	15.00	25.00	65.00	1,000.00
1839 Type of '40	(included above)	14.00	22.00	35.00	375.00

BRAIDED HAIR CENT

BRAIDED HAIR TYPE

	Mintage (in thousands)	Good	Fine	V. Fine	Unc.
1840	2,463	14.00	20.00	32.00	300.00
1841	1,597	14.00	20.00	32.00	325.00
1842	2,383	14.00	20.00	32.00	250.00
1843 Obverse and Reverse of 1842, All Kinds	2,428	14.00	20.00	32.00	250.00
1843 Obverse of 1842, Reverse of '44	—	16.00	40.00	100.00	1,000.00
1843 Obverse and Reverse of 1844	—	14.00	24.00	40.00	300.00
1844, All Kinds	2,399	14.00	20.00	30.00	275.00
1844/81	—	16.00	40.00	65.00	1,100.00
1845	3,895	14.00	20.00	27.00	175.00
1846	4,121	14.00	20.00	27.00	175.00
1847	6,184	14.00	20.00	30.00	175.00
1848	6,416	14.00	24.00	30.00	200.00
1849	4,179	14.00	24.00	30.00	275.00
1850	4,427	14.00	24.00	30.00	175.00
1851	9,890	14.00	24.00	30.00	175.00
1851/81	—	14.00	30.00	60.00	650.00
1852	5,063	14.00	24.00	30.00	175.00
1853	6,641	14.00	24.00	30.00	175.00
1854	4,236	14.00	24.00	30.00	175.00
1855	1,575	14.00	20.00	28.00	175.00
1856	2,690	14.00	20.00	30.00	175.00
1857	333	27.00	50.00	65.00	300.00

FLYING EAGLE CENTS: 1856–1858
COPPER-NICKEL

	Mintage (in thousands)	Good	Fine	V. Fine	Unc.	Proof
1856	1	4,300.00	5,150.00	5,600.00	9,000.00	12,500.00
1857	17,450	18.00	27.00	40.00	425.00	11,000.00
1858 Large Letters	24,600	18.00	27.00	45.00	450.00	10,000.00
1858 Small Letters .....(included above)		18.00	27.00	45.00	425.00	11,000.00

1859 COPPER NICKEL INDIAN CENT **COPPER NICKEL INDIAN CENT WITH SHIELD**

INDIAN HEAD CENTS: 1859–1909
1859–1864 COPPER-NICKEL

		Good	Fine	V. Fine	Unc.	Proof
1859	36,400	11.00	16.00	40.00	285.00	2,000.00
1860	20,566	8.00	13.00	15.00	140.00	1,500.00
1861	10,100	16.00	30.00	40.00	175.00	2,750.00
1862	28,075	7.00	10.00	15.00	110.00	875.00
1863	49,840	7.00	9.00	11.00	95.00	1,000.00
1864	13,740	14.00	27.00	40.00	140.00	1,000.00

BRONZE INDIAN CENT

1864–1909 BRONZE

	Mintage (in thousands)	Good	Fine	V. Fine	Unc.	Proof
1864 No L, All Kinds	39,234	6.00	18.00	30.00	85.00	2,000.00
1864 L on ribbon	—	47.00	95.00	115.00	350.00	40,000.00
1865	35,429	6.00	17.00	20.00	95.00	550.00
1866	9,827	37.00	55.00	85.00	250.00	375.00
1867	9,821	35.00	65.00	95.00	250.00	375.00
1868	10,267	33.00	47.00	75.00	225.00	375.00
1869, All Kinds	6,420	52.00	175.00	225.00	425.00	475.00
1869 over 9	—	110.00	210.00	290.00	500.00	—
1870	5,275	40.00	150.00	210.00	375.00	375.00
1871	3,930	52.00	215.00	260.00	485.00	450.00
1872	4,042	62.00	265.00	285.00	525.00	475.00
1873	11,677	18.00	43.00	47.00	200.00	325.00
1874	14,188	14.00	27.00	41.00	180.00	325.00
1875	13,528	14.00	42.00	45.00	180.00	375.00
1876	7,944	25.00	42.00	60.00	225.00	325.00
1877	853	470.00	775.00	925.00	2,650.00	3,000.00
1878	5,800	24.00	45.00	80.00	250.00	250.00
1879	16,231	6.00	13.00	28.00	90.00	225.00
1880	38,965	3.00	6.00	9.00	85.00	225.00
1881	39,212	3.00	6.00	7.00	55.00	225.00
1882	38,581	3.00	5.00	8.00	70.00	225.00
1883	45,598	3.00	4.00	6.00	55.00	225.00
1884	23,262	3.00	6.00	11.00	95.00	225.00
1885	11,265	6.00	11.00	21.00	135.00	225.00
1886	17,654	3.00	15.00	40.00	170.00	250.00
1887	45,226	2.00	3.00	5.00	50.00	225.00
1888	37,494	2.00	4.00	6.00	90.00	225.00
1889	48,869	2.00	3.00	5.00	50.00	225.00
1890	57,183	2.00	3.00	4.00	50.00	225.00
1891	47,072	2.00	3.00	5.00	50.00	225.00
1892	37,650	2.00	3.00	5.00	50.00	225.00
1893	46,642	2.00	3.00	5.00	50.00	225.00
1894	16,572	3.00	8.00	12.00	60.00	225.00
1895	38,344	2.00	3.00	4.00	40.00	225.00
1896	39,057	2.00	3.00	4.00	40.00	225.00
1897	50,466	2.00	2.00	4.00	40.00	200.00
1898	49,823	2.00	3.00	4.00	40.00	200.00

	Mintage (in thousands)	Good	Fine	V. Fine	Unc.	Proof
1899	53,600	2.00	2.00	3.00	40.00	200.00
1900	66,834	1.00	2.00	3.00	30.00	200.00
1901	79,611	1.00	2.00	3.00	30.00	200.00
1902	87,377	1.00	2.00	3.00	30.00	200.00
1903	85,094	1.00	2.00	3.00	30.00	200.00
1904	61,328	1.00	2.00	3.00	30.00	200.00
1905	80,719	1.00	2.00	3.00	30.00	200.00
1906	96,022	1.00	2.00	3.00	30.00	200.00
1907	108,139	1.00	2.00	3.00	30.00	225.00
1908	32,328	1.00	2.00	3.00	30.00	200.00
1908S	1,115	50.00	65.00	70.00	240.00	—
1909	14,371	3.00	4.00	4.00	35.00	210.00
1909S	309	265.00	320.00	365.00	475.00	—

LINCOLN CENT WITH WHEAT EARS

LINCOLN HEAD CENTS: 1909–DATE

	Mintage (in thousands)	Good	Fine	Ex. Fine	Unc.	Proof
1909 V D B	27,995	4.00	4.00	5.00	10.00	3,000.00
1909 S. V D B	484	450.00	575.00	600.00	850.00	—
1909	72,703	2.00	2.00	3.00	15.00	300.00
1909S	1,825	40.00	62.00	110.00	160.00	—
1910	146,801	—	—	3.00	20.00	275.00
1910S	6,045	7.00	8.00	21.00	65.00	—
1911	101,178	—	1.00	5.00	27.00	275.00
1911D	12,672	5.00	8.00	36.00	95.00	—
1911S	4,026	15.00	18.00	40.00	185.00	—
1912	68,153	2.00	2.00	10.00	35.00	320.00
1912D	10,411	5.00	7.00	42.00	160.00	—
1912S	4,431	10.00	15.00	42.00	130.00	—
1913	76,532	1.00	2.00	13.00	30.00	300.00
1913D	15,804	3.00	4.00	26.00	100.00	—
1913S	6,101	6.00	8.00	32.00	170.00	—
1914	75,238	—	2.00	10.00	40.00	275.00
1914D	1,193	100.00	175.00	465.00	1,500.00	—
1914S	4,137	9.00	12.00	45.00	325.00	—
1915	29,092	2.00	4.00	36.00	75.00	275.00
1915D	22,050	2.00	2.00	11.00	70.00	—
1915S	4,833	6.00	8.00	35.00	180.00	—
1916	131,834	—	—	4.00	20.00	450.00
1916D	35,956	—	1.00	9.00	75.00	—
1916S	22,510	1.00	2.00	10.00	85.00	—

	Mintage (in thousands)	Good	Fine	Ex. Fine	Unc.	Proof
1917	196,430	—	—	4.00	20.00	—
1917D	55,120	—	1.00	8.00	75.00	—
1917S	32,620	—	1.00	7.00	100.00	—
1918	288,103	—	—	4.00	20.00	—
1918D	47,830	—	1.00	7.00	85.00	—
1918S	34,680	—	1.00	8.00	100.00	—
1919	392,021	—	—	2.00	18.00	—
1919D	57,154	—	1.00	5.00	70.00	—
1919S	139,760	—	1.00	3.00	55.00	—
1920	310,165	—	—	2.00	15.00	—
1920D	49,280	—	1.00	8.00	70.00	—
1920S	46,220	—	1.00	7.00	140.00	—
1921	39,157	—	1.00	5.00	50.00	—
1921S	15,274	1.00	2.00	16.00	145.00	—
1922D, All Kinds	7,160	8.00	10.00	23.00	75.00	—
1922 No "D"	—	360.00	500.00	1,475.00	9,500.00	—
1923	74,723	—	—	3.00	17.00	—
1923S	8,700	2.00	3.00	21.00	250.00	—
1924	75,178	—	—	3.00	30.00	—
1924D	2,520	9.00	13.00	80.00	250.00	—
1924S	11,698	1.00	2.00	12.00	135.00	—
1925	139,949	—	—	2.00	15.00	—
1925D	22,580	—	1.00	8.00	55.00	—
1925S	26,380	—	1.00	6.00	100.00	—
1926	157,088	—	—	2.00	11.00	—
1926D	28,020	—	1.00	6.00	65.00	—
1926S	4,550	2.00	5.00	13.00	160.00	—
1927	144,440	—	—	2.00	12.00	—
1927D	27,170	—	1.00	4.00	60.00	—
1927S	14,276	1.00	2.00	9.00	80.00	—
1928	134,116	—	—	1.00	11.00	—
1928D	31,170	—	—	3.00	40.00	—
1928S	17,266	—	1.00	4.00	65.00	—
1929	185,262	—	—	1.00	10.00	—
1929D	41,730	—	—	3.00	25.00	—
1929S	50,148	—	—	3.00	15.00	—
1930	157,415	—	—	1.00	5.00	—
1930D	40,100	—	—	2.00	18.00	—
1930S	24,286	—	—	1.00	11.00	—
1931	19,396	—	1.00	2.00	22.00	—
1931D	4,480	3.00	4.00	8.00	65.00	—
1931S	866	37.00	45.00	55.00	80.00	—
1932	9,062	1.00	2.00	3.00	20.00	—
1932D	10,500	1.00	2.00	2.00	22.00	—
1933	14,360	1.00	2.00	3.00	20.00	—
1933D	6,200	2.00	3.00	5.00	17.00	—
1934	219,080	—	—	1.00	7.00	—

	Mintage (in thousands)	Good	Fine	Ex. Fine	Unc.	Proof
1934D	28,446	—	—	1.00	20.00	—
1935	345,388	—	—	1.00	5.00	—
1935D	47,000	—	—	1.00	5.00	—
1935S	38,702	—	—	1.00	22.00	—
1936	309,638	—	—	1.00	2.00	200.00
1936D	40,620	—	—	1.00	4.00	—
1936S	29,130	—	—	1.00	4.00	—
1937	309,179	—	—	1.00	2.00	75.00
1937D	56,430	—	—	1.00	3.00	—
1937S	34,500	—	—	1.00	4.00	—
1938	157,697	—	—	1.00	3.00	45.00
1938D	20,010	—	—	1.00	4.00	—
1938S	15,180	—	—	1.00	4.00	—
1939	316,480	—	—	—	2.00	45.00
1939D	15,160	—	—	1.00	4.00	—
1939S	52,079	—	—	1.00	4.00	—
1940	586,826	—	—	—	1.00	30.00
1940D	81,390	—	—	—	2.00	—
1940S	112,940	—	—	—	3.00	—
1941	887,039	—	—	—	2.00	30.00
1941D	128,700	—	—	—	3.00	—

	Mintage (in thousands)	Unc.	Proof
1941S	92,360	4.00	—
1942	657,827	1.00	30.00
1942D	206,688	1.00	—
1942S	85,590	8.00	—
1943 Steel	684,629	1.00	—
1943D Steel	217,660	2.00	—
1943S Steel	191,550	5.00	—
1944 Copper Resumed	1,435,400	1.00	—
1944D	430,578	1.00	—
1944S	282,760	1.00	—
1945	1,040,515	1.00	—
1945D	226,268	1.00	—
1945S	181,770	1.00	—
1946	991,655	1.00	—
1946D	315,690	1.00	—
1946S	198,100	1.00	—
1947	190,555	1.00	—
1947D	194,750	1.00	—
1947S	99,000	1.00	—
1948	317,570	1.00	—
1948D	172,638	1.00	—
1948S	81,735	1.00	—
1949	217,775	1.00	—

	Mintage (in thousands)	Unc.	Proof
1949D	153,133	1.00	—
1949S	64,290	2.00	—
1950	272,686	—	30.00
1950D	334,950	—	—
1950S	118,550	1.00	—
1951	284,634	1.00	30.00
1951D	625,355	—	—
1951S	136,010	1.00	—
1952	186,857	1.00	20.00
1952D	746,130	—	—
1952S	137,800	2.00	—
1953	256,884	—	15.00
1953D	700,515	—	—
1953S	181,835	—	—
1954	71,873	—	5.00
1954D	251,553	—	—
1954S	96,190	—	—
1955	330,958	—	5.00

	Mintage (in thousands)	Fine	Ex. Fine	Unc.	Proof
1955 Double Die Obverse	—	450.00	600.00	1,450.00	—
1955D	563,258	—	—	—	—
1955S	44,610	—	—	1.00	—
1956	421,414	—	—	—	2.00
1956D	1,098,201	—	—	—	—
1957	283,788	—	—	—	1.00
1957D	1,051342	—	—	—	—
1958	253,401	—	—	—	1.00
1958D	800,953	—	—	—	—

LINCOLN CENT WITH MEMORIAL REVERSE

MEMORIAL REVERSE TYPE

	Mintage (in thousands)	Fine	Ex. Fine	Unc.	Proof
1959	610,864	—	—	—	1.00
1959D	1,279,760	—	—	—	—
1960 Large Date, All Kinds	588,097	—	—	—	1.00
1960 Small Date	—	—	1.00	3.00	10.00
1960D Large Date, All Kinds	1,580,884	—	—	—	—
1960D Small Date	—	—	—	—	—
1961	756,373	—	—	—	1.00

	Mintage (in thousands)	Fine	V. Fine	Unc.	Proof
1961D	1,753,267	—	—	—	—
1962	609,263	—	—	—	1.00
1962D	1,793,148	—	—	—	
1963	757,186	—	—	—	1.00
1963D	1,774,020	—	—		
1964	2,652,526	—	—	—	1.00
1964D	3,799,072	—	—	—	
1965	1,497,225	—	—	—	
1966	2,188,148	—	—	—	
1967	3,048,667	—	—	—	
1968	1,707,881	—	—	—	
1968D	2,886,270	—	—	—	
1968S	261,312	—	—	—	1.00
1969	1,136,910	—	—	—	
1969D	4,1102,832	—	—	—	
1969S	547,310	—	—	—	1.00
1970	1,898,315	—	—	—	
1970D	2,891,439	—	—	—	
1970S Large Date	693,193	—	—	—	1.00
1970S Small Date	(included above)	—	5.00	28.00	50.00
1971	1,919,490	—	—	—	
1971D	2,911,046	—	—	—	
1971S	528,354	—	—	—	1.00
1972	2,933,255	—	—	—	
1972 Double Die Obverse		135.00	150.00	250.00	
1972D	2,665,071	—	—	—	
1972S	380,200	—	—	—	1.00
1973	3,728,245	—	—	—	
1973D	3,549,577	—	—	—	
1973S	3,191,938	—	—	—	1.00
1974	4,232,141	—	—	—	
1974D	4,335,098	—	—	—	
1974S	412,039	—	—	—	1.00
1975	5,451,476	—	—	—	
1975D	4,505,245	—	—	—	
1975S Proof only	2,909	—	—	—	4.00
1976 P&D	8,895,885	—	—	—	
1976S Proof only	4,150	—	—	—	3.00
1977 P&D	8,663,992	—	—	—	
1977S Proof only	3,251	—	—	—	2.00
1978 P&D	9,838,838	—	—	—	
1978S Proof only	3,128	—	—	—	2.00
1979 P&D	10,157,872	—	—	—	
1979S Proof only, Type I	3,677	—	—	—	3.00
1979S Proof only, Type II, Sharp Mint Mark	—	—	—	—	3.00

	Mintage (in thousands)	Fine	V. Fine	Unc.	Proof
1980 P&D	12,554,803	—	—	—	—
1980S Proof only	3,555	—	—	—	1.00
1981 P&D	12,864,985	—	—	—	—
1981S Proof only	4,063	—	—	—	2.00
1982 P&D	16,725,504	—	—	—	—
1982S Proof only	3,857	—	—	—	3.00
1983 P&D	14,219,554	—	—	—	—
1983 Doubled Die Reverse	—	—	—	200.00	—
1983S Proof only	3,279	—	—	—	3.00
1984 P&D	13,710,218	—	—	—	—
1984 Double Ear	—	—	—	150.00	—
1984S Proof only	3,065	—	—	—	3.00
1985 P&D	10,935,889	—	—	—	—
1985S Proof only	3,367	—	—	—	5.00
1986 P&D	8,934,262	—	—	—	—
1986S Proof only	3,010	—	—	—	6.00
1987 P&D	9,561,856	—	—	—	—
1987S Proof only	4,228	—	—	—	3.00
1988 P&D	11,346,550	—	—	—	—
1988S Proof only	3,263	—	—	—	11.00
1989 P&D	12,606,002	—	—	—	—
1989S Proof only	3,220	—	—	—	11.00
1990 P&D	11,774,660	—	—	—	—
1990S Proof only	3,300	—	—	—	5.00
1990 Proof without S	—	—	—	—	2,500.00
1991 P&D	9,324,382	—	—	—	—
1991S Proof only	2,868	—	—	—	20.00
1992 P&D	9,007,578	—	—	—	—
1992S Proof only	4,177	—	—	—	4.00
1993 P&D	12,111,356	—	—	—	—
1993S Proof only	3,395	—	—	—	6.00
1994 P&D	13,632,615	—	—	—	—
1994S Proof only	3,270	—	—	—	6.00
1995 P&D	13,540,000	—	—	—	—
1995 Doubled Die Obverse	—	—	—	40.00	—
1995S Proof only	—	—	—	—	7.00
1996 P&D	13,123,260	—	—	—	—
1996S Proof only	—	—	—	—	3.00
1997 P&D	9,199,355	—	—	—	—
1997S Proof only	1,975	—	—	—	9.00
1998 P&D	10,257,509	—	—	—	—
1998S Proof only	—	—	—	—	8.00
1999 P&D	11,597,665	—	—	—	—
1999S Proof only	—	—	—	—	4.00
2000 P&D	14,277,420	—	—	—	—
2000S Proof Only	—	—	—	—	3.00
2001 P&D	—	—	—	—	—
2001S Proof Only	—	—	—	—	3.00

31
TWO-CENT PIECES: 1864–1873

TWO-CENT PIECE

	Mintage (in thousands)	Good	Fine	Unc.	Proof
1864 Small Motto	19,848	60.00	110.00	800.00	30,000.00
1864 Large Motto	(included above)	12.00	20.00	115.00	750.00
1865	13,460	12.00	20.00	115.00	500.00
1866	3,177	13.00	20.00	125.00	500.00
1867	2,939	13.00	20.00	135.00	500.00
1868	2,804	13.00	20.00	150.00	500.00
1869	1,547	13.00	20.00	125.00	500.00
1870	861	13.00	22.00	200.00	500.00
1871	721	13.00	24.00	225.00	500.00
1872	65	110.00	200.00	1,050.00	575.00
1873	1	850.00	925.00	—	1,400.00

Note: Uncirculated two-cent pieces with full, original "mint red" color sell at a premium price.

32
NICKEL THREE-CENT PIECES: 1865–1889

NICKEL THREE-CENT PIECE

	Mintage (in thousands)	Good	Fine	Unc.	Proof
1865	11,382	11.00	14.00	110.00	1,750.00
1866	4,801	11.00	14.00	110.00	450.00
1867	3,915	11.00	14.00	110.00	450.00
1868	3,252	11.00	14.00	110.00	475.00

	Mintage (in thousands)	Good	Fine	Unc.	Proof
1869	1,604	11.00	14.00	120.00	375.00
1870	1,335	11.00	14.00	130.00	400.00
1871	604	11.00	14.00	140.00	400.00
1872	862	11.00	14.00	160.00	325.00
1873	1,173	11.00	14.00	130.00	325.00
1874	790	11.00	14.00	135.00	360.00
1875	228	11.00	14.00	150.00	400.00
1876	162	12.00	17.00	175.00	325.00
1877	1	850.00	900.00	—	1,250.00
1878	2	425.00	450.00	—	485.00
1879	4	45.00	70.00	285.00	300.00
1880	25	70.00	95.00	300.00	300.00
1881	1,681	11.00	14.00	130.00	300.00
1882	25	70.00	90.00	300.00	300.00
1883	11	135.00	190.00	525.00	300.00
1884	6	280.00	425.00	800.00	300.00
1885	5	350.00	500.00	725.00	325.00
1886	4	240.00	250.00	—	300.00
1887, All Kinds	8	225.00	250.00	425.00	310.00
1887 over 6	—	280.00	300.00	—	400.00
1888	4	35.00	47.00	275.00	300.00
1889	2	63.00	95.00	300.00	300.00

33
NICKEL FIVE-CENT PIECES: 1866 AND FORWARD

SHIELD TYPE

SHIELD NICKEL WITH RAYS 1866–1867

	Mintage (in thousands)	Good	Fine	Unc.	Proof
1866	14,743	17.00	24.00	285.00	2,250.00
1867 Rays	2,019	18.00	27.00	375.00	40,000.00

SHIELD NICKEL, NO RAYS 1867–1883

	Mintage	Good	Fine	Unc.	Proof
1867 Without Rays	28,891	13.00	17.00	130.00	575.00
1868	28,817	13.00	17.00	130.00	475.00
1869	16,395	13.00	17.00	130.00	375.00
1870	4,806	13.00	20.00	175.00	365.00
1871	561	38.00	55.00	375.00	365.00
1872	6,036	13.00	17.00	185.00	350.00
1873	4,550	13.00	20.00	185.00	325.00
1874	3,538	14.00	26.00	200.00	360.00
1875	2,097	15.00	33.00	250.00	425.00
1876	2,530	14.00	25.00	170.00	350.00
1877	1	925.00	1,050.00	—	1,400.00
1878	2	425.00	470.00	—	500.00
1879	29	250.00	385.00	600.00	425.00
1880	20	280.00	425.00	1,600.00	350.00
1881	72	145.00	250.00	625.00	325.00
1882	11,476	13.00	17.00	130.00	325.00
1883	1,457	14.00	18.00	130.00	325.00
1883 over 2	—	75.00	135.00	600.00	—

Note: Choice, well-struck uncirculated shield nickels, especially 1866–74, are worth more than the listed prices

LIBERTY HEAD TYPE

LIBERTY HEAD NICKEL

	Mintage (in thousands)	Good	Fine	Unc.	Proof
1883 Without CENTS	5,480	5.00	6.00	35.00	350.00
1883 With CENTS	16,033	9.00	15.00	95.00	225.00
1884	11,274	13.00	19.00	150.00	250.00

	Mintage (in thousands)	Good	Fine	Unc.	Proof
1885	1,476	300.00	400.00	875.00	675.00
1886	3,330	110.00	160.00	600.00	290.00
1887	15,264	8.00	22.00	115.00	225.00
1888	10,720	15.00	25.00	165.00	225.00
1889	15,881	6.00	17.00	110.00	225.00
1890	16,259	6.00	17.00	130.00	225.00
1891	16,834	5.00	12.00	125.00	225.00
1892	11,700	5.00	14.00	110.00	225.00
1893	13,370	4.00	13.00	100.00	225.00
1894	5,413	8.00	60.00	225.00	225.00
1895	9,980	3.00	17.00	120.00	225.00
1896	8,843	5.00	20.00	140.00	225.00
1897	20,429	3.00	9.00	100.00	225.00
1898	12,532	2.00	9.00	125.00	225.00
1899	26,029	2.00	5.00	90.00	225.00
1900	27,256	2.00	5.00	95.00	225.00
1901	26,480	2.00	5.00	75.00	225.00
1902	31,490	2.00	4.00	75.00	225.00
1903	28,007	2.00	4.00	75.00	225.00
1904	21,405	2.00	4.00	75.00	250.00
1905	29,827	2.00	4.00	75.00	225.00
1906	38,614	2.00	3.00	75.00	225.00
1907	39,215	2.00	3.00	75.00	225.00
1908	22,686	2.00	3.00	75.00	225.00
1909	11,591	3.00	3.00	80.00	225.00
1910	30,169	2.00	3.00	75.00	225.00
1911	39,559	2.00	3.00	75.00	225.00
1912	26,237	2.00	3.00	75.00	225.00
1912D	8,474	2.00	6.00	235.00	—
1912S	238	65.00	110.00	950.00	—
1913 Liberty Head	(5 struck)	—	—	—	—

INDIAN HEAD OR BUFFALO TYPE

Type I Buffalo nickel 1913

	Mintage (in thousands)	Good	Fine	Unc.	Matte Proof
1913 Var. 1	30,994	7.00	8.00	35.00	1,250.00
1913D Var. 1	5,337	9.00	13.00	50.00	—
1913S Var. 1	2,105	18.00	26.00	85.00	—

TYPE II BUFFALO NICKEL 1913–1938

	Mintage (in thousands)	Good	Fine	Unc.	Matte Proof
1913 Var. 2	29,859	8.00	9.00	40.00	875.00
1913D Var. 2	4,156	52.00	80.00	190.00	
1913S Var. 2	1,209	135.00	210.00	450.00	—
1914	20,666	14.00	15.00	60.00	825.00
1914D	3,912	52.00	75.00	285.00	—
1914S	3,470	14.00	23.00	225.00	—
1915	20,987	5.00	6.00	50.00	825.00
1915D	7,570	12.00	25.00	225.00	—
1915S	1,505	18.00	48.00	550.00	—
1916	63,498	4.00	5.00	45.00	1,100.00
1916 Doubled Die Obverse	—	1750.00	6250.00	45,000.00	—
1916D	13,333	8.00	16.00	165.00	—
1916S	11,860	5.00	12.00	185.00	—
1917	51,224	4.00	5.00	75.00	7,500.00
1917D	9,911	9.00	25.00	400.00	—
1917S	4,193	14.00	36.00	500.00	—
1918	32,086	3.00	5.00	145.00	—
1918D, All Kinds	8,362	8.00	27.00	500.00	—
1918D over 7	—	375.00	1,250.00	25,000.00	—
1918S	4,882	8.00	29.00	725.00	—
1919	60,868	1.00	2.00	65.00	—
1919D	8,006	9.00	32.00	700.00	—
1919S	7,521	5.00	28.00	625.00	—
1920	63,093	1.00	2.00	70.00	—
1920D	9,418	6.00	25.00	700.00	—
1920S	9,689	3.00	20.00	625.00	—
1921	10,663	2.00	3.00	145.00	—
1921S	1,557	32.00	95.00	1,500.00	—
1923	35,715	2.00	3.00	70.00	—
1923S	6,142	4.00	10.00	500.00	—
1924	21,620	1.00	2.00	75.00	—
1924D	5,258	4.00	16.00	525.00	—
1924S	1,437	8.00	65.00	2,350.00	—
1925	35,565	2.00	3.00	55.00	—
1925D	4,450	6.00	30.00	385.00	—
1925S	6,256	4.00	15.00	625.00	—
1926	44,693	1.00	2.00	35.00	—
1926D	5,638	4.00	20.00	300.00	—
1926S	970	13.00	50.00	4,750.00	—

118

	Mintage (in thousands)	Good	Fine	Unc.	Proof
1927	37,981	1.00	2.00	45.00	—
1927D	5,730	2.00	6.00	185.00	—
1927S	3,430	2.00	5.00	725.00	—
1928	23,411	1.00	2.00	35.00	—
1928D	6,436	1.00	4.00	60.00	—
1928S	6,936	2.00	3.00	285.00	—
1929	36,446	1.00	2.00	40.00	—
1929D	8,370	1.00	2.00	70.00	—
1929S	7,754	1.00	1.00	50.00	—
1930	22,849	1.00	1.00	40.00	—
1930S	5,435	1.00	1.00	60.00	—
1931S	1,200	10.00	11.00	55.00	—
1934	20,213	1.00	1.00	40.00	—
1934D	7,480	1.00	2.00	60.00	—
1935	58,264	1.00	1.00	25.00	—
1935D	12,092	1.00	2.00	55.00	—
1935S	10,300	1.00	1.00	50.00	—
1936	119,001	1.00	1.00	23.00	825.00
1936D	24,814	1.00	1.00	30.00	—
1936S	14,930	1.00	1.00	30.00	—
1937	79,486	1.00	1.00	17.00	775.00
1937D, All Kinds	17,826	1.00	1.00	25.00	—
1937D, 3-Legged Var	—	180.00	300.00	1,750.00	—
1937S	5,635	1.00	1.00	25.00	—
1938D, All Kinds	7,020	1.00	2.00	18.00	—
1938D/S	—	5.00	9.00	50.00	—

JEFFERSON NICKEL

JEFFERSON TYPE

	Mintage (in thousands)	Fine	Ex. Fine	Unc.	Proof
1938	19,515	—	1.00	6.00	45.00
1938D	5,376	1.00	2.00	5.00	—
1938S	4,105	2.00	3.00	6.00	—
1939	120,628	—	—	2.00	40.00
1939D	3,514	5.00	12.00	55.00	—
1939S	6,630	1.00	4.00	23.00	—
1940	176,499	—	—	1.00	35.00
1940D	43,540	—	—	2.00	—

	Mintage (in thousands)	Fine	Ex. Fine	Unc.	Proof
1940S	39,690	—	1.00	3.00	—
1941	203,284	—	—	1.00	33.00
1941D	53,432	—	—	3.00	—
1941S	43,445	—	1.00	4.00	—
1942	49,819	—	—	7.00	40.00
1942D	13,938	—	3.00	35.00	—
1942P Wartime Silver Nickels ...	57,901	1.00	2.00	8.00	100.00
1942S	32,900	1.00	2.00	8.00	—
1943P	271,165	1.00	2.00	6.00	—
1943D	15,294	1.00	2.00	7.00	—
1943S	104,060	1.00	2.00	4.00	—
1944P	119,150	1.00	2.00	7.00	—
1944D	32,309	1.00	2.00	9.00	—
1944S	21,640	1.00	2.00	5.00	—
1945P	119,408	1.00	2.00	5.00	—
1945D	37,158	1.00	2.00	5.00	—
1945S	58,939	1.00	2.00	5.00	—
1946 Regular Nickels, Resumed .	161,116	—	—	2.00	—
1946D	45,292	—	—	2.00	—
1946S	13,560	—	—	1.00	—
1947	95,000	—	—	1.00	—
1947D	37,822	—	—	1.00	—
1947S	24,720	—	—	1.00	—
1948	89,348	—	—	1.00	—
1948D	44,734	—	—	1.00	—
1948S	11,300	—	—	2.00	—
1949	60,652	—	—	3.00	—
1949D	36,498	—	—	2.00	—
1949S	9,716	—	1.00	2.00	—
1950	9,847	—	—	2.00	30.00
1950D	2,630	5.00	7.00	8.00	—

	Mintage (in thousands)	Unc.	Proof
1951	28,610	3.00	23.00
1951D	20,460	4.00	—
1951S	7,776	2.00	—
1952	64,070	1.00	15.00
1952D	30,638	3.00	—
1952S	20,572	1.00	—
1953	46,773	—	10.00
1953D	59,873	—	—
1953S	19,211	1.00	—
1954	47,914	1.00	7.00
1954D	117,183	—	—
1954S	29,384	2.00	—
1955	8,266	1.00	5.00

	Mintage (in thousands)	Unc.	Proof
1955D	74,464	—	—
1956	35,885	—	2.00
1956D	67,223	—	—
1957	39,656	—	1.00
1957D	136,829	—	—
1958	17,964	—	2.00
1958D	168,249	—	—
1959	28,397	—	1.00
1959D	160,738	—	—
1960	57,108	—	1.00
1960D	192,343	—	—
1961	76,668	—	1.00
1961D	229,343	—	—
1962	100,602	—	1.00
1962D	280,196	—	—
1963	178,852	—	1.00
1963D	276,829	—	—
1964	1,028,623	—	1.00
1964D	1,787,297	—	—
1965	136,131	—	—
1966	156,208	—	—
1967	107,326	—	—
1968D	91,228	—	—
1968S	103,438	—	1.00
1969D	202,808	—	—
1969S	123,100	—	1.00
1970D	515,485	—	—
1970S	241,465	—	1.00
1971	106,884	—	—
1971D	316,145	—	—
1971S Proof only	3,224	—	2.00
1972	202,036	—	—
1972D	351,695	—	—
1972S Proof only	3,268	—	2.00
1973	384,396	—	—
1973D	261,405	—	—
1973S Proof only	2,770	—	2.00
1974	601,752	—	—
1974D	277,373	—	—
1974S Proof only	2,617	—	2.00
1975	181,772	—	—
1975D	401,875	—	—
1975S Proof only	2,909	—	2.00
1976 P-D	931,088	—	—
1976S Proof only	4,150	—	2.00
1977 P&D	882,689	—	—
1977S Proof only	3,251	—	2.00

	Mintage (in thousands)	Unc.	Proof
1978 P&D	704,402	—	—
1978S Proof only	3,128	—	2.00
1979 P&D	819,056	—	—
1979S Type I Proof only	3,677	—	1.00
1979S Type Two Proof only	—	—	2.00
1980 P&D	1,095,327	—	—
1980S Proof only	3,555	—	1.00
1981 P&D	1,022,306	—	—
1981S Proof only	4,063	—	2.00
1982 P&D	666,082	2.00	—
1982S Proof only	3,857	—	3.00
1983 P&D	1,098,341	2.00	—
1983S Proof only	3,279	—	3.00
1984 P&D	1,264,444	—	—
1984S Proof only	3,065	—	4.00
1985 P&D	10,935,889	—	—
1985S Proof only	3,363	—	3.00
1986 P&D	8,934,262	1.00	—
1986S Proof only	3,010	—	7.00
1987 P&D	9,561,856	—	—
1987S Proof only	4,228	—	3.00
1988 P&D	11,346,550	—	—
1988S Proof only	3,263	—	6.00
1989 P&D	1,469,654	—	—
1989S Proof only	3,220	—	4.00
1990 P&D	1,325,575	—	—
1990S Proof only	3,300	—	4.00
1991 P&D	1,050,601	—	—
1991S Proof only	2,868	—	4.00
1992 P&D	850,107	1.00	—
1992S Proof only	4,177	—	2.00
1993 P&D	818,160	—	—
1993S Proof only	3,395	—	3.00
1994 P&D	1,437,922	—	—
1994 Special Frosted Unc.	168	65.00	—
1994S Proof only	3,270	—	3.00
1995 P&D	1,662,268	—	—
1995S Proof only	—	—	4.00
1996 P&D	1,647,068	—	—
1996S Proof only	—	—	2.00
1997 P&D	937,612	—	—
1997 Special Frosted Unc.	25	150.00	—
1997S Proof only	—	—	4.00
1998 P&D	1,323,632	—	—
1998S Proof only	—	—	3.00
1999 P&D	2,278,720	—	—

	Mintage (in thousands)	Unc.	Proof
1999S Proof only	—	—	3.00
2000 P&D	2,355,760	—	—
2000S Proof only	—	—	2.00
2001 P&D	1,303,384	—	—
2001S Proof only	—	—	2.00
2002 P&D	—	—	—
2002 Proof only	—	—	3.00

34
SILVER THREE-CENT PIECES: 1851–1873

THREE-CENT SILVER PIECE

	Mintage (in thousands)	Good	Fine	Unc.	Proof
1851	5,447	22.00	26.00	175.00	—
1851O	720	24.00	35.00	325.00	—
1852	18,664	22.00	26.00	175.00	—
1853	11,400	22.00	26.00	175.00	—
1854	671	22.00	26.00	400.00	16,000.00
1855	139	24.00	50.00	575.00	7,500.00
1856	1,458	22.00	26.00	350.00	5,000.00
1857	1,042	22.00	26.00	360.00	4,250.00
1858	1,604	22.00	26.00	285.00	3,250.00
1859	365	20.00	26.00	175.00	550.00
1860	287	20.00	26.00	200.00	625.00
1861	498	20.00	26.00	175.00	500.00
1862	344	20.00	26.00	175.00	475.00
1863	21	275.00	310.00	675.00	500.00
1864	12	275.00	310.00	625.00	500.00
1865	9	325.00	375.00	725.00	550.00
1866	23	275.00	310.00	625.00	500.00
1867	5	325.00	375.00	750.00	525.00
1868	4	325.00	375.00	775.00	500.00
1869	5	325.00	375.00	650.00	500.00
1870	4	275.00	325.00	725.00	500.00
1871	4	325.00	375.00	650.00	525.00
1872	2	350.00	400.00	850.00	675.00
1873	1	550.00	625.00	—	850.00

HALF DIME WITH FLOWING HAIR

FLOWING HAIR TYPE

	Mintage (in thousands)	Good	Fine	Unc.
1794	86	825.00	1,350.00	9,250.00
1795	(included above)	600.00	1,050.00	7,250.00

DRAPED BUST HALF DIME WITH SMALL EAGLE

DRAPED BUST TYPE

	Mintage	Good	Fine	Unc.
1796 over 5, All Kinds	10	825.00	1,575.00	18,500.00
1796 Normal Date	—	750.00	1,500.00	11,500.00
1796 LIKERTY	—	750.00	1,500.00	13,500.00
1797 15 Stars, All Kinds	45	700.00	1,375.00	8,250.00
1797 16 Stars	—	700.00	1,375.00	8,750.00
1797 13 Stars	—	700.00	1,375.00	22,500.00

DRAPED BUST HALF DIME WITH HERALDIC EAGLE

	Mintage	Good	Fine	Unc.
1800, All Kinds	24	400.00	950.00	8,750.00
1800 LIBEKTY	—	400.00	1,050.00	9,000.00
1801	34	550.00	1,150.00	10,250.00
1802	13	12,500.00	27,500.00	—
1803 Large 8	38	550.00	1,000.00	9,250.00
1803 Small 8	—	675.00	1,350.00	10,500.00
1805	16	650.00	1,050.00	15,500.00

CAPPED BUST HALF DIME

CAPPED BUST TYPE

	Mintage (in thousands)	Good	Fine	Unc.
1829	1,230	23.00	35.00	350.00
1830	1,240	22.00	35.00	350.00
1831	1,243	21.00	32.00	350.00
1832	965	21.00	32.00	350.00
1833	1,370	21.00	33.00	350.00
1834	1,480	21.00	32.00	350.00
1835	2,760	21.00	35.00	350.00
1836	1,900	21.00	37.00	350.00
1837	871	22.00	40.00	375.00

HALF DIME, NO STARS 1837–1838

LIBERTY SEATED TYPE

	Mintage (in thousands)	Good	Fine	Unc.
1837 No Stars	1,705	25.00	55.00	650.00
1838O No Stars	70	70.00	210.00	2,650.00

HALF DIME WITH STARS 1838–1859

	Mintage (in thousands)	Good	Fine	Unc.
1838 No Drapery at Elbow	2,255	11.00	15.00	275.00
1839 No Drapery at Elbow	1,069	11.00	15.00	285.00
1839O No Drapery at Elbow	1,034	11.00	16.00	675.00
1840 No Drapery at Elbow	1,344	11.00	16.00	275.00
1840O No Drapery at Elbow, All Kinds	695	11.00	18.00	825.00
1840 Drapery at Elbow	310	18.00	50.00	475.00
1840O Drapery at Elbow	240	27.00	90.00	3,250.00
1841	1,150	11.00	14.00	175.00
1841O	815	12.00	23.00	675.00
1842	815	11.00	14.00	175.00

	Mintage (in thousands)	Good	Fine	Unc.
1842O	350	25.00	60.00	1,450.00
1843	1,165	11.00	14.00	190.00
1844	430	11.00	14.00	190.00
1844O	220	65.00	185.00	6,500.00
1845	1,564	11.00	14.00	190.00
1846	27	210.00	475.00	9,000.00
1847	1,274	11.00	14.00	190.00
1848	668	11.00	14.00	260.00
1848O	600	12.00	25.00	435.00
1849, All Kinds	1,309	11.00	14.00	240.00
1849 over 48, All Kinds	—	12.00	25.00	450.00
1849 over 46	—	11.00	20.00	475.00
1849O	140	22.00	75.00	2,400.00
1850	955	11.00	14.00	200.00
1850O	690	11.00	23.00	850.00
1851	781	11.00	14.00	190.00
1851O	860	11.00	23.00	525.00
1852	1,001	11.00	14.00	190.00
1852O	260	23.00	65.00	950.00
1853 No Arrows	135	25.00	60.00	650.00
1853O No Arrows	160	135.00	300.00	6,000.00

	Mintage (in thousands)	Good	Fine	Unc.	Proof
1853 With Arrows	13,210	11.00	13.00	210.00	21,500.00
1853O	2,200	11.00	14.00	325.00	—
1854	5,740	11.00	13.00	210.00	10,000.00
1854O	1,560	11.00	16.00	300.00	—
1855	1,750	11.00	13.00	225.00	9,000.00
1855O	600	13.00	28.00	650.00	—
1856 No Arrows	4,880	11.00	14.00	190.00	4,850.00
1856O	1,100	11.00	18.00	625.00	—
1857	7,280	11.00	14.00	190.00	3,250.00
1857O	1,380	11.00	17.00	335.00	—
1858	3,500	11.00	14.00	190.00	1,650.00
1858O	1,660	11.00	18.00	275.00	—
1859	340	11.00	21.00	240.00	1,500.00
1859O	560	12.00	23.00	260.00	—

HALF DIME WITH LEGEND 1860–1873

	Mintage (in thousands)	Good	Fine	Unc.	Proof
1860	799	11.00	13.00	145.00	525.00
1860O	1,060	11.00	13.00	210.00	—
1861	3,361	11.00	13.00	145.00	625.00

	Mintage (in thousands)	Good	Fine	Unc.	Proof
1862	1,493	11.00	13.00	145.00	500.00
1863	18	140.00	200.00	625.00	600.00
1863S	100	20.00	33.00	700.00	—
1864	48	275.00	425.00	950.00	625.00
1864S	90	35.00	80.00	725.00	—
1865	14	225.00	350.00	800.00	550.00
1865S	120	22.00	40.00	1,175.00	—
1866	11	210.00	345.00	725.00	475.00
1866S	120	22.00	37.00	450.00	—
1867	9	340.00	500.00	875.00	550.00
1867S	120	19.00	32.00	625.00	—
1868	89	45.00	95.00	585.00	475.00
1868S	280	11.00	20.00	325.00	—
1869	209	11.00	16.00	225.00	450.00
1869S	230	11.00	15.00	375.00	—
1870	537	11.00	14.00	145.00	435.00
1871	1,874	11.00	14.00	145.00	—
1871S	161	13.00	28.00	285.00	435.00
1872	2,948	11.00	14.00	145.00	435.00
1872S Mint Mark within Wreath	837	11.00	14.00	145.00	—
1872S Mint Mark below Wreath .	—	11.00	14.00	145.00	—
1873	713	11.00	15.00	145.00	—
1873S	324	11.00	14.00	145.00	—

36
DIMES: 1796 AND FORWARD

DRAPED BUST SMALL EAGLE DIME

DRAPED BUST TYPE

	Mintage (in thousands)	Good	Fine	Unc.
1796	22	1,150.00	2,050.00	10,500.00
1797 16 Stars, All Kinds	25	1,175.00	2,100.00	11,500.00
1797 13 Stars	—	1,175.00	2,100.00	10,750.00

DRAPED BUST HERALDIC EAGLE DIME

	Mintage (in thousands)	Good	Fine	Unc.
1798 over 97, 13 Stars on Reverse, All Kinds	28	1,100.00	2,750.00	—
1798 over 97, 16 Stars on Reverse	—	485.00	875.00	7,250.00
1798	—	460.00	800.00	7,250.00
1800	22	450.00	850.00	7,750.00
1801	35	450.00	1,050.00	—
1802	11	725.00	1,400.00	18,500.00
1803	33	450.00	850.00	—
1804 13 Stars on Reverse, All Kinds	8	1,100.00	2,500.00	—
1804 14 Stars on Reverse	—	1,200.00	2,900.00	—
1805	121	375.00	675.00	5,500.00
1807	165	375.00	675.00	5,750.00

CAPPED BUST DIME, LARGE SIZE

CAPPED BUST TYPE

1809	51	100.00	275.00	3,250.00
1811 over 9	65	60.00	235.00	3,100.00
1814	422	27.00	55.00	1,200.00
1820	943	22.00	50.00	1,200.00
1821	1,187	22.00	50.00	1,200.00
1822	100	350.00	825.00	10,000.00
1823 over 22, All Kinds	440	22.00	40.00	1,325.00
1824 over 22	—	23.00	90.00	1,950.00
1825	510	22.00	40.00	1,250.00
1827	1,215	22.00	40.00	1,200.00
1828 Large Date, Curl Base 2	125	35.00	115.00	2,150.00

CAPPED BUST DIME, REDUCED SIZE

	Mintage (in thousands)	Good	Fine	Unc.
1828 Small Date, Square Base 2	(included above)	25.00	75.00	1,150.00
1829	770	22.00	32.00	850.00
1830	510	22.00	30.00	775.00
1831	771	22.00	30.00	775.00
1832	523	22.00	30.00	775.00
1833	485	22.00	30.00	775.00
1834	635	22.00	30.00	775.00
1835	1,410	22.00	30.00	775.00
1836	1,190	22.00	30.00	775.00
1837	360	22.00	30.00	850.00

LIBERTY SEATED TYPE

LIBERTY SEATED DIME, NO STARS

1837 No Stars	683	27.00	75.00	1,250.00
1838O No Stars	406	32.00	110.00	3,200.00

LIBERTY SEATED DIME WITH STARS

1838 With Stars, All Kinds	1,993	11.00	15.00	375.00
1838 With Partial Drapery	—	20.00	50.00	750.00
1839	1,053	10.00	16.00	375.00
1839O	1,323	10.00	16.00	500.00
1840 No Drapery	982	10.00	13.00	375.00
1840 With Drapery	378	27.00	85.00	1,250.00
1840O No Drapery	1,175	11.00	20.00	1,100.00
1841	1,623	10.00	13.00	325.00
1841O	2,008	10.00	20.00	875.00
1842	1,888	10.00	13.00	315.00
1842O	2,020	11.00	23.00	2,850.00
1843	1,370	10.00	14.00	375.00
1843O	150	30.00	110.00	2,375.00
1844	73	200.00	425.00	2,750.00
1845	1,755	10.00	13.00	375.00
1845O	230	16.00	55.00	2,650.00
1846	31	65.00	160.00	4,750.00

	Mintage (in thousands)	Good	Fine	Unc.	
1847	245	13.00	30.00	1,050.00	
1848	452	12.00	20.00	525.00	
1849	839	12.00	16.00	385.00	
1849O	300	12.00	40.00	2,900.00	
1850	1,932	12.00	14.00	325.00	
1850O	510	12.00	23.00	1,175.00	
1851	1,027	12.00	14.00	425.00	
1851O	400	12.00	32.00	2,250.00	

	Mintage (in thousands)	Good	Fine	Unc.	Proof
1852	1,536	10.00	13.00	325.00	—
1852O	430	14.00	40.00	1,650.00	—
1853 No Arrows	95	40.00	110.00	675.00	—
1853 With Arrows	12,078	10.00	13.00	350.00	27,500.00
1853O	1,100	11.00	14.00	1,275.00	—
1854	4,470	10.00	13.00	350.00	13,500.00
1854O	1,770	10.00	13.00	375.00	—
1855	2,075	10.00	13.00	400.00	13,500.00
1856 No Arrows	5,780	10.00	13.00	300.00	4,500.00
1856O	1,180	11.00	14.00	750.00	—
1856S	70	90.00	285.00	2,850.00	—
1857	5,580	10.00	13.00	300.00	3,500.00
1857O	1,540	10.00	14.00	425.00	—
1858	1,540	10.00	13.00	300.00	1,575.00
1858O	290	13.00	40.00	575.00	—
1858S	60	80.00	160.00	3,250.00	—
1859	430	10.00	14.00	300.00	1,150.00
1859O	480	10.00	14.00	375.00	—
1859S	60	65.00	185.00	7,000.00	—
1860S	140	22.00	55.00	1,950.00	—

LIBERTY SEATED DIME WITH LEGEND 1860–1891

	Mintage	Good	Fine	Unc.	Proof
1860	607	10.00	14.00	185.00	450.00
1860O	40	265.00	725.00	11,000.00	—
1861	1,884	10.00	13.00	150.00	460.00
1861S	173	30.00	95.00	1,575.00	—
1862	848	12.00	14.00	160.00	475.00
1862S	181	30.00	65.00	1,375.00	—
1863	14	250.00	460.00	925.00	525.00
1863S	158	26.00	50.00	1,150.00	—
1864	11	170.00	335.00	900.00	625.00

	Mintage (in thousands)	Good	Fine	Unc.	Proof
1864S	230	20.00	40.00	875.00	—
1865	11	210.00	460.00	975.00	700.00
1865S	175	18.00	42.00	2,450.00	—
1866	9	235.00	500.00	1,100.00	500.00
1866S	135	32.00	65.00	1,350.00	—
1867	7	335.00	685.00	1,200.00	550.00
1867S	140	23.00	65.00	1,150.00	—
1868	465	10.00	21.00	335.00	500.00
1868S	260	12.00	30.00	420.00	—
1869	257	13.00	32.00	450.00	450.00
1869S	450	10.00	17.00	385.00	—
1870	472	10.00	13.00	225.00	450.00
1870S	50	200.00	300.00	1,250.00	—
1871	908	10.00	13.00	260.00	475.00
1871CC	20	900.00	1,850.00	17,000.00	—
1871S	320	18.00	45.00	625.00	—
1872	2,396	10.00	12.00	150.00	475.00
1872CC	24	300.00	1,050.00	27,000.00	—
1872S	190	14.00	70.00	1,400.00	—
1873 No Arrows .,,...........	1,569	10.00	13.00	150.00	450.00
1873CC No Arrows (Unique) ...	12	—	—	—	—

LIBERTY SEATED DIME WITH ARROWS AT DATE

	Mintage (in thousands)	Good	Fine	Unc.	Proof
1873 Arrows at Date	2,379	10.00	20.00	525.00	1,600.00
1873CC Arrows at Date	19	750.00	2,500.00	19,000.00	—
1873S	455	12.00	28.00	950.00	—
1874	2,941	10.00	17.50	550.00	1,600.00
1874CC	11	1,250.00	4,500.00	35,000.00	—
1874S	240	18.00	60.00	925.00	—
1875 Arrows at Date Removed ..	10,351	10.00	13.00	140.00	450.00
1875CC Under Wreath, All Kinds	4,645	10.00	14.00	235.00	—
1875CC In Wreath	—	10.00	14.00	210.00	—
1875S Under Wreath, All Kinds .	9,070	10.00	13.00	140.00	—
1875S In Wreath	—	10.00	13.00	140.00	—
1876	11,461	10.00	13.00	140.00	450.00
1876CC	8,270	10.00	13.00	210.00	—
1876S	10,420	11.00	15.00	145.00	—
1877	7,311	10.00	13.00	140.00	425.00
1877CC	7,700	10.00	14.00	210.00	—
1877S	2,340	11.00	15.00	140.00	—
1878	1,679	10.00	13.00	145.00	425.00

	Mintage (in thousands)	Good	Fine	Unc.	Proof
1878CC	200	45.00	100.00	1,000.00	—
1879	15	150.00	230.00	425.00	425.00
1880	37	100.00	210.00	525.00	425.00
1881	25	120.00	200.00	400.00	425.00
1882	3,911	10.00	13.00	140.00	425.00
1883	7,676	10.00	13.00	140.00	425.00
1884	3,366	10.00	13.00	140.00	425.00
1884S	565	15.00	27.00	675.00	—
1885	2,533	10.00	13.00	145.00	425.00
1885S	44	335.00	750.00	5,350.00	
1886	6,378	10.00	13.00	140.00	425.00
1886S	207	23.00	45.00	550.00	—
1887	11,284	10.00	13.00	140.00	425.00
1887S	4,454	10.00	13.00	150.00	—
1888	5,496	10.00	13.00	140.00	425.00
1888S	1,720	10.00	13.00	250.00	—
1889	7,381	10.00	13.00	140.00	425.00
1889S	973	10.00	22.00	425.00	—
1890	9,912	10.00	13.00	140.00	425.00
1890S	1,423	10.00	25.00	335.00	—
1891	15,311	10.00	13.00	140.00	425.00
1891O	4,540	10.00	13.00	160.00	—
1891S	3,196	10.00	13.00	150.00	—

BARBER HEAD DIME

BARBER OR LIBERTY HEAD TYPE

	Mintage (in thousands)	Good	Fine	Unc.	Proof
1892	12,121	4.00	15.00	100.00	475.00
1892O	3,842	7.00	25.00	150.00	—
1892S	991	47.00	160.00	375.00	—
1893	3,341	7.00	16.00	145.00	475.00
1893O	1,760	24.00	100.00	325.00	—
1893S	2,491	9.00	24.00	300.00	—
1894	1,331	16.00	95.00	260.00	475.00
1894O	720	47.00	175.00	1,300.00	—
1894S (Very rare)	24 Pieces	—	—	—	—
1895	691	65.00	280.00	675.00	600.00
1895O	440	230.00	625.00	3,750.00	—
1895S	1,120	33.00	110.00	550.00	—
1896	2,001	9.00	46.00	165.00	475.00
1896O	610	52.00	230.00	1,100.00	—
1896S	575	65.00	235.00	775.00	—

	Mintage (in thousands)	Good	Fine	Unc.	Proof
1897	10,869	2.00	7.00	120.00	475.00
1897O	666	50.00	235.00	925.00	—
1897S	1,343	13.00	82.00	450.00	—
1898	16,321	2.00	7.00	100.00	475.00
1898O	2,130	8.00	72.00	465.00	—
1898S	1,703	5.00	23.00	385.00	—
1899	19,581	3.00	6.00	100.00	475.00
1899O	2,650	6.00	62.00	425.00	—
1899S	1,867	6.00	18.00	325.00	—
1900	17,601	3.00	6.00	100.00	475.00
1900O	2,010	14.00	90.00	585.00	—
1900S	5,168	4.00	10.00	185.00	—
1901	18,860	3.00	6.00	100.00	475.00
1901O	5,620	3.00	12.00	465.00	—
1901S	593	65.00	300.00	975.00	—
1902	21,381	3.00	5.00	100.00	475.00
1902O	4,500	3.00	13.00	425.00	—
1902S	2,070	6.00	45.00	425.00	—
1903	19,501	3.00	4.00	110.00	475.00
1903O	8,180	3.00	10.00	275.00	—
1903S	613	60.00	320.00	1,100.00	—
1904	14,601	3.00	6.00	110.00	475.00
1904S	800	32.00	130.00	775.00	—
1905	14,552	2.00	5.00	100.00	475.00
1905O	3,400	3.00	27.00	260.00	—
1905S	6,855	3.00	6.00	210.00	—
1906	19,958	2.00	4.00	100.00	475.00
1906D	4,060	3.00	6.00	185.00	—
1906O	2,610	5.00	41.00	200.00	—
1906S	3,137	2.00	10.00	265.00	—
1907	22,221	2.00	3.00	100.00	475.00
1907D	4,080	2.00	8.00	325.00	—
1907O	5,058	3.00	27.00	225.00	—
1907S	3,178	3.00	10.00	385.00	—
1908	10,601	2.00	3.00	100.00	475.00
1908D	7,490	2.00	5.00	145.00	—
1908O	1,789	5.00	39.00	310.00	—
1908S	3,220	2.00	9.00	350.00	—
1909	10,241	2.00	3.00	100.00	475.00
1909D	954	6.00	55.00	500.00	—
1909O	2,287	3.00	10.00	225.00	—
1909S	1,000	7.00	75.00	550.00	—
1910	11,521	2.00	4.00	100.00	475.00
1910D	3,490	2.00	8.00	235.00	—
1910S	1,240	4.00	45.00	425.00	—
1911	18,871	2.00	3.00	100.00	475.00
1911D	17,209	2.00	3.00	100.00	—

	Mintage (in thousands)	Good	Fine	Unc.	Proof
1911S	3,520	2.00	7.00	200.00	—
1912	19,351	2.00	3.00	100.00	475.00
1912D	11,760	2.00	3.00	100.00	—
1912S	3,420	2.00	5.00	165.00	—
1913	19,761	2.00	3.00	100.00	475.00
1913S	510	11.00	70.00	460.00	—
1914	17,361	2.00	3.00	100.00	475.00
1914D	11,908	2.00	4.00	100.00	—
1914S	2,100	2.00	7.00	150.00	—
1915	5,620	2.00	3.00	100.00	475.00
1915S	960	5.00	28.00	260.00	—
1916	18,490	2.00	3.00	100.00	—
1916S	5,820	2.00	4.00	100.00	—

MERCURY TYPE DIME

MERCURY TYPE

	Mintage (in thousands)	Good	Fine	Ex. Fine	Unc.
1916	22,180	3.00	6.00	10.00	35.00
1916D	264	565.00	1,250.00	2,600.00	5,100.00
1916S	10,450	4.00	7.00	17.00	45.00
1917	55,230	2.00	3.00	8.00	45.00
1917D	9,402	4.00	10.00	40.00	185.00
1917S	27,330	2.00	3.00	10.00	90.00
1918	26,680	2.00	5.00	25.00	75.00
1918D	22,675	3.00	4.00	23.00	135.00
1918S	19,300	2.00	3.00	15.00	135.00
1919	35,740	2.00	3.00	11.00	60.00
1919D	9,939	3.00	11.00	32.00	235.00
1919S	8,850	3.00	8.00	30.00	240.00
1920	59,030	2.00	2.00	7.00	45.00
1920D	19,171	2.00	4.00	17.00	175.00
1920S	13,820	2.00	4.00	15.00	160.00
1921	1,230	28.00	80.00	425.00	1,050.00
1921D	1,080	38.00	125.00	475.00	1,150.00
1923	50,130	1.00	2.00	7.00	30.00
1923S	6,440	2.00	7.00	58.00	240.00
1924	24,010	2.00	3.00	12.00	50.00
1924D	6,810	2.00	6.00	42.00	225.00
1924S	7,120	3.00	4.00	42.00	250.00
1925	25,610	1.00	2.00	8.00	40.00

	Mintage (in thousands)	Good	Fine	Ex. Fine	Unc.
1925D	5,117	4.00	13.00	100.00	425.00
1925S	5,850	2.00	6.00	60.00	250.00
1926	32,160	1.00	2.00	5.00	35.00
1926D	6,828	3.00	4.00	23.00	150.00
1926S	1,520	7.00	21.00	200.00	875.00
1927	28,080	1.00	2.00	5.00	30.00
1927D	4,812	3.00	6.00	58.00	200.00
1927S	4,770	2.00	5.00	22.00	315.00
1928	19,480	1.00	2.00	5.00	30.00
1928D	4,161	3.00	8.00	42.00	190.00
1928S	7,400	2.00	3.00	16.00	150.00
1929	25,970	2.00	2.00	5.00	22.00
1929D	5,034	2.00	3.00	15.00	28.00
1929S	4,730	2.00	2.00	7.00	34.00
1930	6,770	2.00	2.00	7.00	30.00
1930S	1,843	3.00	5.00	14.00	75.00
1931	3,150	2.00	3.00	9.00	40.00
1931D	1,260	5.00	10.00	30.00	80.00
1931S	1,800	2.00	4.00	12.00	75.00
1934	24,080	1.00	1.00	3.00	24.00
1934D	6,772	1.00	2.00	6.00	45.00
1935	58,830	1.00	1.00	2.00	11.00
1935D	10,447	1.00	2.00	6.00	37.00
1935S	15,840	1.00	1.00	4.00	24.00

	Mintage (in thousands)	Good	Fine	Ex. Fine	Unc.	Proof
1936	87,504	1.00	1.00	3.00	10.00	800.00
1936D	16,132	1.00	2.00	6.00	25.00	—
1936S	9,210	1.00	1.00	3.00	20.00	—
1937	56,866	1.00	1.00	2.00	10.00	425.00
1937D	14,146	1.00	1.00	3.00	22.00	—
1937S	9,740	1.00	1.00	3.00	23.00	—
1938	22,199	1.00	1.00	3.00	14.00	225.00
1938D	5,537	1.00	2.00	4.00	16.00	—
1938S	8,090	1.00	1.00	3.00	20.00	—
1939	67,749	1.00	1.00	3.00	10.00	225.00
1939D	24,934	1.00	1.00	3.00	9.00	—
1939S	10,540	1.00	1.00	3.00	21.00	—
1940	65,362	1.00	1.00	2.00	7.00	185.00
1940D	21,198	1.00	1.00	2.00	9.00	—
1940S	21,560	1.00	1.00	2.00	9.00	—
1941	175,107	1.00	1.00	2.00	7.00	185.00
1941D	45,634	1.00	1.00	2.00	9.00	—
1941S	43,090	1.00	1.00	2.00	8.00	—
1942	205,432	1.00	1.00	2.00	8.00	185.00
1942 2 over 1	—	250.00	325.00	410.00	2,000.00	—

	Mintage (in thousands)	Good	Fine	Ex. Fine	Unc.	Proof
1942D	60,740	1.00	1.00	2.00	10.00	—
1942D 2 over 1	—	260.00	375.00	525.00	2,250.00	—
1942S	49,300	1.00	1.00	2.00	11.00	—
1943	191,710	1.00	1.00	2.00	8.00	—
1943D	71,949	1.00	1.00	2.00	9.00	—
1943S	60,400	1.00	1.00	2.00	10.00	—
1944	231,410	1.00	1.00	2.00	8.00	—
1944D	62,224	1.00	1.00	2.00	11.00	—
1944S	49,490	1.00	1.00	2.00	10.00	—
1945	159,130	1.00	1.00	2.00	7.00	—
1945D	40,245	1.00	1.00	2.00	8.00	—
1945S	41,920	1.00	1.00	2.00	8.00	—
1945S Micro S	—	1.00	2.00	4.00	25.00	—

ROOSEVELT DIME

ROOSEVELT TYPE

	Mintage (in thousands)	Fine	Ex. Fine	Unc.	Proof
1946	255,250	—	1.00	2.00	—
1946D	61,044	—	1.00	2.00	—
1946S	27,900	—	1.00	5.00	—
1947	121,520	—	1.00	3.00	—
1947D	46,835	—	1.00	5.00	—
1947S	34,840	—	1.00	4.00	—
1948	74,950	—	1.00	4.00	—
1948D	52,841	—	1.00	4.00	—
1948S	35,520	—	1.00	3.00	—
1949	30,940	1.00	2.00	21.00	—
1949D	26,034	1.00	1.00	9.00	—
1949S	13,510	1.00	3.00	30.00	—
1950	50,182	—	1.00	7.00	23.00
1950D	46,803	—	1.00	5.00	—
1950S	20,440	1.00	1.00	32.00	—
1951	103,938	—	1.00	2.00	20.00
1951D	56,529	—	1.00	2.00	—
1951S	31,630	1.00	1.00	10.00	—
1952	99,122	—	1.00	2.00	17.00
1952D	122,100	—	1.00	2.00	—
1952S	44,420	1.00	1.00	6.00	—
1953	53,619	—	1.00	2.00	11.00
1953D	136,433	—	1.00	2.00	—

	Mintage (in thousands)	Fine	Ex. Fine	Unc.	Proof
1953S	39,180	—	1.00	2.00	—
1954	114,244	—	1.00	1.00	6.00
1954D	106,397	—	1.00	1.00	—
1954S	22,860	—	1.00	2.00	—
1955	12,828	—	1.00	1.00	5.00
1955D	13,959	—	1.00	1.00	—
1955S	18,510	—	1.00	1.00	—
1956	109,309	—	1.00	1.00	2.00
1956D	108,015	—	1.00	1.00	—
1957	167,408	—	1.00	1.00	2.00
1957D	133,354	—	1.00	2.00	—
1958	32,786	—	1.00	1.00	2.00
1958D	136,565	—	1.00	1.00	—
1959	86,929	—	1.00	1.00	1.00
1959D	164,920	—	1.00	1.00	—
1960	72,082	—	1.00	1.00	1.00
1960D	200,160	—	1.00	1.00	—
1961	96,758	—	1.00	1.00	1.00
1961D	209,147	—	1.00	1.00	—
1962	75,668	—	1.00	1.00	1.00
1962D	334,948	—	1.00	1.00	—
1963	126,726	—	1.00	1.00	1.00
1963D	421,477	—	1.00	1.00	—
1964	933,311	—	1.00	1.00	1.00
1964D	1,357,517	—	1.00	1.00	—
1965 ...., ...	1,652,141	—	—	—	—
1966	1,382,735	—	—	—	—
1967	2,244,007	—	—	—	—
1968	424,470	—	—	—	—
1968D	480,748	—	—	—	—
1968S Proof only	3,042	—	—	—	1.00
1969	145,790	—	—	1.00	—
1969D	563,324	—	—	—	—
1969S Proof only	2,935	—	—	—	1.00
1970	345,570	—	—	—	—
1970D	754,942	—	—	—	—
1970S Proof only	2,633	—	—	—	1.00
1971	162,690	—	—	—	—
1971D	377,914	—	—	—	—
1971S Proof only	3,224	—	—	—	1.00
1972	431,540	—	—	—	—
1972D	330,290	—	—	—	—
1972S Proof only	3,268	—	—	—	1.00
1973	315,670	—	—	—	—
1973D	455,032	—	—	—	—
1973S Proof only	2,770	—	—	—	1.00
1974	470,248	—	—	—	—

	Mintage (in thousands)	Fine	Ex. Fine	Unc.	Proof
1974D	521,083	—	—	—	—
1974S Proof only	2,617	—	—	—	1.00
1975	585,678	—	—	—	—
1975D	313,705	—	—	—	—
1975S Proof only	2,909	—	—	—	2.00
1976 P&D	1,263,983	—	—	—	—
1976S Proof only	4,150	—	—	—	1.00
1977 P&D	1,173,537	—	—	—	—
1977S Proof only	3,251	—	—	—	2.00
1978 P&D	946,828	—	—	—	—
1978S Proof only	3,128	—	—	—	1.00
1979 P&D	706,361	—	—	—	—
1979S Proof only	3,677	—	—	—	1.00
1979S Type Two, Proof only, Sharp	—	—	—	—	2.00
1980 P&D	1,554,524	—	—	—	—
1980S Proof only	3,555	—	—	—	1.00
1981 P&D	1,388,934	—	—	—	—
1981S Proof only	4,063	—	—	—	1.00
1982 P	519,475	—	—	3.00	—
1982 D	542,714	—	—	2.00	—
1982S Proof only	3,857	—	—	—	2.00
1983 P&D	1,377,154	—	—	2.00	—
1983S Proof only	3,279	—	—	—	1.00
1984 P&D	1,561,473	—	—	—	—
1984S Proof only	3,065	—	—	—	2.00
1985 P&D	1,293,181	—	—	—	—
1985S Proof only	3,363	—	—	—	1.00
1986 P&D	1,155,976	—	—	1.00	—
1986S Proof only	3,010	—	—	—	3.00
1987 P&D	1,415,913	—	—	—	—
1987S Proof only	4,228	—	—	—	2.00
1988 P&D	1,992,935	—	—	—	—
1988S Proof only	3,263	—	—	—	3.00
1989 P&D	2,194,936	—	—	—	—
1989S Proof only	3,220	—	—	—	3.00
1990 P&D	1,874,336	—	—	—	—
1990S Proof only	3,300	—	—	—	2.00
1991 P&D	1,528,461	—	—	—	—
1991S Proof only	2,868	—	—	—	3.00
1992 P&D	1,209,774	—	—	—	—
1992S Proof only	2,859	—	—	—	3.00
1992S Silver Proof	1,318	—	—	—	5.00
1993 P&D	1,516,290	—	—	—	—
1993S Proof only	2,633	—	—	—	6.00
1993S Silver Proof	761	—	—	—	7.00
1994 P&D	2,492,268	—	—	—	—
1994S Proof only	2,485	—	—	—	5.00
1994S Silver Proof	785	—	—	—	7.00

	Mintage (in thousands)	Fine	Ex. Fine	Unc.	Proof
1995 P&D	2,400,390	—	—	—	—
1995S Proof only	2,010	—	—	—	16.00
1995S Silver Proof	839	—	—	—	18.00
1996 P&D	2,821,463	—	—	—	—
1996S Proof only	1,750	—	—	—	3.00
1996S Silver Proof	775	—	—	—	7.00
1996W	1457	—	—	7.00	—
1997 P&D	1,971,450	—	—	—	—
1997S Proof only	1,975	—	—	—	8.00
1997S Silver Proof	742	—	—	—	18.00
1998 P&D	2,335,250	—	—	—	—
1998S Proof only	—	—	—	—	3.00
1998S Silver Proof	879	—	—	—	6.00
1999 P&D	3,561,750	—	—	—	—
1999S Proof only	—	—	—	—	2.00
1999S Silver Proof	800	—	—	—	5.00
2000 P&D	3,661,200	—	—	—	—
2000S Proof only	2,969	—	—	—	1.00
2000S Silver Proof	856	—	—	—	5.00
2001 P&D	2,782,390	—	—	—	—
2001S Proof only	—	—	—	—	1.00
2001S Silver Proof	—	—	—	—	5.00
2002 P&D	—	—	—	—	—
2002S Proof only	—	—	—	—	1.00
2002S Silver Proof	—	—	—	—	5.00

37
TWENTY-CENT PIECES: 1875–1878

TWENTY-CENT PIECE

	Mintage (in thousands)	Good	Fine	V. Fine	Unc.	Proof
1875	40	55.00	75.00	115.00	700.00	2,750.00
1875CC	133	55.00	85.00	140.00	850.00	—
1875S	1,155	55.00	75.00	110.00	625.00	—
1876	16	90.00	165.00	225.00	750.00	2,650.00
1876CC (Very Rare) ...	10	—	—	—	—	—
1877	1	1,150.00	1,400.00	1,575.00	—	3,350.00
1878	1	900.00	1,150.00	1,250.00	—	3,100.00

139

38

QUARTER DOLLARS: 1796–1998

DRAPED BUST TYPE

1796 DRAPED BUST QUARTER WITH SMALL EAGLE

DRAPED BUST QUARTER
WITH HERALDIC EAGLE

	Mintage (in thousands)	Good	Fine	Unc.
1796	6	4,150.00	8,750.00	27,500.00
1804	7	1,850.00	3,350.00	45,000.00
1805	121	200.00	425.00	5,500.00
1806, All Kinds	206	200.00	425.00	5,000.00
1806 over 5	—	210.00	460.00	7,500.00
1807	221	200.00	425.00	5,000.00

CAPPED BUST TYPE

CAPPED BUST QUARTER, LARGE SIZE

	Mintage (in thousands)	Good	Fine	Unc.
1815	89	55.00	125.00	2,500.00
1818, All Kinds	361	55.00	135.00	2,500.00
1818 over 15	(included above)	55.00	135.00	2,500.00
1819	144	55.00	125.00	2,500.00
1820	127	55.00	125.00	2,500.00
1821	217	55.00	125.00	2,500.00
1822, All Kinds	64	60.00	160.00	3,350.00
1822 25 over 50c	—	1,375.00	4,250.00	35,000.00
1823 over 22	18	7,000.00	16,500.00	—
1824 over 2	168	90.00	260.00	6,250.00

	Mintage (in thousands)	Good	Fine	Unc.
1825 over 22, All Kinds	168	75.00	165.00	2,750.00
1825 over 23	(included above)	55.00	110.00	2,500.00
1825 over 24	(included above)	55.00	110.00	2,500.00
1827 Original, curled base 2 in 25c	4	—	—	—
1827 Restrike, square base 2 in 25c	—	—	—	—
1828, All Kinds	102	55.00	110.00	3,250.00
1828 25 over 50c	—	135.00	450.00	8,000.00

CAPPED BUST QUARTER, REDUCED SIZE

1831	398	45.00	60.00	1,000.00
1832	320	45.00	60.00	1,000.00
1833	156	48.00	65.00	1,450.00
1834	286	45.00	60.00	1,000.00
1835	1,952	45.00	60.00	1,000.00
1836	472	45.00	60.00	1,000.00
1837	252	45.00	60.00	1,000.00
1838	366	45.00	60.00	1,050.00

LIBERTY SEATED QUARTER, NO MOTTO

LIBERTY SEATED TYPE

	Mintage (in thousands)	Good	Fine	Unc.
1838 No Drapery	466	15.00	32.00	1,650.00
1839 No Drapery	491	15.00	32.00	1,650.00
1840O No Drapery	390	16.00	42.00	1,700.00
1840 Drapery	188	18.00	55.00	1,000.00
1840O Drapery	43	20.00	60.00	1,275.00
1841	120	45.00	85.00	850.00
1841O	452	15.00	40.00	775.00
1842	88	65.00	140.00	1,400.00
1842O	769	15.00	30.00	1,275.00

	Mintage (in thousands)	Good	Fine	Unc.
1843	646	16.00	30.00	500.00
1843O	968	17.00	45.00	1,675.00
1844	421	16.00	30.00	525.00
1844O	740	18.00	32.00	1,150.00
1845	922	16.00	27.00	500.00
1846	510	16.00	28.00	550.00
1847	734	16.00	28.00	525.00
1847O	368	22.00	55.00	2,250.00
1848	146	25.00	75.00	1,350.00
1849	340	16.00	40.00	800.00
1849O	—	360.00	800.00	7,850.00
1850	191	25.00	60.00	850.00
1850O	412	18.00	55.00	1,450.00
1851	160	35.00	80.00	875.00
1851O	88	150.00	400.00	5,000.00
1852	177	40.00	80.00	500.00
1852O	96	150.00	350.00	10,000.00
1853 No Arrows or Rays, Recut Date	44	235.00	475.00	2,500.00

1853 LIBERTY SEATED QUARTER WITH ARROWS AND RAYS

	Mintage (in thousands)	Good	Fine	Unc.	Proof
1853 Arrows and Rays	15,210	16.00	30.00	1,250.00	45,000.00
1853O	1,332	16.00	35.00	3,600.00	—

LIBERTY SEATED QUARTER, NO MOTTO WITH ARROWS

	Mintage	Good	Fine	Unc.	Proof
1854 Arrows, no Rays	12,380	16.00	27.00	585.00	15,000.00
1854O	1,484	16.00	28.00	850.00	—
1855	2,857	16.00	27.00	585.00	17,500.00
1855O	176	35.00	90.00	2,850.00	—
1855S	396	30.00	60.00	2,250.00	—
1856 No Arrows	7,264	16.00	27.00	350.00	6,000.00

	Mintage (in thousands)	Good	Fine	Unc.	Proof
1856O	968	16.00	30.00	1,000.00	—
1856S	286	30.00	80.00	2,300.00	—
1857	9,644	16.00	30.00	350.00	4,500.00
1857O	1,180	16.00	30.00	1,250.00	—
1857S	82	45.00	165.00	2,600.00	—
1858	7,368	16.00	30.00	335.00	2,000.00
1858O	520	16.00	32.00	1,400.00	—
1858S	121	35.00	135.00	6,000.00	—
1859	1,344	16.00	30.00	450.00	1,600.00
1859O	260	17.00	35.00	1,350.00	—
1859S	80	80.00	175.00	14,000.00	—
1860	805	16.00	30.00	425.00	1,600.00
1860O	388	16.00	33.00	1,150.00	—
1860S	56	140.00	370.00	8,500.00	—
1861	4,855	16.00	30.00	325.00	1,700.00
1861S	96	45.00	165.00	5,000.00	—
1862	933	16.00	30.00	350.00	1,700.00
1862S	67	50.00	110.00	2,350.00	—
1863	192	25.00	55.00	500.00	1,600.00
1864	94	52.00	95.00	650.00	1,600.00
1864S	20	250.00	575.00	6,600.00	—
1865	59	52.00	95.00	675.00	1,600.00
1865S	41	70.00	165.00	2,150.00	—
1866 No Motto	One known	—	—	—	—

LIBERTY SEATED QUARTER WITH MOTTO

	Mintage (in thousands)	Good	Fine	Unc.	Proof
1866 with Motto	18	300.00	510.00	1,750.00	700.00
1866S	28	160.00	460.00	2,500.00	—
1867	21	160.00	325.00	850.00	725.00
1867S	48	115.00	325.00	2,250.00	—
1868	30	95.00	175.00	725.00	725.00
1868S	96	65.00	135.00	2,100.00	—
1869	17	200.00	340.00	1,375.00	725.00
1869S	76	75.00	165.00	2,350.00	—
1870	87	40.00	95.00	775.00	725.00
1870CC	8	1,750.00	6,150.00	36,000.00	—
1871	119	30.00	55.00	525.00	700.00
1871CC	11	1,350.00	3,750.00	32,500.00	—
1871S	31	250.00	425.00	2,500.00	—

	Mintage (in thousands)	Good	Fine	Unc.	Proof
1872	183	25.00	60.00	550.00	675.00
1872CC	23	475.00	1,350.00	14,500.00	—
1872S	83	675.00	925.00	6,000.00	—
1873 No Arrows	213	30.00	55.00	400.00	675.00

LIBERTY SEATED QUARTER WITH ARROWS AND MOTTO

	Mintage (in thousands)	Good	Fine	Unc.	Proof
1873 Arrows	1,272	16.00	31.00	850.00	2,450.00
1873CC	12	1,350.00	4,500.00	40,000.00	—
1873S	156	20.00	55.00	1,275.00	—
1874	472	16.00	30.00	850.00	2,450.00
1874S	392	16.00	55.00	875.00	—
1875 Arrows Removed	4,294	16.00	26.00	260.00	700.00
1875CC	140	55.00	150.00	1,600.00	—
1875S	680	27.00	65.00	675.00	—
1876	17,817	16.00	26.00	260.00	700.00
1876CC	4,944	17.00	30.00	375.00	—
1876S	8,596	16.00	26.00	260.00	—
1877	10,912	16.00	26.00	260.00	700.00
1877CC	4,192	17.00	28.00	350.00	—
1877S	8,996	16.00	26.00	260.00	—
1878	2,261	16.00	26.00	260.00	700.00
1878CC	996	20.00	50.00	485.00	—
1878S	140	90.00	225.00	1,350.00	—
1879	15	110.00	185.00	475.00	675.00
1880	15	110.00	185.00	500.00	675.00
1881	13	130.00	225.00	525.00	675.00
1882	16	125.00	200.00	535.00	675.00
1883	15	120.00	210.00	525.00	675.00
1884	9	225.00	325.00	565.00	675.00
1885	15	125.00	210.00	550.00	675.00
1886	6	260.00	425.00	775.00	675.00
1887	11	190.00	315.00	625.00	675.00
1888	11	185.00	285.00	575.00	675.00
1888S	1,216	16.00	26.00	285.00	—
1889	13	135.00	195.00	525.00	675.00
1890	81	50.00	85.00	475.00	675.00
1891	3,921	16.00	26.00	260.00	675.00
1891O	68	120.00	265.00	2,750.00	—
1891S	2,216	16.00	27.00	260.00	—

BARBER OR LIBERTY HEAD TYPE

	Mintage (in thousands)	Good	Fine	Ex. Fine	Unc.	Proof
1892	8,237	5.00	21.00	75.00	185.00	675.00
1892O	2,640	6.00	28.00	80.00	285.00	—
1892S	964	15.00	55.00	125.00	475.00	—
1893	5,445	5.00	21.00	75.00	210.00	675.00
1893O	3,396	5.00	25.00	80.00	285.00	—
1893S	1,455	9.00	45.00	125.00	485.00	—
1894	3,433	5.00	26.00	80.00	260.00	675.00
1894O	2,852	5.00	33.00	95.00	350.00	—
1894S	2,649	6.00	30.00	95.00	325.00	—
1895	4,441	5.00	22.00	75.00	250.00	675.00
1895O	2,816	6.00	35.00	95.00	425.00	—
1895S	1,765	8.00	42.00	100.00	385.00	—
1896	3,875	5.00	22.00	75.00	250.00	675.00
1896O	1,484	8.00	75.00	350.00	900.00	—
1896S	188	325.00	750.00	2,350.00	5,500.00	—
1897	8,141	5.00	20.00	75.00	185.00	675.00
1897O	1,415	8.00	75.00	350.00	825.00	—
1897S	542	26.00	165.00	350.00	975.00	—
1898	11,101	5.00	21.00	75.00	185.00	675.00
1898O	1,868	7.00	55.00	230.00	675.00	—
1898S	1,021	6.00	40.00	80.00	425.00	—
1899	12,625	4.00	19.00	75.00	185.00	675.00
1899O	2,644	5.00	30.00	100.00	425.00	—
1899S	708	11.00	55.00	110.00	450.00	—
1900	10,017	5.00	19.00	70.00	185.00	675.00
1900O	3,416	8.00	52.00	140.00	550.00	—
1900S	1,859	7.00	36.00	75.00	400.00	—
1901	8,893	6.00	19.00	70.00	185.00	675.00
1901O	1,612	26.00	95.00	350.00	875.00	—
1901S	73	2,150.00	5,450.00	9,250.00	18,750.00	—
1902	12,198	5.00	16.00	65.00	185.00	675.00
1902O	4,748	5.00	35.00	100.00	465.00	—
1902S	1,525	8.00	36.00	85.00	575.00	—
1903	9,670	5.00	16.00	65.00	210.00	675.00
1903O	3,500	5.00	32.00	85.00	450.00	—
1903S	1,036	10.00	38.00	100.00	475.00	—
1904	9,589	5.00	17.00	65.00	185.00	675.00

	Mintage (in thousands)	Good	Fine	Ex. Fine	Unc.	Proof
1904O	2,456	7.00	45.00	175.00	825.00	—
1905	4,968	5.00	22.00	65.00	200.00	675.00
1905O	1,230	10.00	70.00	200.00	515.00	—
1905S	1,884	7.00	34.00	90.00	375.00	—
1906	3,656	5.00	18.00	70.00	185.00	675.00
1906D	3,280	5.00	24.00	70.00	240.00	—
1906O	2,056	5.00	35.00	85.00	300.00	—
1907	7,193	5.00	18.00	65.00	185.00	675.00
1907D	3,484	5.00	24.00	80.00	285.00	—
1907O	4,560	5.00	18.00	65.00	225.00	—
1907S	1,360	6.00	37.00	100.00	485.00	—
1908	4,233	4.00	19.00	65.00	210.00	750.00
1908D	5,788	4.00	18.00	70.00	235.00	—
1908O	6,244	4.00	18.00	70.00	200.00	—
1908S	784	11.00	65.00	215.00	725.00	—
1909	9,269	4.00	18.00	65.00	185.00	675.00
1909D	5,114	4.00	18.00	65.00	200.00	—
1909O	712	13.00	75.00	265.00	800.00	—
1909S	1,348	5.00	28.00	65.00	310.00	—
1910	2,245	5.00	23.00	65.00	200.00	675.00
1910D	1,500	6.00	36.00	100.00	375.00	—
1911	3,721	5.00	18.00	75.00	185.00	675.00
1911D	934	6.00	75.00	265.00	675.00	—
1911S	988	6.00	45.00	130.00	385.00	—
1912	4,401	5.00	18.00	65.00	185.00	800.00
1912S	708	5.00	40.00	100.00	400.00	—
1913	485	10.00	60.00	360.00	850.00	825.00
1913D	1,451	6.00	30.00	80.00	260.00	—
1913S	40	525.00	1,875.00	3,700.00	5,100.00	—
1914	6,245	4.00	16.00	60.00	185.00	775.00
1914D	3,046	4.00	16.00	60.00	185.00	—
1914S	264	50.00	145.00	360.00	850.00	—
1915	3,480	4.00	16.00	65.00	185.00	825.00
1915D	3,694	4.00	16.00	65.00	185.00	—
1915S	708	5.00	25.00	75.00	250.00	—
1916	1,788	4.00	16.00	60.00	185.00	—
1916D	6,541	4.00	16.00	60.00	185.00	—

STANDING LIBERTY TYPE I QUARTER

STANDING LIBERTY TYPE

	Mintage (in thousands)	Good	Fine	Ex. Fine	Unc.
1916	52	1,750.00	3,000.00	4,500.00	6,500.00
1917 Type I	8,792	23.00	37.00	65.00	215.00
1917D	1,509	23.00	37.00	90.00	235.00
1917S	1,952	23.00	38.00	130.00	260.00

STANDING LIBERTY TYPE II QUARTER

	Mintage	Good	Fine	Ex. Fine	Unc.
1917 Type 2	13,880	15.00	21.00	42.00	140.00
1917D	6,224	34.00	60.00	90.00	200.00
1917S	5,552	36.00	53.00	75.00	190.00
1918	14,240	15.00	25.00	47.00	140.00
1918D	7,380	28.00	43.00	80.00	225.00
1918S, All Kinds	11,072	17.00	30.00	45.00	200.00
1918S, 8 over 7	—	1,100.00	1,850.00	4,500.00	15,000.00
1919	11,324	33.00	46.00	65.00	140.00
1919D	1,944	80.00	130.00	300.00	675.00
1919S	1,836	80.00	140.00	370.00	775.00
1920	27,860	15.00	25.00	40.00	145.00
1920D	3,586	45.00	65.00	100.00	325.00
1920S	6,380	21.00	28.00	55.00	325.00
1921	1,916	105.00	155.00	300.00	550.00
1923	9,716	15.00	25.00	37.00	140.00
1923S	1,360	290.00	365.00	450.00	650.00
1924	10,920	14.00	21.00	35.00	145.00
1924D	3,112	50.00	67.00	95.00	160.00
1924S	2,860	24.00	34.00	90.00	375.00
1925	12,280	3.00	6.00	30.00	135.00
1926	11,316	3.00	6.00	30.00	135.00

	Mintage (in thousands)	Good	Fine	Ex. Fine	Unc.
1926D	1,716	7.00	14.00	50.00	145.00
1926S	2,700	4.00	13.00	100.00	375.00
1927	11,912	3.00	5.00	30.00	135.00
1927D	976	7.00	19.00	85.00	160.00
1927S	396	11.00	55.00	1,000.00	3,675.00
1928	6,336	3.00	5.00	30.00	135.00
1928D	1,628	4.00	7.00	40.00	140.00
1928S	2,644	4.00	6.00	30.00	140.00
1929	11,140	3.00	5.00	30.00	135.00
1929D	1,358	4.00	7.00	32.00	140.00
1929S	1,764	4.00	6.00	30.00	140.00
1930	5,632	3.00	5.00	30.00	135.00
1930S	1,556	4.00	6.00	30.00	135.00

WASHINGTON QUARTER

WASHINGTON HEAD TYPE

	Mintage (in thousands)	Good	Fine	Ex. Fine	Unc.	Proof
1932	5,404	5.00	7.00	10.00	35.00	—
1932D	437	75.00	95.00	165.00	1,000.00	—
1932S	408	75.00	85.00	115.00	475.00	—
1934	31,912	2.00	3.00	5.00	25.00	—
1934D	3,527	5.00	7.00	19.00	215.00	—
1935	32,484	2.00	3.00	4.00	25.00	—
1935D	5,780	3.00	5.00	20.00	220.00	—
1935S	5,660	3.00	5.00	15.00	85.00	—
1936	41,304	2.00	3.00	4.00	25.00	675.00
1936D	5,374	4.00	5.00	42.00	410.00	—
1936S	3,828	2.00	4.00	15.00	100.00	—
1937	19,702	2.00	4.00	5.00	25.00	300.00
1937D	7,190	3.00	4.00	14.00	55.00	—
1937S	1,652	3.00	5.00	21.00	110.00	—
1938	9,480	5.00	6.00	15.00	65.00	150.00
1938S	2,832	5.00	6.00	15.00	70.00	—
1939	33,549	2.00	3.00	4.00	16.00	130.00
1939D	7,992	2.00	4.00	9.00	34.00	—
1939S	2,628	3.00	4.00	15.00	75.00	—
1940	35,715	2.00	3.00	3.00	17.00	95.00

	Mintage (in thousands)	Good	Fine	Ex. Fine	Unc.	Proof
1940D	2,798	3.00	7.00	18.00	100.00	—
1940S	8,244	3.00	5.00	7.00	23.00	—
1941	79,047	1.00	2.00	3.00	9.00	80.00
1941D	16,715	1.00	2.00	4.00	35.00	—
1941S	16,080	1.00	2.00	3.00	26.00	—
1942	102,117	1.00	2.00	3.00	5.00	70.00
1942D	17,487	1.00	2.00	3.00	15.00	—
1942S	19,384	1.00	2.00	8.00	65.00	—
1943	99,700	1.00	2.00	3.00	6.00	—
1943D	16,096	1.00	2.00	4.00	25.00	—
1943S	21,700	1.00	2.00	5.00	28.00	—
1944	104,956	1.00	2.00	2.00	4.00	—
1944D	14,601	1.00	2.00	3.00	14.00	—
1944S	12,560	1.00	2.00	3.00	15.00	—
1945	74,372	1.00	2.00	2.00	4.00	—
1945D	12,342	1.00	2.00	3.00	20.00	—
1945S	17,004	1.00	2.00	2.00	10.00	—
1946	53,436	1.00	2.00	2.00	5.00	—
1946D	9,073	1.00	2.00	2.00	5.00	—
1946S	4,204	1.00	2.00	2.00	7.00	—
1947	22,556	1.00	2.00	2.00	9.00	—
1947D	15,338	1.00	2.00	2.00	8.00	—
1947S	5,532	1.00	2.00	2.00	8.00	—
1948	35,196	1.00	2.00	2.00	5.00	—
1948D	16,767	1.00	2.00	2.00	6.00	—
1948S	15,960	1.00	2.00	2.00	6.00	—
1949	9,312	1.00	2.00	4.00	38.00	—
1949D	10,068	1.00	2.00	3.00	17.00	—
1950	24,972	1.00	2.00	3.00	9.00	45.00
1950D	21,076	1.00	2.00	3.00	8.00	—
1950S	10,284	1.00	2.00	3.00	13.00	—
1951	43,506	1.00	1.00	2.00	12.00	40.00
1951D	35,355	1.00	1.00	2.00	10.00	—
1951S	9,048	1.00	1.00	2.00	28.00	—
1952	38,862	1.00	1.00	2.00	11.00	30.00
1952D	49,795	1.00	1.00	2.00	10.00	—
1952S	13,708	1.00	1.00	2.00	26.00	—
1953	18,665	1.00	1.00	2.00	12.00	24.00
1953D	56,112	1.00	1.00	2.00	7.00	—
1953S	14,016	1.00	1.00	2.00	10.00	—
1954	54,646	1.00	1.00	2.00	11.00	10.00
1954D	46,306	1.00	1.00	2.00	10.00	—
1954S	11,835	1.00	1.00	2.00	8.00	—
1955	18,558	1.00	1.00	2.00	5.00	9.00
1955D	3,182	1.00	1.00	2.00	4.00	—
1956	44,813	1.00	1.00	2.00	8.00	4.00
1956D	32,335	1.00	1.00	2.00	5.00	—

	Mintage (in thousands)	Good	Fine	Ex. Fine	Unc.	Proof
1957	47,780	1.00	1.00	2.00	5.00	3.00
1957D	77,924	1.00	1.00	2.00	3.00	—
1958	7,236	1.00	1.00	2.00	3.00	4.00
1958D	78,125	1.00	1.00	2.00	3.00	—
1959	25,533	1.00	1.00	2.00	3.00	3.00
1959D	62,054	1.00	1.00	2.00	3.00	—
1960	30,856	1.00	1.00	2.00	3.00	3.00
1960D	63,000	1.00	1.00	2.00	3.00	—
1961	40,064	1.00	1.00	2.00	3.00	3.00
1961D	83,657	1.00	1.00	2.00	3.00	—
1962	39,374	1.00	1.00	2.00	2.00	3.00
1962D	127,555	1.00	1.00	2.00	2.00	—
1963	77,392	1.00	1.00	1.00	2.00	3.00
1963D	135,288	1.00	1.00	1.00	2.00	—
1964	564,341	1.00	1.00	1.00	2.00	3.00
1964D	704,136	1.00	1.00	1.00	2.00	—
1965	1,819,718	—	—	—	1.00	—
1966	821,102	—	—	—	1.00	—
1967	1,524,032	—	—	—	1.00	—
1968	220,732	—	—	—	1.00	—
1968D	101,534	—	—	—	1.00	—
1968S Proof only	3,042	—	—	—	—	1.00
1969	176,212	—	—	—	3.00	—
1969D	114,372	—	—	—	2.00	—
1969S Proof only	2,935	—	—	—	—	1.00
1970	136,420	—	—	—	1.00	—
1970D	417,341	—	—	—	1.00	—
1970S Proof only	2,633	—	—	—	—	1.00
1971	109,284	—	—	—	1.00	—
1971D	258,634	—	—	—	1.00	—
1971S Proof only	3,224	—	—	—	—	1.00
1972	215,048	—	—	—	1.00	—
1972D	311,068	—	—	—	1.00	—
1972S Proof only	3,268	—	—	—	—	1.00
1973	346,924	—	—	—	1.00	—
1973D	232,977	—	—	—	1.00	—
1973S Proof only	2,770	—	—	—	—	1.00
1974	801,456	—	—	—	1.00	—
1974D	353,160	—	—	—	1.00	—
1974S Proof only	2,617	—	—	—	—	1.00
1976 P&D	725,081	—	—	—	1.00	—
1976S Proof only	4,150	—	—	—	—	1.00
1976S Silver	15,000	—	—	—	3.00	3.00
1977 P&D	725,081	—	—	—	—	—
1977S Proof only	3,251	—	—	—	—	1.00
1978 P&D	808,825	—	—	—	—	—
1978S Proof only	3,128	—	—	—	—	1.00
1979 P-D	1,005,498	—	—	—	—	—

	Mintage (in thousands)	Good	Fine	Ex. Fine	Unc.	Proof
1979S Type I, Proof only	3,677	—	—	—	—	1.00
1979S Type II, Proof only, Sharp Mint Mark	—	—	—	—	—	2.00
1980 P&D	1,154,159	—	—	—	—	—
1980S Proof only	3,555	—	—	—	—	1.00
1981 P&D	1,177,439	—	—	—	—	—
1981S Proof only	4,063	—	—	—	—	1.00
1982 P	500,931	—	—	—	6.00	—
1982 D	480,043	—	—	—	3.00	—
1982S Proof only	3,857	—	—	—	—	2.00
1983 P	673,535	—	—	—	20.00	—
1983 D	617,806	—	—	—	12.00	—
1983S Proof only	3,278	—	—	—	—	3.00
1984 P&D	1,223,028	—	—	—	1.00	—
1984S Proof only	3,065	—	—	—	—	3.00
1985 P&D	1,295,782	—	—	—	1.00	—
1985S Proof only	3,363	—	—	—	—	2.00
1986 P&D	1,055,498	—	—	—	4.00	—
1986S Proof only	3,010	—	—	—	—	3.00
1987 P&D	1,238,094	—	—	—	—	—
1987S Proof only	4,228	—	—	—	—	2.00
1988 P&D	1,158,863	—	—	—	1.00	—
1988S Proof only	3,263	—	—	—	—	2.00
1989 P&D	1,409,404	—	—	—	1.00	—
1989S Proof only	3,220	—	—	—	—	2.00
1990 P&D	1,541,430	—	—	—	1.00	—
1990S Proof only	3,300	—	—	—	—	6.00
1991 P&D	1,201,935	—	—	—	1.00	—
1991S Proof only	2,868	—	—	—	—	3.00
1992 P&D	774,541	—	—	—	1.00	—
1992S Proof only	2,859	—	—	—	—	3.00
1992S Silver Proof	1,318	—	—	—	—	4.00
1993 P&D	1,284,752	—	—	—	1.00	—
1993S Proof only	2,633	—	—	—	—	5.00
1993S Silver Proof	761	—	—	—	—	6.00
1994 P&D	1,705,634	—	—	—	1.00	—
1994S Proof only	2,485	—	—	—	—	4.00
1994S Silver Proof	785	—	—	—	—	11.00
1995 P&D	2,107,552	—	—	—	1.00	—
1995S Proof only	2,010	—	—	—	—	15.00
1995S Silver Proof	839	—	—	—	—	17.00
1996 P&D	1,831,908	—	—	—	1.00	—
1996S Proof only	1,750	—	—	—	—	4.00
1996S Silver Proof	775	—	—	—	—	11.00
1997 P&D	1,195,420	—	—	—	1.00	—
1997S Proof only	1,975	—	—	—	—	9.00
1997S Silver Proof	742	—	—	—	—	15.00
1998 P&D	1,717,268	—	—	—	1.00	—

	Mintage (in thousands)	Good	Fine	Ex. Fine	Unc.	Proof
1998S Proof only	—	—	—	—	—	10.00
1998S Silver Proof	879	—	—	—	—	9.00

(Note: No 1975 dated quarters were minted.)

39
STATEHOOD QUARTERS

1999 DELAWARE QUARTER

	Mintage (in thousands)	Ex. Fine	Unc.	Proof
1999P Delaware	373,400	.50	1.50	—
1999D Delaware	400,832	.50	1.50	—
1999S Delaware Proof only	—	—	—	6.00
1999S Delaware Silver Proof	800	—	—	14.00

1999 PENNSYLVANIA QUARTER

1999P Pennsylvania	349,000	.50	1.00	—
1999D Pennsylvania	358,332	.50	1.00	—
1999S Pennsylvania Proof only	—	—	—	5.00
1999S Pennsylvania Silver Proof	800	—	—	14.00

1999 NEW JERSEY QUARTER

	Mintage (in thousands)	Ex. Fine	Unc.	Proof
1999P New Jersey	363,200	—	.50	—
1999D New Jersey	299,028	—	1.00	—
1999S New Jersey Proof only	—	—	—	5.00
1999S New Jersey Silver Proof	800	—	—	12.00

1999 GEORGIA QUARTER

1999P Georgia	451,188	—	.50	—
1999D Georgia	488,744	—	.50	—
1999S Georgia Proof only	—	—	—	5.00
1999S Georgia Silver Proof	800	—	—	12.00

1999 CONNECTICUT QUARTER

1999P Connecticut	688,744	—	.50	—
1999D Connecticut	657,489	—	.50	—
1999S Connecticut Proof only	—	—	—	5.00
1999S Connecticut Silver Proof	800	—	—	12.00

2000 MASSACHUSETTS QUARTER

2000P Massachusetts	628,600	—	.50	—
2000D Massachusetts	535,184	—	.50	—
2000S Massachusetts Proof only	938	—	—	4.00
2000S Massachusetts Silver Proof	854	—	—	6.00

2000 MARYLAND QUARTER

	Mintage (in thousands)	Ex. Fine	Unc.	Proof
2000P Maryland	678,200	—	.50	—
2000D Maryland	556,532	—	.50	—
2000S Maryland Proof only	938	—	—	4.00
2000S Maryland Silver Proof	856	—	—	6.00

2000 SOUTH CAROLINA QUARTER

2000P South Carolina	742,576	—	.50	—
2000D South Carolina	566,208	—	.50	—
2000S South Carolina Proof only	938	—	—	4.00
2000S South Carolina Silver Proof	856	—	—	6.00

2000 NEW HAMPSHIRE QUARTER

2000P New Hampshire	673,040	—	.50	—
2000D New Hampshire	495,976	—	.50	—
2000S New Hampshire Proof only	938	—	—	4.00
2000S New Hampshire Silver Proof	856	—	—	6.00

2000 Virginia quarter

	Mintage (in thousands)	Ex. Fine	Unc.	Proof
2000P Virginia	943,000	—	.50	—
2000D Virginia	651,616	—	.50	—
2000S Virginia Proof only	938	—	—	4.00
2000S Virginia Silver Proof	856	—	—	6.00

2001 New York quarter

2001P New York	655,400	—	.50	—
2001D New York	619,640	—	.50	—
2001S New York Proof only	—	—	—	4.00
2001S New York Silver Proof	—	—	—	7.00

2001 North Carolina quarter

2001P North Carolina	627,600	—	.50	—
2001D North Carolina	427,876	—	.50	—
2001S North Carolina Proof only	—	—	—	4.00
2001S North Carolina Silver Proof	—	—	—	7.00

2001 RHODE ISLAND QUARTER

	Mintage (in thousands)	Ex. Fine	Unc.	Proof
2001P Rhode Island	423,000	—	.50	—
2001D Rhode Island	447,100	—	.50	—
2001S Rhode Island Proof only	—	—	—	4.00
2001S Rhode Island Silver Proof	—	—	—	7.00

2001 VERMONT QUARTER

2001P Vermont	423,400	—	.50	—
2001D Vermont	459,404	—	.50	—
2001S Vermont Proof only	—	—	—	4.00
2001S Vermont Silver Proof	—	—	—	7.00

2001 KENTUCKY QUARTER

2001P Kentucky	353,000	—	.50	—
2001D Kentucky	370,564	—	.50	—
2001S Kentucky Proof only	—	—	—	4.00
2001S Kentucky Silver Proof...........	—	—	—	7.00

2002 TENNESSEE QUARTER

	Mintage (in thousands)	Ex. Fine	Unc.	Proof
2002P Tennessee	—	—	—	—
2002D Tennessee	—	—	—	—
2002S Tennessee Proof only	—	—	—	3.00
2002S Tennessee Silver Proof	—	—	—	5.00

2002 OHIO QUARTER

	Mintage	Ex. Fine	Unc.	Proof
2002P Ohio	—	—	—	—
2002D Ohio	—	—	—	—
2002S Ohio Proof only	—	—	—	3.00
2002S Ohio Silver Proof	—	—	—	5.00

2002 LOUISIANA QUARTER

	Mintage	Ex. Fine	Unc.	Proof
2002P Louisiana	—	—	—	—
2002D Louisiana	—	—	—	—
2002S Louisiana Proof only	—	—	—	3.00
2002S Louisiana Silver Proof	—	—	—	5.00

2002 INDIANA QUARTER

	Mintage (in thousands)	Ex. Fine	Unc.	Proof
2002P Indiana	—	—	—	—
2002D Indiana	—	—	—	—
2002S Indiana Proof only	—	—	—	3.00
2002S Indiana Silver Proof	—	—	—	5.00

2002 MISSISSIPPI QUARTER

	Mintage	Ex. Fine	Unc.	Proof
2002P Mississippi	—	—	—	—
2002D Mississippi	—	—	—	—
2002S Mississippi Proof only	—	—	—	3.00
2002S Mississippi Silver Proof	—	—	—	5.00

FLOWING HAIR HALF DOLLAR

FLOWING HAIR TYPE

	Mintage (in thousands)	Good	Fine	V. Fine	Unc.
1794	23	1,375.00	3,650.00	6,500.00	65,000.00
1795	300	485.00	1,250.00	2,450.00	20,000.00

DRAPED BUST HALF DOLLAR, SMALL EAGLE

DRAPED BUST TYPE

	Mintage (in thousands)	Good	Fine	V. Fine	Unc.
1796 15 Stars	4	11,750.00	19,250.00	27,500.00	100,000.00
1796 16 Stars	(included above)	13,500.00	22,750.00	32,500.00	125,000.00
1797	(included above)	11,250.00	19,500.00	28,500.00	85,000.00

DRAPED BUST HALF DOLLAR, HERALDIC EAGLE

	Mintage (in thousands)	Good	Fine	V. Fine	Unc.
1801	30	225.00	550.00	900.00	22,000.00
1802	30	200.00	525.00	825.00	21,000.00
1803	188	160.00	260.00	450.00	7,000.00
1805, All Kinds	212	150.00	240.00	375.00	7,000.00
1805 over 4	—	170.00	500.00	700.00	20,000.00
1806, All Kinds	840	150.00	240.00	350.00	6,750.00
1806 over 5, All Kinds	—	150.00	265.00	375.00	7,000.00
1806 over Inverted 6	—	170.00	600.00	925.00	12,000.00
1807	301	150.00	240.00	350.00	6,500.00

CAPPED BUST HALF DOLLAR, LETTERED EDGE

CAPPED BUST TYPE

	Mintage (in thousands)	Good	Fine	Unc.
1807, All Kinds	751	65.00	185.00	3,750.00
1807 50 over 20	—	50.00	130.00	3,500.00
1808, All Kinds	1,369	50.00	65.00	1,500.00
1808 over 7	—	50.00	85.00	2,400.00
1809	1,406	50.00	65.00	1,650.00
1810	1,276	50.00	65.00	1,650.00
1811	1,204	50.00	65.00	1,000.00
1812, All Kinds	1,628	45.00	65.00	850.00
1812 over 11	—	50.00	90.00	2,750.00
1813	1,242	45.00	65.00	1,175.00

	Mintage (in thousands)	Good	Fine	Unc.
1814, All Kinds	1,039	50.00	65.00	1,050.00
1814 over 13	—	50.00	90.00	2,350.00
1815 over 12	47	750.00	1,300.00	10,000.00
1817, All Kinds	1,216	50.00	60.00	1,100.00
1817 over 13	—	75.00	160.00	3,650.00
1817 over 14 (Rare)	—	45,000.00	110,000.00	—
1818, All Kinds	1,960	50.00	60.00	925.00
1818 over 17	—	50.00	60.00	1,500.00
1819 over 18	—	50.00	65.00	1,375.00
1819, All Kinds	2,208	45.00	55.00	975.00
1820, All Kinds	251	45.00	70.00	1,200.00
1820 over 19	—	50.00	75.00	1,750.00
1821	1,306	45.00	65.00	1,175.00
1822, All Kinds	1,560	45.00	55.00	625.00
1822 over 1	—	50.00	80.00	1,150.00
1823, All Kinds	1,694	45.00	55.00	750.00
1823 Broken 3	—	50.00	85.00	1,300.00
1823 Patched 3	—	50.00	80.00	1,150.00

	Mintage (in thousands)	Good	Fine	V. Fine	Unc.
1824	3,505	45.00	50.00	60.00	475.00
1824 over 21, All Kinds	—	45.00	60.00	75.00	1,100.00
1824 over Various Dates	—	50.00	65.00	85.00	1,175.00
1825	2,943	45.00	50.00	60.00	475.00
1826	4,004	45.00	50.00	60.00	475.00
1827	5,493	45.00	50.00	60.00	475.00
1827 over 6, All Kinds	—	45.00	55.00	75.00	1,050.00
1828	3,075	45.00	50.00	60.00	500.00
1829, All Kinds	3,712	45.00	50.00	60.00	475.00
1829 over 27, All Kinds	—	45.00	65.00	75.00	1,250.00
1830	4,765	45.00	50.00	60.00	475.00
1831	5,874	45.00	50.00	60.00	475.00
1832	4,797	45.00	50.00	60.00	475.00
1833	5,206	45.00	50.00	60.00	475.00
1834	6,412	45.00	50.00	60.00	475.00
1835	5,352	45.00	50.00	60.00	475.00
1836 (Lettered Edge), All Kinds .	6,545	45.00	50.00	60.00	475.00
1836 50 over 00	—	50.00	65.00	110.00	1,600.00

CAPPED BUST HALF DOLLAR, REEDED EDGE

	Mintage (in thousands)	Good	Fine	V. Fine	Unc.
1836 Reeded Edge	1	675.00	1,050.00	1,250.00	6,750.00
1837	3,630	45.00	60.00	90.00	785.00
1838	3,546	45.00	60.00	90.00	785.00
1838O (Very rare)	20 Pieces	—	—	—	120,000.00
1839	3,335	45.00	60.00	95.00	1,150.00
1839O	179	125.00	235.00	335.00	2,850.00

LIBERTY SEATED TYPE

LIBERTY SEATED HALF DOLLAR, NO MOTTO

	Mintage (in thousands)	Good	Fine	V. Fine	Unc.
1839 No Drapery from Elbow ...	—	45.00	130.00	360.00	5,750.00
1839 With Drapery	1,972	25.00	60.00	85.00	575.00
1840	1,435	27.00	55.00	75.00	500.00
1840O	855	25.00	50.00	85.00	550.00
1841	310	40.00	85.00	135.00	1,350.00
1841O	401	22.00	50.00	80.00	675.00
1842	2,013	22.00	48.00	70.00	750.00
1842O	957	21.00	45.00	65.00	1,350.00
1843	3,844	21.00	45.00	60.00	500.00
1843O	2,268	21.00	48.00	60.00	525.00
1844	1,766	21.00	45.00	55.00	475.00
1844O	2,005	21.00	45.00	55.00	625.00
1845	589	27.00	60.00	120.00	850.00
1845O, All Kinds	2,094	21.00	45.00	60.00	550.00
1845O, No Drapery	—	28.00	75.00	110.00	1,400.00
1846, All Kinds	2,210	22.00	45.00	60.00	525.00

	Mintage (in thousands)	Good	Fine	V. Fine	Unc.
1846 over Horizontal 6	—	135.00	235.00	360.00	3,750.00
1846O	2,304	22.00	45.00	55.00	1,100.00
1847	1,156	20.00	45.00	60.00	500.00
1847 7 over 6	—	1,750.00	3,000.00	4,250.00	—
1847O	2,584	20.00	45.00	60.00	675.00
1848	580	40.00	85.00	150.00	1,050.00
1848O	3,180	21.00	45.00	65.00	750.00
1849	1,252	30.00	60.00	85.00	900.00
1849O	2,310	22.00	45.00	65.00	785.00
1850	227	210.00	425.00	525.00	1,750.00
1850O	2,456	22.00	45.00	65.00	550.00
1851	201	285.00	450.00	525.00	1,650.00
1851O	402	25.00	60.00	80.00	525.00
1852	77	350.00	575.00	775.00	1,475.00
1852O	144	60.00	150.00	250.00	2,000.00
1853O No Rays & Arrows ..... (Very rare)	—	—	—	—	—

1853 LIBERTY SEATED HALF DOLLAR WITH ARROWS AND RAYS

	Mintage (in thousands)	Good	Fine	V. Fine	Unc.
1853 Arrows & Rays	3,533	22.00	55.00	90.00	1,650.00
1853O	1,328	23.00	65.00	150.00	2,500.00

LIBERTY SEATED HALF DOLLAR WITH ARROWS

	Mintage (in thousands)	Good	Fine	V. Fine	Unc.	Proof
1854 Arrows at Date ...	2,982	20.00	45.00	65.00	675.00	—
1854O	5,240	20.00	45.00	65.00	675.00	—
1855	760	25.00	45.00	67.00	775.00	20,000.00
1855 over 54	—	75.00	175.00	275.00	2,500.00	—
1855O	3,688	20.00	45.00	65.00	675.00	—
1855S	130	300.00	675.00	1,300.00	—	—
1856 No Arrows	938	20.00	45.00	55.00	465.00	9,500.00
1856O	2,658	20.00	45.00	55.00	465.00	—
1856S	211	45.00	130.00	250.00	3,850.00	—
1857	1,988	20.00	45.00	55.00	465.00	5,000.00
1857O	818	20.00	45.00	55.00	1,275.00	—
1857S	158	55.00	135.00	240.00	4,250.00	—
1858	4,226	20.00	45.00	55.00	465.00	3,500.00
1858O	7,294	20.00	45.00	55.00	465.00	—
1858S	476	22.00	55.00	125.00	1,150.00	—
1859	748	30.00	60.00	85.00	485.00	1,800.00
1859O	2,834	20.00	45.00	55.00	465.00	—
1859S	566	22.00	55.00	95.00	975.00	—
1860	304	22.00	45.00	57.00	625.00	1,675.00
1860O	1,290	20.00	45.00	55.00	465.00	—
1860S	472	22.00	45.00	55.00	875.00	—
1861	2,888	20.00	45.00	55.00	500.00	1,675.00
1861O	2,533	20.00	45.00	55.00	475.00	—
1861S	940	20.00	45.00	55.00	725.00	—
1862	254	30.00	65.00	115.00	550.00	1,675.00
1862S	1,325	20.00	45.00	55.00	625.00	—
1863	504	22.00	55.00	75.00	550.00	1,675.00
1863S	916	20.00	45.00	55.00	600.00	—
1864	380	25.00	60.00	95.00	475.00	1,675.00
1864S	658	20.00	45.00	60.00	925.00	—
1865	512	25.00	55.00	85.00	500.00	1,675.00
1865S	675	20.00	45.00	55.00	675.00	—
1866 No Motto	Unique	—	—	—	—	—
1866S No Motto, ... All Kinds	1,054	75.00	200.00	350.00	4,250.00	—

LIBERTY SEATED HALF DOLLAR WITH MOTTO

	Mintage (in thousands)	Good	Fine	V. Fine	Unc.	Proof
1866 Motto	746	21.00	45.00	65.00	575.00	975.00
1866S Motto	—	20.00	43.00	55.00	650.00	—
1867	450	27.00	65.00	115.00	575.00	975.00
1867S	1,196	20.00	45.00	55.00	650.00	—
1868	418	40.00	90.00	130.00	600.00	975.00
1868S	1,160	20.00	45.00	65.00	625.00	—
1869	796	22.00	50.00	67.00	500.00	975.00
1869S	656	20.00	45.00	70.00	1,000.00	—
1870	635	23.00	47.00	70.00	500.00	975.00
1870CC	55	500.00	1,500.00	3,600.00	35,000.00	—
1870S	1,004	20.00	45.00	75.00	1,050.00	—
1871	1,205	20.00	45.00	60.00	450.00	975.00
1871CC	150	130.00	410.00	700.00	11,500.00	—
1871S	2,178	20.00	45.00	55.00	575.00	—
1872	882	20.00	45.00	55.00	600.00	975.00
1872CC	252	70.00	200.00	360.00	4,750.00	—
1872S	580	30.00	70.00	125.00	1,200.00	—
1873	802	27.00	65.00	100.00	675.00	975.00
1873CC No Arrows	123	130.00	325.00	600.00	11,000.00	—
1873 Arrows	1,816	21.00	50.00	100.00	1,150.00	2,450.00
1873CC Arrows	215	135.00	360.00	775.00	6,850.00	—
1873S	228	55.00	130.00	250.00	2,750.00	—
1874	2,360	21.00	50.00	100.00	1,150.00	2,450.00
1874CC	59	275.00	750.00	1,250.00	12,000.00	—
1874S	394	32.00	85.00	190.00	2,000.00	—
1875 No Arrows	6,028	20.00	45.00	55.00	450.00	975.00
1875CC	1,008	27.00	55.00	80.00	675.00	—
1875S	3,200	20.00	45.00	65.00	375.00	—
1876	8,419	20.00	42.00	55.00	375.00	975.00
1876CC	1,956	22.00	50.00	70.00	675.00	—
1876S	4,528	20.00	42.00	55.00	375.00	—
1877	8,305	20.00	42.00	55.00	375.00	975.00
1877CC	1,420	22.00	45.00	70.00	700.00	—
1877S	5,356	20.00	42.00	55.00	375.00	—
1878	1,378	25.00	55.00	85.00	485.00	975.00

	Mintage (in thousands)	Good	Fine	V. Fine	Unc.	Proof
1878CC	62	300.00	575.00	900.00	5,500.00	—
1878S	12	10,000.00	15,000.00	17,500.00	37,500.00	—
1879	6	225.00	300.00	335.00	650.00	975.00
1880	10	180.00	250.00	285.00	650.00	975.00
1881	11	180.00	250.00	285.00	675.00	975.00
1882	6	245.00	325.00	350.00	675.00	975.00
1883	9	230.00	285.00	325.00	675.00	975.00
1884	5	290.00	350.00	375.00	700.00	975.00
1885	6	300.00	325.00	350.00	725.00	975.00
1886	6	330.00	430.00	485.00	750.00	975.00
1887	6	410.00	550.00	580.00	875.00	975.00
1888	13	185.00	240.00	285.00	675.00	975.00
1889	13	185.00	265.00	300.00	675.00	975.00
1890	13	195.00	240.00	310.00	685.00	975.00
1891	201	45.00	100.00	115.00	450.00	975.00

BARBER-TYPE HALF DOLLAR

BARBER OR LIBERTY HEAD TYPE

	Mintage (in thousands)	Good	Fine	V. Fine	Unc.	Proof
1892	935	23.00	48.00	90.00	450.00	975.00
1892O	390	150.00	285.00	315.00	875.00	—
1892S	1,029	130.00	235.00	300.00	950.00	—
1893	1,827	14.00	50.00	85.00	550.00	975.00
1893O	1,389	23.00	70.00	125.00	550.00	—
1893S	740	100.00	185.00	300.00	1,250.00	—
1894	1,149	18.00	70.00	100.00	500.00	975.00
1894O	2,138	14.00	63.00	95.00	525.00	—
1894S	4,049	14.00	48.00	80.00	500.00	—
1895	1,835	11.00	50.00	85.00	575.00	975.00
1895O	1,766	13.00	55.00	100.00	625.00	—
1895S	1,108	20.00	75.00	135.00	600.00	—
1896	951	18.00	60.00	100.00	550.00	975.00
1896O	924	24.00	100.00	150.00	1,350.00	—
1896S	1,141	65.00	125.00	210.00	1,300.00	—
1897	2,481	10.00	35.00	75.00	475.00	975.00
1897O	632	55.00	350.00	650.00	1,600.00	—
1897S	934	115.00	260.00	400.00	1,400.00	—

	Mintage (in thousands)	Good	Fine	V. Fine	Unc.	Proof
1898	2,957	9.00	30.00	71.00	450.00	975.00
1898O	874	20.00	110.00	185.00	975.00	—
1898S	2,359	11.00	42.00	86.00	925.00	—
1899	5,539	10.00	28.00	71.00	450.00	975.00
1899O	1,724	10.00	50.00	90.00	650.00	—
1899S	1,686	13.00	50.00	88.00	775.00	—
1900	4,763	9.00	28.00	71.00	425.00	975.00
1900O	2,744	9.00	40.00	90.00	900.00	—
1900S	2,560	9.00	42.00	95.00	675.00	—
1901	4,269	9.00	28.00	67.00	425.00	975.00
1901O	1,124	10.00	53.00	115.00	1,450.00	—
1901S	847	19.00	110.00	245.00	1,600.00	—
1902	4,923	9.00	28.00	67.00	425.00	975.00
1902O	2,526	9.00	40.00	80.00	775.00	—
1902S	1,461	9.00	50.00	90.00	725.00	—
1903	2,279	8.00	42.00	75.00	500.00	975.00
1903O	2,100	9.00	42.00	75.00	700.00	—
1903S	1,921	9.00	42.00	75.00	650.00	—
1904	2,993	9.00	28.00	65.00	450.00	975.00
1904O	1,118	11.00	55.00	115.00	1,150.00	—
1904S	553	19.00	150.00	360.00	3,350.00	—
1905	663	12.00	55.00	85.00	575.00	975.00
1905O	505	15.00	85.00	150.00	750.00	—
1905S	2,494	9.00	38.00	79.00	675.00	—
1906	2,639	8.00	27.00	65.00	425.00	975.00
1906D	4,028	8.00	30.00	72.00	460.00	—
1906O	2,446	8.00	40.00	75.00	625.00	—
1906S	1,740	9.00	44.00	75.00	600.00	—
1907	2,599	8.00	26.00	65.00	425.00	975.00
1907D	3,856	8.00	27.00	65.00	425.00	—
1907O	3,947	8.00	28.00	70.00	585.00	—
1907S	1,250	9.00	65.00	125.00	1,475.00	—
1908	1,355	8.00	30.00	72.00	425.00	975.00
1908D	3,280	8.00	30.00	72.00	440.00	—
1908O	5,360	8.00	30.00	72.00	550.00	—
1908S	1,645	9.00	47.00	78.00	775.00	—
1909	2,369	8.00	30.00	65.00	425.00	975.00
1909O	925	10.00	45.00	90.00	750.00	—
1909S	1,764	8.00	33.00	75.00	600.00	—
1910	419	11.00	65.00	120.00	650.00	975.00
1910S	1,948	9.00	32.00	72.00	675.00	—
1911	1,407	9.00	28.00	65.00	450.00	975.00
1911D	695	8.00	36.00	70.00	560.00	—
1911S	1,272	8.00	35.00	75.00	575.00	—
1912	1,551	8.00	26.00	65.00	425.00	975.00
1912D	2,301	8.00	26.00	65.00	450.00	—
1912S	1,370	8.00	32.00	72.00	550.00	—

	Mintage (in thousands)	Good	Fine	V. Fine	Unc.	Proof
1913	189	21.00	115.00	185.00	975.00	975.00
1913D	534	8.00	35.00	72.00	475.00	—
1913S	604	8.00	44.00	90.00	650.00	—
1914	125	31.00	170.00	325.00	975.00	1,050.00
1914S	992	8.00	34.00	72.00	575.00	—
1915	138	22.00	90.00	210.00	1,050.00	1,000.00
1915D	1,170	8.00	27.00	65.00	425.00	—
1915S	1,604	8.00	30.00	65.00	425.00	—

LIBERTY WALKING HALF DOLLAR

LIBERTY WALKING TYPE

	Mintage (in thousands)	Good	Fine	Ex. Fine	Unc.
1916	608	30.00	57.00	160.00	300.00
1916D on Obverse	1,014	24.00	43.00	145.00	400.00
1916S on Obverse	508	90.00	140.00	525.00	1,150.00
1917	12,292	4.00	10.00	35.00	125.00
1917D on Obverse	765	15.00	43.00	150.00	575.00
1917D on Reverse	1,940	10.00	28.00	210.00	875.00
1917S on Obverse	952	18.00	55.00	665.00	2,450.00
1917S on Reverse	5,554	6.00	14.00	55.00	475.00
1918	6,634	5.00	16.00	145.00	600.00
1918D	3,853	7.00	22.00	155.00	1,000.00
1918S	10,282	6.00	14.00	60.00	575.00
1919	962	17.00	50.00	450.00	1,250.00
1919D	1,165	13.00	55.00	585.00	3,750.00
1919S	1,552	15.00	40.00	750.00	2,675.00
1920	6,372	5.00	13.00	65.00	360.00
1920D	1,551	10.00	35.00	375.00	1,450.00
1920S	4,624	6.00	15.00	200.00	875.00
1921	246	100.00	195.00	1,400.00	3,150.00
1921D	208	150.00	275.00	2,000.00	3,350.00
1921S	548	27.00	110.00	4,150.00	12,000.00
1923S	2,178	9.00	24.00	210.00	1,450.00
1927S	2,392	5.00	11.00	90.00	875.00
1928S	1,940	5.00	13.00	100.00	875.00
1929D	1,001	6.00	13.00	75.00	385.00

	Mintage (in thousands)	Good	Fine	Ex. Fine	Unc.
1929S	1,902	5.00	10.00	80.00	425.00
1933S	1,786	6.00	10.00	45.00	675.00
1934	6,964	3.00	4.00	10.00	75.00
1934D	2,361	5.00	6.00	25.00	165.00
1934S	3,652	4.00	4.00	25.00	465.00
1935	9,162	3.00	4.00	7.00	50.00
1935D	3,004	4.00	5.00	25.00	165.00
1935S	3,854	3.00	4.00	25.00	325.00

	Mintage (in thousands)	Good	Fine	Ex. Fine	Unc.	Proof
1936	12,618	3.00	4.00	7.00	45.00	2,450.00
1936D	4,252	3.00	4.00	17.00	90.00	—
1936S	3,884	3.00	4.00	20.00	150.00	—
1937	9,528	3.00	4.00	7.00	45.00	675.00
1937D	1,676	5.00	6.00	28.00	210.00	—
1937S	2,090	4.00	5.00	18.00	155.00	—
1938	4,118	4.00	5.00	10.00	85.00	600.00
1938D	492	28.00	35.00	90.00	390.00	—
1939	6,821	3.00	4.00	7.00	45.00	550.00
1939D	4,267	3.00	4.00	9.00	45.00	—
1939S	2,552	4.00	6.00	13.00	110.00	—
1940	9,167	3.00	4.00	6.00	40.00	485.00
1940S	4,550	3.00	4.00	7.00	40.00	—
1941	24,207	3.00	4.00	6.00	35.00	425.00
1941D	11,248	3.00	4.00	6.00	40.00	—
1941S	8,098	3.00	4.00	7.00	80.00	—
1942	47,839	3.00	4.00	6.00	35.00	425.00
1942D	10,974	3.00	4.00	6.00	50.00	—
1942S	12,708	3.00	4.00	6.00	45.00	—

	Mintage (in thousands)	Good	Fine	Ex. Fine	Unc.
1943	53,190	3.00	4.00	6.00	35.00
1943D	11,346	3.00	4.00	6.00	50.00
1943S	13,450	3.00	4.00	6.00	40.00
1944	28,206	3.00	4.00	6.00	35.00
1944D	9,769	3.00	4.00	6.00	43.00
1944S	9,904	3.00	4.00	6.00	40.00
1945	31,502	3.00	4.00	6.00	35.00
1945D	9,967	3.00	4.00	6.00	40.00
1945S	10,156	3.00	4.00	6.00	40.00
1946	12,118	3.00	4.00	6.00	35.00
1946D	2,151	4.00	6.00	10.00	40.00
1946S	3,724	3.00	4.00	6.00	40.00
1947	4,094	3.00	4.00	8.00	40.00
1947D	3,901	3.00	4.00	8.00	40.00

FRANKLIN HALF DOLLAR

FRANKLIN TYPE

	Mintage (in thousands)	Ex. Fine	Unc.	Proof
1948	3,007	5.00	17.00	—
1948D	4,029	5.00	12.00	—
1949	5,614	6.00	40.00	—
1949D	4,121	7.00	40.00	—
1949S	3,748	10.00	55.00	—
1950	7,794	5.00	25.00	260.00
1950D	8,032	4.00	25.00	—
1951	16,860	4.00	12.00	210.00
1951D	9,475	4.00	24.00	—
1951S	13,696	4.00	22.00	—
1952	21,274	3.00	11.00	95.00
1952D	25,396	3.00	9.00	—
1952S	5,526	4.00	37.00	—
1953	2,797	6.00	16.00	75.00
1953D	20,900	3.00	8.00	—
1953S	4,148	4.00	22.00	—
1954	13,422	3.00	8.00	55.00
1954D	25,446	3.00	8.00	—
1954S	4,993	3.00	8.00	—
1955	2,876	6.00	11.00	32.00
1956	4,701	3.00	8.00	15.00
1957	6,362	3.00	8.00	16.00
1957D	19,967	3.00	6.00	—
1958	4,918	3.00	6.00	16.00
1958D	23,962	3.00	6.00	—
1959	7,349	3.00	6.00	14.00
1959D	13,054	3.00	6.00	—
1960	7,716	3.00	6.00	10.00
1960D	18,216	3.00	6.00	—
1961	11,318	3.00	6.00	10.00
1961D	20,276	3.00	6.00	—
1962	12,932	3.00	6.00	10.00
1962D	35,473	3.00	6.00	—

	Mintage (in thousands)	Ex. Fine	Unc.	Proof
1963	25,240	3.00	6.00	10.00
1963D	67,069	3.00	6.00	—

KENNEDY HALF DOLLAR

KENNEDY TYPE

	Mintage (in thousands)	Unc.	Proof
1964	277,255	4.00	8.00
1964D	156,205	4.00	—
1965	65,879	2.00	—
1966	108,985	2.00	—
1967	295,047	2.00	—
1968D	246,952	2.00	—
1968S Proof only	3,042	—	4.00
1969D	129,882	2.00	—
1969S Proof only	2,935	—	4.00
1970D	2,150	17.00	—
1970S Proof only	2,633	—	11.00
1971	155,164	2.00	—
1971D	302,097	1.00	—
1971S Proof only	3,224	—	3.00
1972	153,180	2.00	—
1972D	141,890	2.00	—
1972S Proof only	3,268	—	3.00
1973	64,964	2.00	—
1973D	83,171	2.00	—
1973S Proof only	2,770	—	2.50
1974	201,596	2.00	—
1974D	79,066	2.00	—
1974S Proof only	2,617	—	3.00
1976 P&D*	521,873	2.00	—
1976S Proof only*	7,059	—	2.00
1976S Silver*	15,000	4.00	5.00
1977 P&D	75,047	2.00	—
1977S Proof only	3,251	—	3.00

*Bicentennial coinage dated 1776–1976, with reverses showing Independence Hall in Philadelphia. No 1975 dated half dollars were struck.

	Mintage (in thousands)	Unc.	Proof
1978 P&D	28,116	2.00	—
1978S Proof only	3,128	—	2.00
1979 P&D	84,127	2.00	—
1979S Type I, Proof only	3,677	—	2.00
1979S Type II, Proof only, Sharp Mint Mark	—	—	13.00
1980 P&D	77,590	1.00	—
1980S Proof only	3,555	—	2.00
1981 P&D	57,384	2.00	—
1981S Proof only	4,063	—	3.00
1982 P&D	23,959	3.00	—
1982S Proof only	3,857	—	2.00
1983 P&D	66,611	4.00	—
1983S Proof only	3,279	—	4.00
1984 P&D	52,291	2.00	—
1984S Proof only	3,065	—	5.00
1985 P&D	38,521	3.00	—
1985S Proof only	3,363	—	3.00
1986 P&D	28,444	6.00	—
1986S	3,010	—	9.00
1987 P&D	5,781	5.00	—
1987S	4,228	—	3.00
1988 P&D	25,626	4.00	—
1988S	3,263	—	7.00
1989 P&D	47,542	2.00	—
1989S Proof only	3,220	—	7.00
1990 P&D	42,364	3.00	—
1990S Proof only	3,300	—	6.00
1991 P&D	29,929	3.00	—
1991S Proof only	2,868	—	12.00
1992 P&D	34,628	2.00	—
1992S Proof only	2,859	—	7.00
1992S Silver Proof	1,318	—	14.00
1993 P&D	30,510	2.00	—
1993S Proof only	2,633	—	13.00
1993S Silver Proof	761	—	23.00
1994 P&D	47,546	1.00	—
1994S Proof only	2,485	—	6.00
1994S Silver Proof	785	—	34.00
1995 P&D	52,784	—	—
1995S Proof only	2,010	—	29.00
1995S Silver Proof	839	—	95.00
1996 P&D	49,186	—	—
1996S Proof only	1,750	—	8.00
1996S Silver Proof	775	—	44.00
1997 P&D	40,758	1.00	—
1997S Proof only	1,975	—	21.00
1997S Silver Proof	742	—	88.00

	Mintage (in thousands)	Unc.	Proof
1998 P&D	30,710	—	—
1998S Proof only	—	—	12.00
1998S Silver Proof	879	—	26.00
1998S Silver Matte Proof	—	—	250.00
1999 P&D	19,582	—	—
1999S Proof only	—	—	10.00
1999S Silver Proof	800	—	13.00
2000 P&D	42,066	—	—
2000S Proof only	2,969	—	7.00
2000S Silver Proof	856	—	11.00
2001 P&D	40,704	2.00	—
2001S Proof only	—	—	10.00
2001S Silver Proof	—	—	12.00
2002 P&D	—	—	—
2002S Proof only	—	—	10.00
2002S Silver Proof	—	—	12.00

41

SILVER DOLLARS AND THEIR SUCCESSORS: 1794 AND FORWARD

FLOWING HAIR SILVER DOLLAR

FLOWING HAIR TYPE

	Mintage (in thousands)	Good	Fine	V. Fine	Unc.
1794	2	13,500.00	30,000.00	65,000.00	—
1795	160	800.00	2,350.00	3,950.00	35,000.00

DRAPED BUST SILVER DOLLAR, SMALL EAGLE

DRAPED BUST TYPE

	Mintage (in thousands)	Good	Fine	V. Fine	Unc.
1795	43	800.00	1,850.00	2,950.00	27,500.00
1796	73	725.00	1,800.00	2,900.00	31,000.00
1797 9 Stars Left, 7 Right, ... Large Letter Reverse	8	725.00	1,800.00	2,900.00	30,000.00
1797 9 Stars Left, 7 Right, ... Small Letter Reverse	(included above)	1,250.00	3,000.00	4,850.00	47,500.00
1797 10 Stars Left, 6 Right	(included above)	725.00	1,800.00	2,900.00	30,000.00
1798 13 Stars, All Kinds	328	950.00	1,875.00	3,100.00	32,500.00
1798 15 Stars	(included above)	1,200.00	2,250.00	3,350.00	35,000.00

DRAPED BUST SILVER DOLLAR, HERALDIC EAGLE

1798 Large Eagle	(included above)	525.00	1,175.00	1,800.00	17,500.00
1799 over 98, All Kinds	424	525.00	1,175.00	1,850.00	17,000.00
1799 Stars 7 Left, 6 Right, ... All Kinds	(included above)	525.00	1,175.00	1,800.00	16,500.00

	Mintage (in thousands)	Good	Fine	V. Fine	Unc.
1799 Stars 8 Left, 5 Right, ... All Kinds	(included above)	575.00	1,300.00	1,900.00	21,500.00
1800	221	525.00	1,175.00	1,800.00	17,000.00
1801	54	565.00	1,275.00	1,900.00	25,000.00
1802 over 1, All Kinds	42	525.00	1,175.00	1,850.00	18,500.00
1802, All Kinds	(included above)	525.00	1,200.00	1,850.00	18,500.00
1803	86	525.00	1,175.00	1,850.00	19,500.00
1804 (Very rare)	—	—	—	—	—

GOBRECHT SILVER DOLLAR

GOBRECHT PATTERNS

	Mintage (in thousands)	Proof
1836 C. Gobrecht F. in field below base. Reverse Eagle in field of stars (Rare)	—	28,000.00
1836 Obverse as above. Reverse Eagle flying in plain field (Rare)	—	30,000.00

	Mintage (in thousands)	V. Fine	Proof
1836 C. Gobrecht F. on base	1	4,350.00	14,500.00
1838	about 100 Pieces	6,000.00	22,500.00
1839	about 300 Pieces	5,750.00	17,500.00

LIBERTY SEATED SILVER DOLLAR, NO MOTTO

LIBERTY SEATED TYPE

	Mintage (in thousands)	V. Good	V. Fine	Unc.	Proof
1840	61	180.00	300.00	2,250.00	30,000.00
1841	173	150.00	250.00	1,800.00	30,000.00
1842	185	150.00	240.00	1,350.00	30,000.00
1843	165	150.00	240.00	1,650.00	30,000.00
1844	20	225.00	375.00	2,850.00	32,500.00
1845	25	250.00	325.00	6,500.00	30,000.00
1846	111	150.00	260.00	1,850.00	28,500.00
1846O	59	175.00	325.00	3,200.00	—
1847	141	150.00	240.00	1,100.00	22,500.00
1848	15	275.00	500.00	3,350.00	25,000.00
1849	63	160.00	260.00	1,850.00	32,500.00
1850	8	450.00	775.00	5,250.00	25,000.00
1850O	40	235.00	675.00	7,850.00	—
1851	1	1,250.00	3,600.00	26,000.00	27,500.00
1852	1	1,200.00	3,350.00	24,500.00	25,000.00
1853	46	185.00	385.00	2,750.00	25,000.00
1854	33	1,200.00	2,450.00	7,000.00	17,000.00
1855	26	975.00	1,950.00	7,750.00	17,000.00
1856	64	340.00	550.00	3,850.00	13,500.00
1857	94	335.00	575.00	2,650.00	11,500.00
1858	About 300 Pieces	3,000.00	4,000.00	—	11,000.00
1859	257	240.00	400.00	1,675.00	3,500.00
1859O	360	150.00	240.00	1,250.00	—
1859S	20	300.00	650.00	11,000.00	—
1860	219	210.00	400.00	1,250.00	3,500.00
1860O	515	150.00	240.00	1,250.00	—
1861	79	575.00	825.00	2,950.00	3,750.00
1862	12	475.00	750.00	2,950.00	3,500.00
1863	28	275.00	425.00	2,650.00	3,600.00
1864	31	225.00	425.00	2,650.00	3,500.00
1865	47	210.00	400.00	2,500.00	3,250.00

LIBERTY SEATED SILVER DOLLAR WITH MOTTO

	Mintage (in thousands)	V. Good	V. Fine	Unc.	Proof
1866	50	210.00	390.00	1,750.00	2,750.00
1867	48	200.00	375.00	1,750.00	2,750.00
1868	163	175.00	350.00	2,250.00	2,750.00
1869	424	160.00	275.00	1,825.00	2,750.00
1870	416	150.00	240.00	1,500.00	2,750.00
1870CC	12	350.00	775.00	13,500.00	
1870S (Rare)	—	—	100,000.00	—	—
1871	1,075	150.00	240.00	1,100.00	2,750.00
1871CC	1	2,100.00	5,000.00	55,000.00	—
1872	1,106	150.00	240.00	1,100.00	2,750.00
1872CC	3	1,200.00	2,850.00	21,000.00	—
1872S	9	290.00	575.00	10,000.00	—
1873	294	160.00	260.00	1,475.00	2,750.00
1873CC	2	4,500.00	8,500.00	75,000.00	—
1873S (Unknown)	1	—	—	—	—

MORGAN SILVER DOLLAR

MORGAN OR LIBERTY HEAD TYPE

	Mintage (in thousands)	Ex. Fine	Unc.	Proof
1878 8 Tail Feathers	750	25.00	115.00	2,350.00
1878 7 Tail Feathers over 8 Tail Feathers	9,760	30.00	130.00	—

	Mintage (in thousands)	Ex. Fine	Unc.	Proof
1878 7 Tail Feathers, Reverse of 1878	(included above)	20.00	55.00	2,650.00
1878 7 Tail Feathers, Reverse of 1879	(included above)	20.00	65.00	30,000.00
1878CC	2,212	65.00	165.00	—
1878S	9,774	19.00	45.00	—
1879	14,807	15.00	30.00	1,875.00
1879CC	756	325.00	1,675.00	—
1879O	2,887	15.00	85.00	—
1879S	9,110	15.00	30.00	—
1880	12,601	15.00	30.00	1,875.00
1880CC	591	160.00	325.00	—
1880O	5,305	15.00	85.00	—
1880S	8,990	15.00	27.00	—
1881	9,164	16.00	30.00	1,875.00
1881CC	296	195.00	300.00	—
1881O	5,708	15.00	27.00	—
1881S	12,760	15.00	27.00	—
1882	11,101	15.00	27.00	1,875.00
1882CC	1,133	63.00	130.00	—
1882O	6,090	15.00	26.00	—
1882S	9,250	15.00	27.00	—
1883	12,291	15.00	26.00	1,875.00
1883CC	1,204	63.00	125.00	—
1883O	8,725	15.00	26.00	—
1883S	6,250	32.00	525.00	—
1884	14,071	15.00	26.00	1,875.00
1884CC	1,136	70.00	125.00	—
1884O	9,730	15.00	26.00	—
1884S	3,200	40.00	3,850.00	—
1885	17,788	15.00	26.00	1,875.00
1885CC	228	245.00	325.00	—
1885O	9,185	15.00	26.00	—
1885S	1,497	20.00	175.00	—
1886	19,964	15.00	26.00	1,875.00
1886O	10,710	17.00	450.00	—
1886S	750	50.00	220.00	—
1887	20,291	15.00	26.00	1,875.00
1887O	11,550	15.00	55.00	—
1887S	1,771	20.00	110.00	—
1888	19,184	15.00	26.00	1,875.00
1888O	12,150	15.00	30.00	—
1888S	657	53.00	230.00	—
1889	21,737	15.00	26.00	1,875.00
1889CC	350	1,250.00	8,750.00	—
1889O	11,875	16.00	140.00	—

	Mintage (in thousands)	Ex. Fine	Unc.	Proof
1889S	700	35.00	165.00	—
1890	16,803	15.00	30.00	1,875.00
1890CC	2,309	55.00	300.00	—
1890O	10,701	15.00	45.00	—
1890S	8,230	15.00	55.00	—
1891	8,694	15.00	60.00	1,875.00
1891CC	1,608	55.00	280.00	—
1891O	7,955	15.00	120.00	—
1891S	5,296	17.00	60.00	—
1892	1,037	25.00	160.00	1,875.00
1892CC	1,352	130.00	500.00	—
1892O	2,742	26.00	125.00	—
1892S	1,200	175.00	18,500.00	—
1893	390	165.00	475.00	1,875.00
1893CC	677	575.00	1,800.00	—
1893O	300	225.00	1,700.00	—
1893S	100	4,750.00	50,000.00	—
1894	111	485.00	1,300.00	1,900.00
1894O	1,723	50.00	575.00	—
1894S	1,260	110.00	460.00	—
1895	13	16,500.00	—	26,000.00
1895O	450	325.00	14,000.00	—
1895S	400	450.00	1,850.00	—
1896	9,977	15.00	26.00	1,875.00
1896O	4,900	18.00	875.00	—
1896S	5,000	150.00	900.00	—
1897	2,823	15.00	26.00	1,950.00
1897O	4,004	22.00	750.00	—
1897S	5,825	15.00	55.00	—
1898	5,885	15.00	26.00	1,875.00
1898O	4,440	15.00	26.00	—
1898S	4,102	30.00	175.00	—
1899	331	50.00	95.00	1,875.00
1899O	12,290	15.00	30.00	—
1899S	2,562	35.00	210.00	—
1900	8,831	16.00	30.00	1,875.00
1900O	12,590	18.00	37.00	—
1900S	3,540	35.00	210.00	—
1901	6,963	60.00	1,750.00	1,950.00
1901O	13,320	16.00	30.00	—
1901S	2,284	50.00	300.00	—
1902	7,995	15.00	45.00	1,875.00
1902O	8,636	15.00	26.00	—
1902S	1,530	100.00	250.00	—
1903	4,653	32.00	42.00	1,875.00
1903O	4,450	170.00	300.00	—
1903S	1,241	300.00	2,850.00	—

	Mintage (in thousands)	Ex. Fine	Unc.	Proof
1904	2,789	17.00	85.00	1,875.00
1904O	3,720	17.00	27.00	—
1904S	2,304	200.00	1,200.00	—
1921	44,690	10.00	16.00	4,000.00
1921D	20,345	12.00	40.00	—
1921S	21,695	12.00	32.00	—

PEACE DOLLAR

PEACE TYPE

	Mintage (in thousands)	Ex. Fine	Unc.
1921	1,006	55.00	190.00
1922	51,737	10.00	16.00
1922D	15,063	10.00	27.00
1922S	17,475	12.00	27.00
1923	30,800	10.00	16.00
1923D	6,811	10.00	60.00
1923S	13,020	10.00	32.00
1924	11,811	10.00	16.00
1924S	1,728	24.00	235.00
1925	10,198	10.00	17.00
1925S	1,610	13.00	70.00
1926	1,939	13.00	32.00
1926D	2,349	16.00	65.00
1926S	6,980	11.00	40.00
1927	848	27.00	70.00
1927D	1,269	25.00	145.00
1927S	866	25.00	135.00
1928	361	175.00	230.00
1928S	1,632	24.00	160.00
1934	954	20.00	90.00
1934D	1,570	20.00	100.00
1934S	1,011	150.00	1,600.00
1935	1,576	16.00	65.00
1935S	1,964	23.00	175.00

EISENHOWER DOLLAR

EISENHOWER DOLLAR

	Mintage (in thousands)	Unc.	Proof
1971 Copper-Nickel	47,799	4.00	—
1971D Copper-Nickel	68,587	2.00	—
1971S Silver	11,134	6.00	7.00
1972 Copper-Nickel	75,890	3.00	—
1972D Copper-Nickel	92,549	2.00	—
1972S Silver	4,005	7.00	7.00
1973 Copper-Nickel	2,000	11.00	—
1973D Copper-Nickel	2,000	11.00	—
1973S Copper-Nickel	2,770	—	9.00
1973S Silver	2,889	9.00	26.00
1974 Copper-Nickel	27,366	3.00	—
1974D Copper-Nickel	45,517	3.00	—
1974S Copper-Nickel	2,617	—	7.00
1974S Silver	3,215	7.00	6.00
1976 Copper-Nickel*	117,338	3.00	—
1976D Copper-Nickel*	103,228	3.00	—
1976S Silver*	15,000	13.00	15.00
1976S Copper-Nickel*	6,995	—	7.00
1977 Copper-Nickel	12,596	4.00	—
1977D Copper-Nickel	32,983	3.00	—
1977S Copper-Nickel	3,251	—	8.00
1978 Copper-Nickel	25,702	2.00	—
1978D Copper-Nickel	23,013	3.00	—
1978S Copper-Nickel	3,128	—	8.00

*Bicentennial coinage dated 1776–1976, with reverses showing the Liberty Bell superimposed on the moon. No 1975 dated dollars were struck.

SUSAN B. ANTHONY DOLLAR

ANTHONY DOLLAR

	Mintage (in thousands)	Unc.	Proof
1979P	360,222	2.00	—
1979D	288,016	2.00	—
1979S Type I	113,253	2.00	10.00
1979S Type II, Proof only, Sharp Mint Mark	3,667	—	95.00
1980P	27,610	2.00	—
1980D	41,629	2.00	—
1980S	23,969	2.00	10.00
1981 P&D	6,250	6.00	—
1981S	7,555	6.00	8.00
1999 P&D	41,305	2.00	—
1999P Proof	—	—	9.00

SACAGAWEA GOLDEN DOLLAR

	Mintage (in thousands)	Unc.	Proof
2000 P&D	1,286,056	2.00	—
2000S Proof	—	—	7.00
2001 P&D	133,408	2.00	—
2001S Proof	—	—	7.00

42
TRADE DOLLARS: 1873–1885

TRADE DOLLAR

	Mintage (in thousands)	V. Good	Fine	Ex. Fine	Unc.	Proof
1873	398	75.00	100.00	180.00	550.00	2,400.00
1873CC	125	90.00	170.00	550.00	3,500.00	—
1873S	703	75.00	115.00	215.00	875.00	—
1874	988	75.00	100.00	170.00	550.00	2,350.00
1874CC	1,373	85.00	105.00	250.00	1,300.00	—

183

	Mintage (in thousands)	V. Good	Fine	Ex. Fine	Unc.	Proof
1874S	2,549	75.00	100.00	160.00	500.00	—
1875	219	150.00	285.00	450.00	1,725.00	2,400.00
1875CC	1,574	85.00	120.00	230.00	775.00	—
1875S	4,487	75.00	100.00	160.00	500.00	—
1876	456	75.00	105.00	160.00	500.00	2,400.00
1876CC	509	85.00	125.00	325.00	2,950.00	—
1876S	5,227	75.00	100.00	160.00	500.00	—
1877	3,040	75.00	100.00	160.00	550.00	2,350.00
1877CC	534	140.00	195.00	450.00	1,100.00	
1877S	9,519	75.00	100.00	160.00	500.00	—
1878	1	650.00	750.00	975.00	—	2,300.00
1878CC	97	375.00	575.00	1,675.00	11,500.00	—
1878S	4,162	75.00	100.00	160.00	500.00	—
1879	2	575.00	700.00	850.00	—	2,300.00
1880	2	575.00	700.00	850.00	—	2,300.00
1881	1	625.00	750.00	925.00	—	2,350.00
1882	1	600.00	725.00	900.00	—	2,300.00
1883	1	650.00	750.00	925.00	—	2,350.00
1884 Only 10 Struck . . .	—	—	—	—	—	200,000.00
1885 Only 5 Struck	—	—	—	—	—	600,000.00

Note: Trade dollars with Asian chopmarks (counterstamps) are worth considerably less than quoted values.

43
SILVER COMMEMORATIVE COINS

(Half Dollars unless otherwise specified)

	Mintage (in thousands)	Ex. Fine	Unc.
1892 Columbian Exposition	950	15.00	45.00
1893 Columbian Exposition	1,550	12.00	45.00

1893 ISABELLA QUARTER

1893 Isabella Quarter	24	350.00	625.00

1900 LAFAYETTE DOLLAR

	Mintage (in thousands)	Ex. Fine	Unc.
1900 Lafayette Dollar	36	225.00	725.00

PANAMA-PACIFIC HALF DOLLAR

1915S Panama-Pacific Exposition	27	160.00	450.00
1918 Illinois Centennial	100	65.00	95.00
1920 Maine Centennial	50	65.00	125.00
1920 Pilgrim Tercentenary	152	45.00	75.00
1921 Pilgrim Tercentenary (1921) on obverse . . .	20	80.00	130.00

MISSOURI HALF DOLLAR, WITH 2★4

1921 Missouri Centennial (with 2★4)	5	260.00	600.00

MISSOURI HALF DOLLAR, NO 2★4

	Mintage (in thousands)	Ex. Fine	Unc.
1921 Missouri Centennial (no 2★4)	15	170.00	500.00

ALABAMA HALF DOLLAR 2x2

	Mintage	Ex. Fine	Unc.
1921 Alabama Centennial (with 2x2)	6	120.00	375.00
1921 Alabama Centennial (no 2x2)	59	70.00	275.00
1922 Grant Memorial (with star)	4	500.00	1,300.00
1922 Grant Memorial (no star)	67	65.00	125.00
1923S Monroe Doctrine Centennial	274	23.00	65.00
1924 Huguenot-Walloon Tercentenary	142	75.00	120.00
1925 Lexington-Concord Sesquicentennial	162	45.00	80.00
1925 Stone Mountain Memorial	1,315	33.00	60.00
1925S California Diamond Jubilee	87	80.00	130.00
1925 Fort Vancouver Centennial	15	200.00	325.00
1926 Sesquicentennial of American . . . . Independence	141	45.00	100.00

OREGON TRAIL HALF DOLLAR

	Mintage (in thousands)	Ex. Fine	Unc.
1926 Oregon Trail Memorial	48	75.00	100.00
1926S Oregon Trail Memorial	83	75.00	100.00
1928 Oregon Trail Memorial	6	130.00	160.00
1933D Oregon Trail Memorial	5	200.00	230.00
1934D Oregon Trail Memorial	7	115.00	150.00
1936 Oregon Trail Memorial	10	95.00	115.00
1936S Oregon Trail Memorial	5	100.00	135.00
1937D Oregon Trail Memorial	12	110.00	130.00
1938P-D-S Oregon Trail Memorial .... (set of three)	Each 6	425.00	525.00
1939P-D-S Oregon Trail Memorial .... (set of three)	Each 3	850.00	1,100.00

VERMONT HALF DOLLAR

	Mintage	Ex. Fine	Unc.
1927 Vermont Sesquicentennial	28	130.00	160.00

HAWAIIAN HALF DOLLAR

	Mintage (in thousands)	Ex. Fine	Unc.
1928 Hawaiian Sesquicentennial	10	925.00	1,550.00
1934 Maryland Tercentenary	25	95.00	135.00
1934 Texas Centennial	61	75.00	100.00
1935P-D-S Texas Centennial (set of three)	Each 10	220.00	270.00
1936P-D-S Texas Centennial (set of three)	Each 9	220.00	270.00
1937P-D-S Texas Centennial (set of three)	Each 7	225.00	280.00
1938P-D-S Texas Centennial (set of three)	Each 4	425.00	650.00

BOONE HALF DOLLAR

	Mintage	Ex. Fine	Unc.
1934 Daniel Boone Bicentennial	10	58.00	75.00
1935P-D-S Daniel Boone Bicentennial .... (set of three)	Each 5	185.00	235.00
1935P-D-S Daniel Boone Bicentennial .... (set of three)*	Each 2	475.00	675.00
1936P-D-S Daniel Boone Bicentennial .... (set of three)	Each 5	185.00	225.00
1937P-D-S Daniel Boone Bicentennial .... (set of three)	Each 3	375.00	600.00
1938P-D-S Daniel Boone Bicentennial .... (set of three)	Each 2	625.00	800.00
1935 Connecticut Tercentenary	25	145.00	180.00

*Small "1934" added on Reverse.

	Mintage (in thousands)	Ex. Fine	Unc.
1935P-D-S Arkansas Centennial (set of three) ...	Each 6	175.00	210.00
1936P-D-S Arkansas Centennial (set of three) ...	Each 10	175.00	210.00
1937P-D-S Arkansas Centennial (set of three) ...	Each 6	185.00	240.00
1938P-D-S Arkansas Centennial (set of three) ...	Each 3	225.00	350.00
1939P-D-S Arkansas Centennial (set of three) ...	Each 2	350.00	650.00

HUDSON HALF DOLLAR

1935 Hudson, New York Sesquicentennial	10	375.00	465.00
1935S California-Pacific Exposition	70	50.00	80.00
1936D California-Pacific Exposition	30	52.00	80.00

SPANISH TRAIL HALF DOLLAR

1935 Old Spanish Trail	10	685.00	750.00

RHODE ISLAND HALF DOLLAR

	Mintage (in thousands)	Ex. Fine	Unc.
1936P-D-S Rhode Island Tercentenary .... (set of three)	Each 15	170.00	225.00
1936 Cleveland, Great Lakes Exposition	56	57.00	70.00
1936 Wisconsin Territorial Centennial	25	135.00	160.00
1936P-D-S Cincinnati Musical Center .... (set of three)	Each 5	560.00	650.00

LONG ISLAND HALF DOLLAR

	Mintage	Ex. Fine	Unc.
1936 Long Island Tercentenary	82	48.00	65.00
1936 York County, Maine Tercentenary	25	130.00	150.00
1936 Bridgeport, Connecticut Centennial	25	85.00	120.00
1936 Lynchburg, Virginia Sesquicentennial	20	125.00	155.00
1936 Elgin, Illinois Centennial	20	140.00	165.00
1936 Albany, New York Charter	18	175.00	200.00
1936S San Francisco-Oakland Bay Bridge	71	85.00	110.00
1936P-D-S Columbia, South Carolina .... Sesquicentennial (set of three)	Each 8	440.00	500.00

ROBINSON-ARKANSAS HALF DOLLAR

	Mintage (in thousands)	Ex. Fine	Unc.
1936 Robinson-Arkansas Centennial	25	85.00	100.00
1936 Delaware Tercentenary	21	170.00	200.00
1936 Battle of Gettysburg (1863–1938)	27	225.00	300.00
1936 Norfolk, Virginia, Bicentennial	17	310.00	370.00
1937 Roanoke Island, North Carolina, ... (1587–1937)	29	135.00	200.00

ANTIETAM HALF DOLLAR

	Mintage	Ex. Fine	Unc.
1937 Battle of Antietam (1862–1937)	18	365.00	425.00
1938 New Rochelle, New York, (1688–1938)	15	225.00	270.00
1946 Iowa Centennial	100	55.00	65.00
1946 Booker T. Washington Memorial .... (set of three)	+1,001	30.00	50.00
1947 Booker T. Washington Memorial .... (set of three)	Each 100	33.00	70.00
1948 Booker T. Washington Memorial .... (set of three)	Each 8	48.00	130.00
1949 Booker T. Washington Memorial .... (set of three)	Each 6	115.00	200.00
1950 Booker T. Washington Memorial .... (set of three)	Each 6+	48.00	115.00
1951 Booker T. Washington Memorial .... (set of three)	Each 7+	50.00	115.00
1951 Washington-Carver (set of three)	Each 10	35.00	80.00
1952 Washington-Carver (set of three)	Each 8	35.00	85.00

+Additional quantities struck, beyond sets of three.

	Mintage (in thousands)	Ex. Fine	Unc.
1953 Washington-Carver (set of three)	Each 8	35.00	95.00
1954 Washington-Carver (set of three)	Each 12	32.00	80.00

MODERN COMMEMORATIVE HALF DOLLARS AND SILVER DOLLARS

	Mintage (in thousands)	Unc.	Proof
1982D Geo. Washington—250th Anniversary ... Half Dollar	2,210	6.50	—
1982S Geo. Washington—250th Anniversary ... Half Dollar	4,894	—	6.50
1983P Los Angeles XIII Olympiad Dollar	295	11.00	—
1983D Los Angeles XIII Olympiad Dollar	174	11.00	—
1983S Los Angeles XIII Olympiad Dollar	174	11.00	11.00
1984P Los Angeles XIII Olympiad Dollar	217	13.00	—
1984D Los Angeles XIII Olympiad Dollar	117	20.00	—
1984S Los Angeles XIII Olympiad Dollar	117	21.00	12.00
1986D Statue of Liberty Half Dollar	928	6.00	—
1986S Statue of Liberty Half Dollar	6,926	—	6.50
1986P Statue of Liberty Dollar	724	15.00	—
1986S Statue of Liberty Dollar	6,415	—	15.00
1987P Constitution Dollar	451	12.00	—
1987S Constitution Dollar	2,747	—	12.00
1988D Olympic Dollar	191	12.00	—
1988S Olympic Dollar	1,359	—	11.00
1989D Congressional Half Dollar	164	7.00	—
1989S Congressional Half Dollar	7,679	—	6.50
1989D Congressional Dollar	135	15.00	—
1989S Congressional Dollar	762	—	16.00
1990W Eisenhower Dollar	241	16.00	—
1990P Eisenhower Dollar	1,144	—	19.00
1991D Mount Rushmore Half Dollar	173	11.00	—
1991S Mount Rushmore Half Dollar	753	—	11.00
1991P Mount Rushmore Dollar	133	26.00	—
1991S Mount Rushmore Dollar	738	—	34.00
1991D Korean War Dollar	213	14.00	—
1991P Korean War Dollar	618	—	14.00
1991D USO Dollar	125	15.00	—
1991S USO Dollar	321	—	14.00
1992D Columbus Half Dollar	136	9.00	—
1992S Columbus Half Dollar	390	—	11.00
1992D Columbus Dollar	107	26.00	—
1992P Columbus Dollar	385	—	35.00
1992P Olympic Half Dollar	162	6.00	—
1992S Olympic Half Dollar	520	—	7.50
1992D Olympic Dollar	188	22.00	—
1992S Olympic Dollar	505	—	24.00
1992D White House Dollar	124	34.00	—
1992W White House Dollar	376	—	34.00

	Mintage (in thousands)	Unc.	Proof
1993W Bill of Rights Half Dollar	173	13.50	—
1993S Bill of Rights Half Dollar	560	—	13.00
1993D Bill of Rights Dollar	98	17.00	—
1993S Bill of Rights Dollar	534	—	19.00
1993P World War II Half Dollar	193	14.00	14.00
1993D World War II Dollar	95	22.00	—
1993S World War II Dollar	322	—	29.00
1993P Jefferson Dollar	267	25.00	—
1993S Jefferson Dollar	333	—	26.00
1994D World Cup Half Dollar	53	9.00	—
1994P World Cup Half Dollar	122	—	9.00
1994D World Cup Dollar	82	25.00	—
1994S World Cup Dollar	577	—	27.00
1994W Prisoner of War Dollar	55	55.00	—
1994P Prisoner of War Dollar	220	—	37.00
1994W Vietnam Veterans Dollar	57	50.00	—
1994P Vietnam Veterans Dollar	226	—	53.00
1994W Women in Military Dollar	53	25.00	—
1994P Women in Military Dollar	213	—	24.00
1994D Capitol Dollar	68	20.00	—
1994S Capitol Dollar	279	—	22.00
1995S Civil War Half Dollar	—	27.00	27.00
1995P Civil War Dollar	—	35.00	—
1995S Civil War Dollar	—	—	45.00
1995S Olympic Basketball Half Dollar	341	20.00	15.00
1995S Olympic Baseball Half Dollar	283	20.00	15.00
1995D Olympic Gymnast Dollar	42	55.00	—
1995P Olympic Gymnast Dollar	183	—	27.00
1995D Olympic Blind Runner Dollar	29	78.00	—
1995P Olympic Blind Runner Dollar	138	—	31.00
1995D Olympic Track and Field Dollar	25	55.00	—
1995P Olympic Track and Field Dollar	137	—	25.00
1995D Olympic Cycling Dollar	20	77.00	—
1995P Olympic Cycling Dollar	119	—	31.00
1995W Special Olympics Dollar	—	19.00	—
1995P Special Olympics Dollar	—	—	19.00
1996S Olympic Swimming Half Dollar	—	77.00	15.00
1996S Olympic Soccer Half Dollar	175	37.00	72.00
1996D Olympic Wheelchair Athlete Dollar	14	205.00	—
1996P Olympic Wheelchair Athlete Dollar	82	—	47.00
1996D Olympic Tennis Dollar	16	140.00	—
1996P Olympic Tennis Dollar	92	—	49.00
1996D Olympic Rowing Dollar	16	180.00	—
1996P Olympic Rowing Dollar	152	—	37.00
1996D Olympic High Jump Dollar	16	215.00	—
1996P Olympic High Jump Dollar	125	—	31.00
1996S Community Service Dollar	124	200.00	55.00
1996D Smithsonian Anniversary Dollar	31	86.00	—

	Mintage (in thousands)	Unc.	Proof
1996P Smithsonian Anniversary Dollar	127	—	40.00
1997P Botanic Gardens Dollar	322	34.00	37.00
1997S Jackie Robinson Dollar	140	50.00	36.00
1997P Law Enforcement Dollar	140	105.00	100.00
1998S Robert F. Kennedy Dollar	205	29.00	36.00
1998S Black Patriots Dollar	112	76.00	67.00
1999P Dolly Madison Dollar	296	37.00	39.00
1999P Yellowstone Dollar	207	37.00	37.00
2000W Library of Congress Dollar	—	34.00	—
2000P Library of Congress Dollar	—	—	37.00
2000P Leif Ericson Dollar	171	48.00	44.00
2001D Buffalo Dollar	—	145.00	—
2001P Buffalo Dollar	—	—	150.00
2001P Capitol Visitor Center Half Dollar	—	10.00	15.00
2001P Capitol Visitor Center Dollar	—	41.00	38.00

44
GOLD COMMEMORATIVE COINS

(Dollar unless otherwise specified)

	Mintage (in thousands)	Ex. Fine	Unc.
1903 Louisiana Purchase (Jefferson)	18	300.00	500.00

LA PURCHASE MCKINLEY

1903 Louisiana Purchase (McKinley)	18	285.00	475.00

LEWIS & CLARK EXPO

1904 Lewis and Clark Exposition	10	435.00	1,100.00
1905 Lewis and Clark Exposition	10	425.00	1,300.00

PANAMA-PACIFIC DOLLAR

1915S Panama-Pacific Exposition	15	285.00	400.00

Panama-Pacific $2.50

	Mintage (in thousands)	Ex. Fine	Unc.
1915S Panama-Pacific Exposition ($2.50)	7	1,000.00	1,950.00
1915S Panama-Pacific Exposition Pieces .... ($50.00 round)	483 Pieces	22,500.00	28,500.00
1915S Panama-Pacific Exposition Pieces .... ($50.00 octagonal)	645 Pieces	19,000.00	25,500.00

1916 McKinley

1916 McKinley Memorial	10	245.00	425.00
1917 McKinley Memorial	10	300.00	675.00

Grant with star

1922 Grant Memorial (with star)	5	1,000.00	1,450.00
1922 Grant Memorial (no star)	5	950.00	1,275.00

Sesquicentennial $2.50

1926 Philadelphia Sesquicentennial ($2.50)	46	230.00	375.00

MODERN COMMEMORATIVE GOLD COINS

	Mintage (in thousands)	Unc.	Proof
1984P Olympic ($10.00)	33	—	270.00
1984D Olympic ($10.00)	35	—	270.00
1984S Olympic ($10.00)	49	—	195.00

195

	Mintage (in thousands)	Unc.	Proof
1984W Olympic ($10.00)	437	185.00	185.00
1986W Statue of Liberty ($5.00)	499	100.00	110.00
1987W Constitution ($5.00)	866	100.00	100.00
1988W Olympic ($5.00)	344	100.00	100.00
1989W Congressional ($5.00)	212	105.00	100.00
1991W Mount Rushmore ($5.00)	144	135.00	135.00
1992W Olympic ($5.00)	105	135.00	115.00
1992W Columbus ($5.00)	104	150.00	130.00
1993W Bill of Rights ($5.00)	102	160.00	140.00
1993W World War II ($5..00)	89	160.00	145.00
1994W World Cup ($5.00)	112	145.00	120.00
1995W Civil War ($5.00)	68	350.00	270.00
1995W Olympic Torch Runner ($5.00)	72	210.00	150.00
1995W Olympic Stadium ($5.00)	54	265.00	195.00
1996W Olympic Flag Bearer ($5.00)	42	290.00	260.00
1996W Olympic Cauldron ($5.00)	48	290.00	235.00
1996W Smithsonian ($5.00)	30	370.00	250.00
1997W Jackie Robinson ($5.00)	29	1,050.00	315.00
1997W Franklin Delano Roosevelt ($5.00)	41	235.00	225.00
1999W George Washington ($5.00)	58	235.00	240.00
2000W Library of Congress ($10.00, Bimetallic)	—	925.00	510.00
2000W Capitol Visitor Center ($5.00)	—	570.00	260.00

45
U.S. SILVER EAGLE BULLION COINS

	Mintage (in thousands)	Unc.	Proof
1986	5,393	16.00	—
1986S	1,447	—	26.00
1987	11,442	8.00	—
1987S	904	—	26.00
1988	5,004	10.00	—
1988S	557	—	80.00
1989	5,203	10.00	—
1989S	618	—	26.00
1990	5,840	11.00	—
1990S	696	—	27.00
1991	7,191	8.50	—
1991S	511	—	51.00
1992	5,540	10.00	—
1992S	499	—	31.00
1993	6,764	10.00	—
1993P	404	—	98.00
1994	4,227	13.00	—
1994P	372	—	110.00
1995	4,672	11.00	—

	Mintage (in thousands)	Unc.	Proof
1995P	395	—	100.00
1995W	30	—	2,300.00
1996	3,603	26.00	—
1996P	473	—	45.00
1997	4,295	11.00	—
1997P	430	—	80.00
1998	4,848	8.00	—
1998P	452	—	36.00
1999	9,133	8.50	—
1999P	550	—	65.00
2000	9,239	8.00	—
2000P	(unknown)	—	26.00
2001	(unknown)	8.00	—
2001W	9,002	—	26.00
2002	(unknown)	9.00	—
2002W	(unknown)	—	35.00

46
U.S. GOLD EAGLE BULLION COINS

TENTH-OUNCE GOLD ($5.00)

	Mintage (in thousands)	Unc.	Proof
MCMLXXXVI (1986)	913	45.00	—
MCMLXXXVII (1987)	580	47.00	—
MCMLXXXVIII (1988)	160	160.00	—
MCMLXXXVIII (1988)P	144	—	70.00
MCMLXXXIX (1989)	265	67.00	—
MCMLXXXIX (1989)P	85	—	72.00
MCMXC (1990)	210	50.00	—
MCMXC (1990)P	99	—	63.00
MCMXCI (1991)	165	91.00	—
MCMXCI (1991)P	70	—	62.00
1992	209	45.00	—
1992P	65	—	75.00
1993	211	45.00	—
1993P	59	—	67.00
1994	206	45.00	—
1994W	62	—	60.00
1995	223	45.00	—
1995W	49	—	62.00
1996	402	39.00	—
1996W	57	—	90.00
1997	529	40.00	—
1997W	35	—	115.00
1998	1,345	39.00	—

	Mintage (in thousands)	Unc.	Proof
1998W	40	—	67.00
1999	2,750	39.00	—
1999W	20	—	64.00
2000	569	40.00	—
2000W	—	—	83.00
2001	269	39.00	—
2001W	—	—	90.00
2002	—	39.00	—
2002W	—	—	90.00

QUARTER-OUNCE GOLD ($10.00)

	Mintage (in thousands)	Unc.	Proof
MCMLXXXVI (1986)	726	100.00	—
MCMLXXXVII (1987)	269	115.00	—
MCMLXXXVIII (1988)	49	115.00	—
MCMLXXXVIII (1988)P	98	—	130.00
MCMLXXXIX (1989)	82	110.00	—
MCMLXXXIX (1989)P	54	—	130.00
MCMXC (1990)	41	120.00	—
MCMXC (1990)P	63	—	130.00
MCMXCI (1991)	36	200.00	—
MCMXCI (1991)P	51	—	130.00
1992	60	113.00	—
1992P	46	—	130.00
1993	72	105.00	—
1993P	46	—	130.00
1994	73	105.00	—
1994W	48	—	130.00
1995	84	100.00	—
1995W	47	—	130.00
1996	60	105.00	—
1996W	38	—	130.00
1997	109	100.00	—
1997W	30	—	130.00
1998	310	100.00	—
1998W	30	—	130.00
1999	564	100.00	—
1999W	34	—	130.00
2000	129	100.00	—
2000W	—	—	180.00
2001	71	100.00	—
2001W	—	—	180.00
2002	—	100.00	—
2002W	—	—	160.00

HALF-OUNCE GOLD ($25.00)

	Mintage (in thousands)	Unc.	Proof
MCMLXXXVI (1986)	600	215.00	—
MCMLXXXVII (1987)	131	220.00	—
MCMLXXXVII (1987)P	143	—	260.00
MCMLXXXVIII (1988)	45	225.00	—

	Mintage (in thousands)	Unc.	Proof
MCMLXXXVIII (1988)P	77	—	260.00
MCMLXXXIX (1989)	45	350.00	—
MCMLXXXIX (1989)P	45	—	265.00
MCMXC (1990)	31	350.00	—
MCMXC (1990)P	52	—	265.00
MCMXCI (1991)	24	415.00	—
MCMXCI (1991)P	53	—	260.00
1992	54	260.00	—
1992P	41	—	260.00
1993	73	200.00	—
1993P	43	—	260.00
1994	62	200.00	—
1994W	44	—	260.00
1995	53	220.00	—
1995W	46	—	260.00
1996	39	265.00	—
1996W	35	—	260.00
1997	80	170.00	—
1997W	27	—	260.00
1998	169	200.00	—
1998W	26	—	260.00
1999	263	190.00	—
1999W	30	—	260.00
2000	79	190.00	—
2000W	—	—	345.00
2001	48	285.00	—
2001W	—	—	330.00
2002	—	190.00	—
2002W	—	—	300.00

ONE-OUNCE GOLD ($50.00)

	Mintage (in thousands)	Unc.	Proof
MCMLXXXVI (1986)	1,363	365.00	—
MCMLXXXVI (1986)W	446	—	500.00
MCMLXXXVII (1987)	1,046	365.00	—
MCMLXXXVII (1987)W	147	—	500.00
MCMLXXXVIII (1988)	465	380.00	—
MCMLXXXVIII (1988)W	87	—	500.00
MCMLXXXIX (1989)	416	365.00	—
MCMLXXXIX (1989)W	55	—	500.00
MCMXC (1990)	373	365.00	—
MCMXC (1990)W	62	—	500.00
MCMXCI (1991)	243	380.00	—
MCMXCI (1991)W	50	—	500.00
1992	275	365.00	—
1992W	45	—	500.00
1993	480	365.00	—
1993W	34	—	500.00
1994	222	365.00	—

	Mintage (in thousands)	Unc.	Proof
1994W	46	—	500.00
1995	201	365.00	—
1995W	48	—	500.00
1996	189	365.00	—
1996W	36	—	500.00
1997	665	365.00	—
1997W	28	—	500.00
1998	1,469	365.00	—
1998W	26	—	500.00
1999	1505	365.00	—
1999W	31	—	500.00
2000	433	365.00	—
2000W	—	—	700.00
2001	144	365.00	—
2001W	—	—	600.00
2002	—	365.00	—
2002W	—	—	600.00

47
PROOF SETS

Date and Number of Sets Coined	Proof
1936 (3,837).............................	5,450.00
1937 (5,542).............................	2,700.00
1938 (8,045).............................	1,250.00
1939 (8,795).............................	1,300.00
1940 (11,246)	1,100.00
1941 (15,287)	925.00
1942 (21,120) 6 pieces	1,050.00
1942 (included above) 5 pieces	900.00
1950 (51,386)	525.00
1951 (57,500)	525.00
1952 (81,980)	270.00
1953 (128,800)	280.00
1954 (233,300)	145.00
1955 (378,200)	95.00
1956 (669,384)	50.00
1957 (1,247,952)	18.00
1958 (875,652)	35.00
1959 (1,149,291)	25.00
1960 (1,691,602)	18.00
1960 with small date cent (included above)	35.00
1961 (3,028,244)	10.00
1962 (3,218,039)	10.00
1963 (3,075,045)	13.00
1964 (3,950,962)	11.00
1968S (3,041,509)	8.00

Date and Number of Sets Coined	Proof
1968S with no mint mark on dime	8,000.00
(included above)	
1969S (2,934,631)	8.00
1970S (2,632,810)	13.00
1970S with small date cent (included above)	80.00
1970S with no mint mark on dime	850.00
(included above)	
1971S (3,224,138)	6.00
1971S with no mint mark on nickel	850.00
(Included Above)	
1972S (3,267,667)	5.00
1973S (2,769,624)	13.00
1974S (2,617,350)	11.00
1975S (2,909,369)	16.00
1975S with no mint mark on dime	32,500.00
(Included Above)	
1976S (4,149,730)	10.00
1976S 3-piece 40 percent Silver (3,998,621)	20.00
1977S (3,251,152)	8.00
1978S (3,127,781)	10.00
1979S Type I (3,677,175)	10.00
1979S Type II (each mint mark is sharp and well defined) (Included Above)	110.00
1980S (3,554,806)	10.00
1981S Type I (4,063,083)	8.00
1981S Type II with new mint mark style	335.00
(Included Above)	
1982S (3,857,479)	5.00
1983S (3,138,765)	7.00
1983S with no mint mark on dime	735.00
(included above)	
1983S Prestige Set with Olympic Dollar .... (140,361)	75.00
1984S (2,748,430)	11.00
1984S Prestige Set with Olympic Dollar .... (316,680)	20.00
1985S (3,362,821)	7.00
1986S (2,411,180)	20.00
1986S Prestige Set with Statue of Liberty Half Dollar and Dollar (599,317)	35.00
1987S (3,792,233)	5.00
1987S Prestige Set with Constitution Dollar .... (435,495)	21.00
1988S (3,031,287)	11.00
1988S Prestige Set with Olympic Dollar (231,661)	30.00
1989S (3,009,107)	11.00
1989S Prestige Set with Congressional Half Dollar and Dollar (211,087)	36.00

Date and Number of Sets Coined	Proof
1990S (2,793,433)	15.00
1990S with no mint mark on cent	3,000.00
(included above)	
1990S Prestige Set with Eisenhower Dollar	29.00
(506,126)	
1990S Prestige Set with no mint mark on cent ...	3,500.00
(included above)	
1991S (2,610,833)	24.00
1991S Prestige Set with Mount Rushmore Half Dollar	
and Dollar (256,954)	70.00
1992S (2,675,618)	12.00
1992S Prestige Set with Olympic Half Dollar	
and Dollar (183,293)	39.00
1992S Silver (1,009,586)	15.00
1992S Premier Silver (308,055)	16.00
1993S (2,409,394)	16.00
1993S Prestige Set with Madison Half Dollar	
and Dollar (224,045)	42.00
1993S Silver (570,213)	33.00
1993S Premier Silver (191,140)	38.00
1994S (2,308,701)	19.00
1994S Prestige Set with World Cup Half Dollar	
and Dollar (175,893)	52.00
1994S Silver (636,009)	37.00
1994S Premier Silver (149,320)	41.00
1995S (2.010,384)	49.00
1995S Prestige Set with Civil War Half Dollar	
and Dollar (107,112)	125.00
1995S Silver	92.00
1995S Premier Silver	95.00
1996S (1,695,244)	14.00
1996S Prestige Set with Olympic Half Dollar	
and Dollar (55,000)	230.00
1996S Silver	49.00
1996S Premier Silver	49.00
1997S (1,975,000)	63.00
1997S Prestige Set with Botanic Dollar	160.00
1997S Silver	88.00
1997S Premier Silver	88.00
1998S	35.00
1998S Silver	33.00
1998S Premier Silver	33.00
1999S 9-piece Set with 5 Statehood Quarters	49.00
1999S Statehood Quarter 5-piece Set	43.00
1999S Silver 9-piece Set	150.00
2000S 10-piece Set with 5 Statehood Quarters ...	20.00
2000S Statehood Quarter 5-piece Set	16.00
2000S Silver 10-piece Set	27.00

Date and Number of Sets Coined	Proof
2001S 10-piece Set with 5 Statehood Quarters . . .	30.00
2001S Statehood Quarter 5-piece Set	16.00
2001S Silver 10-piece Set	80.00
2002S 10-piece Set with 5 Statehood Quarters . . .	35.00
2002S Silver 10-piece Set	55.00

48
GOLD DOLLARS: 1849–1889

LIBERTY HEAD TYPE (TYPE I)

TYPE I GOLD DOLLAR

	Mintage (in thousands)	V. Fine	Unc.
1849	689	135.00	500.00
1849C	12	550.00	9,500.00
1849D	22	675.00	5,000.00
1849O	215	160.00	775.00
1850	482	140.00	475.00
1850C	7	650.00	9,250.00
1850D	8	725.00	9,500.00
1850O	14	265.00	3,250.00
1851	3,318	135.00	325.00
1851C	41	475.00	2,850.00
1851D	10	700.00	5,750.00
1851O	290	165.00	950.00
1852	2,045	135.00	325.00
1852C	9	550.00	4,950.00
1852D	6	750.00	9,250.00
1852O	140	145.00	1,350.00
1853	4,076	135.00	325.00
1853C	12	675.00	6,750.00
1853D	7	750.00	10,000.00
1853O	290	160.00	675.00
1854	737	135.00	325.00
1854D	3	1,000.00	15,000.00
1854S	15	325.00	2,350.00

INDIAN HEADDRESS TYPE (TYPE II)

TYPE II GOLD DOLLAR

	Mintage (in thousands)	V. Fine	Unc.
1854	903	285.00	3,500.00
1855	758	285.00	3,500.00
1855C	10	1,475.00	21,000.00
1855D	2	3,750.00	31,500.00
1855O	55	450.00	6,950.00
1856S	25	675.00	7,750.00

LARGER INDIAN HEADDRESS TYPE (TYPE III)

TYPE III GOLD DOLLAR

	Mintage (in thousands)	V. Fine	Unc.	Proof
1856	1,763	140.00	325.00	—
1856D	1	3,750.00	30,000.00	—
1857	775	135.00	325.00	12,000.00
1857C	13	675.00	13,750.00	—
1857D	4	1,050.00	12,750.00	—
1857S	10	500.00	6,750.00	—
1858	118	135.00	350.00	10,000.00
1858D	3	875.00	11,750.00	—
1858S	10	385.00	6,500.00	—
1859	168	135.00	350.00	5,750.00
1859C	5	675.00	14,500.00	—
1859D	5	875.00	11,500.00	—
1859S	15	265.00	5,650.00	—
1860	37	135.00	400.00	5,500.00
1860D	2	2,750.00	26,500.00	—
1860S	13	335.00	2,750.00	—
1861	527	135.00	325.00	5,750.00
1861D	—	6,850.00	36,500.00	—
1862	1,361	135.00	325.00	6,000.00
1863	6	450.00	4,250.00	6,500.00

	Mintage (in thousands)	V. Fine	Unc.	Proof
1864	6	350.00	1,275.00	7,000.00
1865	4	360.00	1,675.00	6,250.00
1866	7	350.00	1,100.00	6,250.00
1867	5	385.00	1,250.00	6,600.00
1868	11	295.00	1,150.00	6,500.00
1869	6	350.00	1,250.00	7,000.00
1870	6	285.00	875.00	6,000.00
1870S	3	475.00	2,650.00	—
1871	4	285.00	775.00	5,750.00
1872	4	290.00	975.00	7,500.00
1873	125	135.00	325.00	10,000.00
1874	199	135.00	325.00	7,500.00
1875	420 Pieces	2,500.00	6,750.00	16,500.00
1876	3	275.00	675.00	5,750.00
1877	4	190.00	650.00	8,000.00
1878	3	230.00	650.00	5,850.00
1879	3	190.00	575.00	6,500.00
1880	2	160.00	475.00	5,500.00
1881	8	160.00	475.00	5,500.00
1882	5	175.00	475.00	4,150.00
1883	11	160.00	475.00	4,150.00
1884	6	155.00	475.00	4,150.00
1885	12	160.00	475.00	4,150.00
1886	6	160.00	475.00	4,150.00
1887	9	160.00	475.00	4,150.00
1888	16	160.00	475.00	4,150.00
1889	31	160.00	375.00	4,150.00

49
QUARTER EAGLES: 1796–1929

($2.50 GOLD PIECES) CAPPED BUST TO RIGHT TYPE

1796 CAPPED BUST TO RIGHT, NO STARS   **CAPPED BUST TO RIGHT WITH STARS ON OBVERSE**

	Mintage (in thousands)	V. Fine	Unc.
1796 No Stars	1	24,500.00	180,000.00
1796 Stars	432 Pieces	14,500.00	135,000.00
1797	427 Pieces	11,500.00	100,000.00

	Mintage (in thousands)	V. Fine	Unc.
1798	1	4,000.00	55,000.00
1802 over 1	3	3,800.00	20,000.00
1804	3	3,900.00	25,000.00
1805	2	3,800.00	24,000.00
1806 over 4	1	3,950.00	26,500.00
1806 over 5	480 Pieces	8,500.00	80,000.00
1807	7	4,100.00	19,000.00

CAPPED BUST TO LEFT TYPE

1808 CAPPED BUST TO LEFT

1808	3	16,000.00	55,000.00

CAPPED HEAD TO LEFT TYPE

CAPPED HEAD TO LEFT, LARGE SIZE

1821	6	3,900.00	20,000.00
1824 over 21	3	3,900.00	16,750.00
1825	4	3,700.00	16,000.00
1826 over 25	760 Pieces	4,400.00	31,500.00
1827	3	5,350.00	17,500.00

CAPPED HEAD TO LEFT, REDUCED SIZE

1829	3	3,850.00	11,750.00
1830	5	3,850.00	11,750.00

	Mintage (in thousands)	V. Fine	Unc.
1831	5	3,850.00	11,750.00
1832	4	3,850.00	11,750.00
1833	4	3,850.00	12,750.00
1834 With Motto	4	10,250.00	32,500.00

CLASSIC HEAD TYPE

CLASSIC HEAD

	Mintage (in thousands)	Ex. Fine	Unc.
1834 No Motto	112	475.00	2,250.00
1835	131	475.00	2,750.00
1836	548	475.00	2,250.00
1837	45	500.00	3,250.00
1838	47	485.00	2,350.00
1838C	8	2,650.00	26,500.00
1839	27	750.00	4,750.00
1839C	18	2,250.00	26,500.00
1839D	14	3,250.00	24,500.00
1839O	18	975.00	6,850.00

CORONET TYPE

LIBERTY HEAD

1840	19	950.00	6,500.00
1840C	13	1,450.00	14,500.00
1840D	4	8,250.00	37,000.00
1840O	34	875.00	13,500.00
1841 Proof (Ex. rare)	—	87,500.00	—
1841C	10	1,675.00	22,000.00
1841D	4	4,250.00	29,000.00
1842	3	2,750.00	22,500.00
1842C	7	3,150.00	27,500.00
1842D	5	3,450.00	38,500.00
1842O	20	1,250.00	13,750.00

	Mintage (in thousands)	Ex. Fine	Unc.
1843	101	225.00	1,375.00
1843C	26	1,350.00	8,750.00
1843D	36	1,450.00	10,000.00
1843O	364	235.00	1,650.00
1844	7	875.00	7,500.00
1844C	12	2,150.00	20,000.00
1844D	17	1,375.00	7,500.00
1845	91	290.00	1,375.00

	Mintage (in thousands)	Ex. Fine	Unc.	Proof
1845D	19	1,375.00	15,000.00	—
1845O	4	2,100.00	16,000.00	—
1846	22	550.00	5,750.00	—
1846C	5	2,450.00	21,000.00	—
1846D	19	1,275.00	13,250.00	—
1846O	66	475.00	6,750.00	—
1847	30	375.00	3,750.00	—
1847C	23	1,225.00	7,250.00	—
1847D	16	1,275.00	9,750.00	—
1847O	124	425.00	3,600.00	—
1848	7	950.00	7,000.00	—
1848 CAL above Eagle	1	14,500.00	36,000.00	—
1848C	17	1,575.00	15,750.00	—
1848D	14	1,400.00	11,500.00	—
1849	23	500.00	2,750.00	—
1849C	10	1,675.00	24,000.00	—
1849D	11	1,475.00	17,500.00	—
1850	253	235.00	1,150.00	—
1850C	9	1,675.00	18,000.00	—
1850D	12	1,350.00	14,250.00	—
1850O	84	485.00	4,850.00	—
1851	1,373	200.00	325.00	—
1851C	15	1,475.00	14,500.00	—
1851D	11	1,400.00	14,000.00	—
1851O	148	250.00	4,750.00	—
1852	1,160	200.00	325.00	—
1852C	8	1,750.00	18,000.00	—
1852D	4	2,450.00	18,500.00	—
1852O	140	310.00	5,250.00	—
1853	1,405	200.00	375.00	—
1853D	3	2,850.00	18,500.00	—
1854	596	200.00	375.00	—
1854C	7	2,100.00	18,000.00	—
1854D	2	5,500.00	28,500.00	—
1854O	153	240.00	1,750.00	—

	Mintage (in thousands)	Ex. Fine	Unc.	Proof
1854S (Rare)	246 Pieces	70,000.00	—	—
1855	235	190.00	425.00	—
1855C	4	3,250.00	27,500.00	—
1855D	1	8,000.00	42,500.00	—
1856	384	190.00	450.00	45,000.00
1856C	10	2,400.00	17,000.00	—
1856D	874 Pieces	11,000.00	50,000.00	—
1856O	21	750.00	7,750.00	—
1856S	71	400.00	4,650.00	—
1857	214	190.00	400.00	40,000.00
1857D	2	2,350.00	16,000.00	—
1857O	34	375.00	4,750.00	—
1857S	69	360.00	6,750.00	—
1858	47	260.00	1,500.00	22,500.00
1858C	9	1,375.00	10,000.00	—
1859	39	260.00	1,500.00	16,000.00
1859D	2	2,850.00	24,500.00	—
1859S	15	1,100.00	7,750.00	—
1860	23	290.00	1,375.00	16,000.00
1860C	7	1,875.00	22,500.00	—
1860S	36	700.00	4,350.00	—
1861	1,248	190.00	375.00	15,000.00
1861S	24	1,000.00	7,750.00	—
1862	99	300.00	1,350.00	15,000.00
1862S	8	2,400.00	18,500.00	—
1863	30 Pieces	—	—	37,500.00
1863S	11	1,500.00	18,500.00	—
1864	3	11,500.00	37,500.00	13,000.00
1865	2	8,500.00	37,500.00	14,000.00
1865S	23	625.00	4,350.00	—
1866	3	3,450.00	18,500.00	11,000.00
1866S	39	725.00	6,500.00	—
1867	3	850.00	5,000.00	11,500.00
1867S	28	700.00	4,750.00	—
1868	4	425.00	1,950.00	12,000.00
1868S	34	330.00	4,500.00	—
1869	4	475.00	3,250.00	10,000.00
1869S	30	475.00	4,500.00	—
1870	5	450.00	4,000.00	10,500.00
1870S	16	450.00	5,000.00	—
1871	5	360.00	2,600.00	10,000.00
1871S	22	325.00	2,600.00	—
1872	3	850.00	4,750.00	10,000.00
1872S	18	425.00	4,600.00	—
1873	178	190.00	325.00	8,250.00
1873S	27	400.00	3,150.00	—

	Mintage (in thousands)	Ex. Fine	Unc.	Proof
1874	4	425.00	2,500.00	12,000.00
1875	420 Pieces	5,250.00	13,750.00	20,000.00
1875S	12	325.00	4,650.00	—
1876	4	650.00	3,650.00	8,000.00
1876S	5	550.00	3,900.00	—
1877	2	775.00	3,450.00	9,000.00
1877S	35	190.00	675.00	—
1878	286	190.00	325.00	11,000.00
1878S	178	190.00	385.00	—
1879	89	190.00	325.00	8,000.00
1879S	44	300.00	2,300.00	—
1880	3	375.00	1,600.00	8,500.00
1881	691 Pieces	2,900.00	8,250.00	6,500.00
1882	4	325.00	750.00	6,500.00
1883	2	425.00	2,300.00	6,250.00
1884	2	410.00	1,675.00	6,250.00
1885	887 Pieces	1,725.00	4,500.00	6,250.00
1886	4	300.00	1,175.00	6,400.00
1887	6	250.00	775.00	6,400.00
1888	16	230.00	350.00	6,000.00
1889	18	210.00	360.00	6,500.00
1890	9	230.00	500.00	6,000.00
1891	11	200.00	450.00	6,500.00
1892	3	250.00	850.00	6,000.00
1893	30	190.00	325.00	5,850.00
1894	4	225.00	850.00	5,600.00
1895	6	210.00	425.00	5,500.00
1896	19	190.00	300.00	5,500.00
1897	30	190.00	300.00	5,500.00
1898	24	190.00	300.00	5,500.00
1899	27	190.00	375.00	5,500.00
1900	67	220.00	300.00	5,500.00
1901	91	190.00	300.00	5,500.00
1902	134	190.00	300.00	5,500.00
1903	201	190.00	300.00	5,500.00
1904	161	190.00	300.00	5,500.00
1905	218	190.00	300.00	5,500.00
1906	176	190.00	300.00	5,500.00
1907	336	190.00	300.00	5,500.00

INDIAN HEAD

	Mintage (in thousands)	Ex. Fine	Unc.	Proof
1908	565	170.00	280.00	8,500.00
1909	442	170.00	325.00	13,000.00
1910	493	170.00	290.00	9,250.00
1911	704	170.00	300.00	8,700.00
1911D	56	1,150.00	3,400.00	—
1912	616	170.00	335.00	8,700.00
1913	722	170.00	300.00	8,700.00
1914	240	200.00	475.00	8,700.00
1914D	448	170.00	325.00	—
1915	606	170.00	290.00	10,000.00
1925D	578	170.00	270.00	—
1926	446	170.00	270.00	—
1927	388	170.00	270.00	—
1928	416	170.00	270.00	—
1929	532	170.00	270.00	—

50
THREE-DOLLAR GOLD PIECES: 1854–1889

	Mintage (in thousands)	$3.00 GOLD PIECE V. Fine	Unc.	Proof
1854	139	550.00	1,950.00	50,000.00
1854D	1	8,250.00	70,000.00	—
1854O	24	925.00	17,500.00	—

	Mintage (in thousands)	V. Fine	Unc.	Proof
1855	51	550.00	2,100.00	—
1855S	7	950.00	25,000.00	—
1856	26	550.00	2,350.00	24,000.00
1856S	35	575.00	9,250.00	—
1857	21	550.00	3,150.00	20,000.00
1857S	14	775.00	16,500.00	—
1858	2	800.00	7,500.00	20,000.00
1859	16	550.00	2,450.00	16,500.00
1860	7	585.00	2,600.00	14,500.00
1860S	7	750.00	15,750.00	—
1861	6	650.00	3,150.00	15,000.00
1862	6	650.00	3,150.00	15,000.00
1863	5	675.00	3,150.00	14,000.00
1864	3	685.00	3,150.00	15,000.00
1865	1	1,000.00	7,500.00	15,000.00
1866	4	700.00	2,950.00	15,000.00
1867	3	700.00	2,800.00	15,000.00
1868	5	650.00	2,600.00	16,000.00
1869	3	750.00	3,500.00	16,000.00
1870	4	625.00	3,750.00	15,000.00
1870S (Unique)	—	—	—	2,000,000.00
1871	1	725.00	3,450.00	19,000.00
1872	2	675.00	3,150.00	14,000.00
1873 Closed 3	—	2,900.00	25,000.00	22,500.00
1873 Open 3	25 Pieces	—	—	27,500.00
1874	42	550.00	1,950.00	16,000.00
1875	20 Pieces	—	—	80,000.00
1876	45 Pieces	—	—	24,000.00
1877	1	1,075.00	12,750.00	16,500.00
1878	82	550.00	1,950.00	16,500.00
1879	3	625.00	2,350.00	13,750.00
1880	1	650.00	2,600.00	13,250.00
1881	554 Pieces	1,200.00	5,250.00	10,250.00
1882	2	800.00	2,675.00	9,750.00
1883	1	700.00	2,800.00	9,750.00
1884	1	1,075.00	2,675.00	9,750.00
1885	1	1,075.00	3,250.00	10,000.00
1886	1	1,000.00	3,600.00	9,750.00
1887	6	600.00	1,975.00	9,750.00
1888	5	600.00	1,950.00	9,750.00
1889	2	600.00	1,975.00	9,750.00

51
"STELLAS": 1879–1880

($4.00 GOLD PIECES)

FLOWING HAIR STELLA

1879 COILED HAIR STELLA

1880 COILED HAIR STELLA

	Mintage (in thousands)	Proof-63	Proof-65
1879 Flowing hair	415 Pieces	76,000.00	105,000.00
1879 Coiled hair (Very rare)	10 Pieces	175,000.00	275,000.00
1880 Flowing hair (Very rare)	15 Pieces	90,000.00	160,000.00
1880 Coiled hair (Very rare)	10 Pieces	285,000.00	475,000.00

52

HALF EAGLES: 1795–1929

($5.00 GOLD PIECES)
CAPPED BUST FACING RIGHT TYPE

$5.00 CAPPED BUST RIGHT, SMALL EAGLE

$5.00 CAPPED BUST RIGHT, HERALDIC EAGLE

	Mintage (in thousands)	V. Fine	Unc.
1795 Small Eagle, All Kinds	9	10,000.00	40,000.00
1795 Large Eagle, All Kinds	*	13,750.00	90,000.00
1796, 6 over 5	6	10,750.00	72,500.00
1797 15 Stars, Small Eagle, All Kinds	4	14,500.00	135,000.00
1797 16 Stars, Small Eagle, All Kinds	(included above)	13,000.00	125,000.00
1797, 7 over 5, Large Eagle	*	13,250.00	150,000.00
1798 Small Eagle (Very rare)	—	160,000.00	—
1798 Large Eagle, 13 star reverse, All Kinds	25	2,650.00	18,000.00
1798 Large Eagle, 14 star reverse, All Kinds	(included above)	3,400.00	40,000.00
1799	7	2,500.00	20,000.00
1800	38	1,850.00	7,500.00
1802 over 1	53	1,850.00	7,750.00
1803 over 2	34	1,850.00	7,600.00

*Mintage is believed to be included with mintage of 1798 Large Eagle, 13 star reverse.

	Mintage (in thousands)	V. Fine	Unc.
1804	30	1,900.00	7,750.00
1805	33	1,950.00	7,350.00
1806	64	1,900.00	6,850.00
1807	32	1,900.00	7,750.00

CAPPED BUST FACING LEFT TYPE

$5.00 CAPPED BUST LEFT

1807	52	1,800.00	6,250.00
1808 over 7, All Kinds	56	2,850.00	11,500.00
1808, All Kinds	56	1,775.00	6,500.00
1809 over 8	34	1,800.00	6,750.00
1810	100	1,775.00	6,000.00
1811	100	1,775.00	6,000.00
1812	58	1,850.00	6,250.00

CAPPED HEAD FACING LEFT TYPE

$5.00 CAPPED HEAD LEFT, LARGE SIZE

1813	95	2,100.00	6,750.00
1814 over 3	15	2,575.00	9,250.00
1815 (Rare)	(635 Pieces)	50,000.00	150,000.00
1818	49	2,375.00	8,250.00
1819	52	16,500.00	40,000.00
1820	264	2,550.00	10,500.00
1821	35	14,000.00	45,000.00
1822 (Very rare)	18	—	—
1823	14	3,200.00	16,500.00
1824	17	9,750.00	28,500.00
1825 5 over 1	29	7,750.00	29,000.00

	Mintage (in thousands)	V. Fine	Unc.
1825 5 over 4 (Very Rare)	(included above)	—	350,000.00
1826	18	7,000.00	24,500.00
1827	25	9,000.00	32,500.00
1828 over 27 (Rare)	28	18,000.00	110,000.00
1828	(included above)	12,500.00	52,500.00
1829, Large Date (Rare)	57	50,000.00	160,000.00

$5.00 CAPPED HEAD LEFT, REDUCED SIZE

	Mintage (in thousands)	V. Fine	Unc.
1829 Small Date (Rare)	(included above)	47,500.00	150,000.00
1830	126	8,000.00	22,500.00
1831	141	8,000.00	24,000.00
1832	157	8,000.00	22,500.00
1833	194	8,000.00	21,500.00
1834	50	8,000.00	24,000.00

CLASSIC HEAD TYPE

$5.00 CLASSIC HEAD

	Mintage (in thousands)	Ex. Fine	Unc.
1834	658	525.00	2,850.00
1835	372	525.00	3,250.00
1836	553	525.00	2,850.00
1837	207	600.00	3,500.00
1838	287	525.00	3,575.00
1838C	17	4,250.00	42,500.00
1838D	21	3,850.00	26,000.00

$5.00 LIBERTY HEAD, NO MOTTO

	Mintage (in thousands)	V. Fine	Ex. Fine	Unc.
1839	118	285.00	435.00	4,000.00
1839C	17	1,200.00	2,850.00	26,000.00
1839D	19	1,100.00	2,350.00	21,500.00
1840	137	225.00	350.00	3,600.00
1840C	19	950.00	2,750.00	26,500.00
1840D	23	900.00	1,850.00	16,500.00
1840O	40	325.00	825.00	11,000.00
1841	16	375.00	850.00	5,600.00
1841C	21	850.00	1,550.00	16,500.00
1841D	29	825.00	1,375.00	15,000.00
1841O	50 Pieces	—	—	—
1842	28	350.00	1,150.00	12,500.00
1842C	28	900.00	1,675.00	17,500.00
1842D	160	825.00	1,450.00	15,500.00
1842O	16	1,050.00	3,250.00	21,500.00
1843	611	210.00	240.00	1,850.00
1843C	44	850.00	1,650.00	14,000.00
1843D	98	775.00	1,350.00	12,750.00
1843O	517	250.00	1,050.00	13,500.00
1844	340	210.00	225.00	1,875.00
1844C	24	975.00	3,000.00	21,000.00
1844D	89	825.00	1,275.00	12,000.00
1844O	365	250.00	375.00	4,500.00
1845	417	210.00	225.00	1,950.00
1845D	90	825.00	1,300.00	12,500.00
1845O	41	425.00	675.00	9,750.00
1846	396	210.00	225.00	2,650.00
1846C	13	1,000.00	3,000.00	23,500.00
1846D	80	825.00	1,475.00	13,500.00
1846O	58	375.00	925.00	13,750.00
1847	916	210.00	230.00	1,500.00
1847C	84	850.00	1,450.00	13,250.00
1847D	64	825.00	1,375.00	8,500.00
1847O	12	1,850.00	6,750.00	24,000.00
1848	261	210.00	235.00	1,500.00

	Mintage (in thousands)	V. Fine	Ex. Fine	Unc.	Proof
1848C	64	825.00	1,375.00	19,000.00	—
1848D	47	925.00	1,475.00	14,500.00	—
1849	133	210.00	260.00	2,500.00	—
1849C	65	825.00	1,350.00	14,000.00	—
1849D	39	825.00	1,375.00	14,500.00	—
1850	64	260.00	575.00	3,500.00	—
1850C	64	825.00	1375.00	13,000.00	—
1850D	44	950.00	1,650.00	26,000.00	—
1851	378	210.00	235.00	2,900.00	—
1851C	49	825.00	1,375.00	16,000.00	—
1851D	63	950.00	1,675.00	15,000.00	—
1851O	41	550.00	1,350.00	11,750.00	—
1852	574	210.00	235.00	1,400.00	—
1852C	73	825.00	1,350.00	6,500.00	—
1852D	92	825.00	1,350.00	13,000.00	—
1853	306	210.00	235.00	1,450.00	—
1853C	66	825.00	1,350.00	8,000.00	—
1853D	90	825.00	1,350.00	6,250.00	—
1854	161	210.00	245.00	2,100.00	—
1854C	39	950.00	1,650.00	15,000.00	—
1854D	56	825.00	1,350.00	9,000.00	—
1854O	46	300.00	525.00	8,000.00	—
1854S (Rare)	268 Pieces	—	—	—	—
1855	117	210.00	235.00	1,650.00	—
1855C	40	975.00	1,750.00	16,000.00	—
1855D	22	850.00	1,425.00	18,000.00	—
1855O	11	650.00	2,100.00	21,500.00	—
1855S	61	400.00	1,000.00	14,500.00	—
1856	198	210.00	235.00	2,150.00	—
1856C	28	825.00	1,450.00	21,000.00	—
1856D	20	825.00	1,475.00	10,000.00	—
1856O	10	625.00	1,300.00	15,500.00	—
1856S	105	310.00	600.00	6,500.00	—
1857	98	210.00	235.00	1,650.00	—
1857C	31	825.00	1,450.00	11,500.00	—
1857D	17	825.00	1,450.00	14,000.00	—
1857O	13	625.00	1,450.00	21,500.00	—
1857S	87	310.00	525.00	12,500.00	—
1858	15	250.00	525.00	3,750.00	—
1858C	39	825.00	1,450.00	12,500.00	—
1858D	15	925.00	1,450.00	14,000.00	—
1858S	19	700.00	2,500.00	26,500.00	—
1859	17	325.00	575.00	6,850.00	—
1859C	32	950.00	1,650.00	15,000.00	—
1859D	10	975.00	1,775.00	14,000.00	—
1859S	13	1,350.00	3,400.00	31,500.00	—

	Mintage (in thousands)	V. Fine	Ex. Fine	Unc.	Proof
1860	20	285.00	575.00	4,000.00	—
1860C	15	1,000.00	2,100.00	14,000.00	—
1860D	15	1,000.00	2,100.00	17,500.00	—
1860S	21	1,150.00	2,100.00	22,500.00	—
1861	688	210.00	235.00	1,250.00	—
1861C	7	1,775.00	3,750.00	27,500.00	—
1861D	2	4,350.00	7,250.00	48,500.00	—
1861S	18	1,100.00	4,350.00	32,500.00	—
1862	4	675.00	1,500.00	19,000.00	—
1862S	10	3,500.00	6,500.00	60,000.00	—
1863	2	1,175.00	3,500.00	26,000.00	—
1863S	17	1,375.00	4,000.00	32,500.00	—
1864	4	625.00	1,875.00	14,500.00	—
1864S	4	4,750.00	14,750.00	48,500.00	—
1865	1	1,350.00	3,850.00	19,500.00	—
1865S	28	1,250.00	2,700.00	16,500.00	—
1866S No Motto	9	1,600.00	3,700.00	36,000.00	—

$5.00 LIBERTY HEAD WITH MOTTO

	Mintage	V. Fine	Ex. Fine	Unc.	Proof
1866 Motto on Reverse	7	750.00	1,450.00	17,500.00	23,500.00
1866S	35	1,150.00	2,750.00	23,500.00	—
1867	7	500.00	1,600.00	9,750.00	23,500.00
1867S	29	1,350.00	2,650.00	26,000.00	—
1868	6	650.00	1,000.00	9,750.00	23,500.00
1868S	52	450.00	1,450.00	21,000.00	—
1869	2	875.00	2,100.00	17,500.00	23,500.00
1869S	31	465.00	1,650.00	24,000.00	—
1870	4	775.00	1,825.00	17,000.00	27,500.00
1870CC	7	4,600.00	12,500.00	100,000.00	—
1870S	17	800.00	2,500.00	26,000.00	—
1871	3	850.00	1,675.00	15,000.00	23,500.00
1871CC	21	1,100.00	3,100.00	55,000.00	—
1871S	25	500.00	950.00	13,500.00	—
1872	2	800.00	1,850.00	13,750.00	23,500.00
1872CC	17	1,100.00	4,000.00	55,000.00	—
1872S	36	425.00	775.00	10,500.00	—
1873	112	170.00	225.00	700.00	25,000.00
1873CC	7	1,950.00	9,250.00	50,000.00	—
1873S	31	525.00	1,350.00	21,000.00	—

	Mintage (in thousands)	V. Fine	Ex. Fine	Unc.	Proof
1874	4	575.00	1,500.00	13,750.00	22,500.00
1874CC	21	725.00	1,650.00	32,500.00	—
1874S	16	550.00	1,900.00	21,000.00	—
1875	220 Pieces	45,000.00	55,000.00	170,000.00	70,000.00
1875CC	12	1,300.00	4,250.00	43,500.00	—
1875S	9	650.00	2,350.00	19,500.00	—
1876	1	1,000.00	2,250.00	11,500.00	16,000.00
1876CC	7	1,050.00	4,250.00	42,500.00	—
1876S	4	1,500.00	3,250.00	27,500.00	—
1877	1	800.00	2,500.00	11,500.00	23,000.00
1877CC	9	950.00	2,750.00	43,500.00	—
1877S	27	375.00	625.00	8,750.00	—
1878	132	135.00	180.00	400.00	23,000.00
1878CC	9	2,750.00	6,750.00	55,000.00	—
1878S	145	135.00	185.00	650.00	—
1879	302	135.00	175.00	360.00	22,000.00
1879CC	17	475.00	1,175.00	19,000.00	—
1879S	426	165.00	210.00	825.00	—
1880	3,166	135.00	145.00	210.00	15,000.00
1880CC	51	385.00	700.00	9,650.00	—
1880S	1,349	135.00	145.00	210.00	—
1881	5,709	135.00	145.00	210.00	14,500.00
1881CC	14	465.00	1,350.00	21,000.00	—
1881S	969	135.00	145.00	210.00	—
1882	2,515	135.00	145.00	210.00	14,500.00
1882CC	83	365.00	500.00	6,750.00	—
1882S	970	135.00	145.00	210.00	—
1883	233	135.00	145.00	265.00	14,500.00
1883CC	13	425.00	950.00	18,500.00	—
1883S	83	180.00	225.00	1,000.00	—
1884	191	160.00	180.00	675.00	14,500.00
1884CC	16	500.00	900.00	16,500.00	—
1884S	177	160.00	180.00	350.00	—
1885	602	135.00	145.00	210.00	12,500.00
1885S	1,212	135.00	145.00	210.00	—
1886	388	135.00	145.00	210.00	12,500.00
1886S	3,268	135.00	145.00	210.00	—
1887	87 Pieces	—	—	—	60,000.00
1887S	1,912	135.00	145.00	210.00	—
1888	18	160.00	210.00	525.00	11,000.00
1888S	294	160.00	180.00	1,200.00	—
1889	8	300.00	425.00	1,050.00	12,500.00
1890	4	400.00	450.00	2,150.00	12,500.00
1890CC	54	300.00	360.00	1,100.00	—
1891	61	160.00	185.00	450.00	11,000.00
1891CC	208	275.00	360.00	725.00	—

	Mintage (in thousands)	V. Fine	Ex. Fine	Unc.	Proof
1892	754	135.00	145.00	210.00	12,500.00
1892CC	83	290.00	390.00	1,400.00	—
1892O	10	475.00	925.00	2,950.00	—
1892S	298	150.00	170.00	625.00	—
1893	1,528	135.00	145.00	210.00	11,000.00
1893CC	60	275.00	425.00	1,350.00	—
1893O	110	225.00	300.00	875.00	—
1893S	224	160.00	175.00	230.00	—
1894	958	135.00	145.00	210.00	11,000.00
1894O	17	210.00	350.00	1,175.00	—
1894S	56	230.00	350.00	2,750.00	—
1895	1,346	135.00	145.00	210.00	10,000.00
1895S	112	200.00	260.00	2,900.00	—
1896	59	135.00	145.00	235.00	10,000.00
1896S	155	200.00	225.00	1,300.00	—
1897	868	135.00	145.00	210.00	10,000.00
1897S	354	175.00	200.00	875.00	—
1898	633	135.00	145.00	235.00	10,000.00
1898S	1,397	135.00	175.00	235.00	—
1899	1,711	135.00	145.00	210.00	10,000.00
1899S	1,545	160.00	165.00	235.00	—
1900	1,406	135.00	145.00	230.00	10,000.00
1900S	329	150.00	175.00	225.00	—
1901	616	135.00	145.00	210.00	10,000.00
1901S	3,648	135.00	145.00	210.00	—
1902	173	135.00	145.00	220.00	10,000.00
1902S	939	135.00	145.00	210.00	—
1903	227	135.00	170.00	210.00	10,000.00
1903S	1,855	135.00	145.00	210.00	—
1904	392	135.00	145.00	215.00	10,000.00
1904S	97	160.00	200.00	950.00	—
1905	302	135.00	145.00	215.00	11,000.00
1905S	881	160.00	175.00	525.00	—
1906	349	135.00	145.00	220.00	10,000.00
1906D	320	135.00	145.00	210.00	—
1906S	598	150.00	165.00	220.00	—
1907	626	135.00	145.00	210.00	10,000.00
1907D	888	135.00	145.00	210.00	—
1908	422	135.00	145.00	210.00	—

$5.00 INDIAN HEAD	Mintage (in thousands)	Ex. Fine	Unc.	Proof
1908	578	195.00	350.00	11,500.00
1908D	148	195.00	325.00	—
1908S	82	400.00	1,350.00	—
1909	627	195.00	350.00	14,000.00
1909D	3,424	195.00	325.00	—
1909O	34	1,150.00	8,000.00	—
1909S	297	230.00	1,700.00	—
1910	604	195.00	325.00	12,500.00
1910D	194	195.00	385.00	—
1910S	770	235.00	1,250.00	—
1911	915	195.00	325.00	12,000.00
1911D	73	400.00	3,750.00	—
1911S	1,416	200.00	650.00	—
1912	790	195.00	325.00	12,000.00
1912S	392	250.00	1,900.00	—
1913	916	195.00	325.00	12,000.00
1913S	408	230.00	1,800.00	—
1914	247	195.00	375.00	12,000.00
1914D	247	200.00	350.00	—
1914S	263	245.00	1,550.00	—
1915	588	210.00	375.00	15,000.00
1915S	164	325.00	2,250.00	—
1916S	240	250.00	600.00	—
1929	662	4,400.00	6,350.00	—

53

EAGLES: 1795–1933

($10.00 GOLD PIECES)
CAPPED BUST TYPE

$10.00 CAPPED BUST RIGHT, SMALL EAGLE

	Mintage (in thousands)	V. Fine	Unc.
1795	6	10,500.00	57,500.00
1796	4	11,250.00	72,500.00
1797 Small Eagle	4	15,000.00	175,000.00

$10.00 CAPPED BUST RIGHT, HERALDIC EAGLE

1797 Large Eagle	11	3,950.00	24,000.00
1798 over 97, 9 Stars Left, 4 Right	1	12,000.00	85,000.00
1798 over 97, 7 Stars Left, 6 Right	1	25,000.00	180,000.00
1799	37	3,750.00	12,000.00
1800	6	4,000.00	18,000.00
1801	44	3,750.00	12,750.00
1803	15	3,850.00	15,000.00
1804	4	4,650.00	28,500.00

1838–39 $10.00 LIBERTY HEAD

	Mintage (in thousands)	Ex. Fine	Unc.
1838	7	3,000.00	32,500.00
1839 Type of 1838, Large Letters	38	2,000.00	24,500.00

$10.00 LIBERTY HEAD, NO MOTTO

1839 Type of 1840, Small Letters	—	3,500.00	31,500.00
1840	47	650.00	13,000.00
1841	63	485.00	7,750.00
1841O	3	4,750.00	32,500.00
1842	82	525.00	15,000.00
1842O	27	525.00	18,000.00
1843	75	450.00	17,500.00
1843O	175	440.00	11,500.00
1844	6	3,000.00	16,500.00
1844O	119	465.00	14,000.00
1845	26	775.00	17,000.00
1845O	48	725.00	13,500.00
1846	20	1,250.00	22,500.00
1846O	82	1,000.00	16,000.00
1847	862	385.00	3,250.00
1847O	572	385.00	5,250.00
1848	145	425.00	5,250.00
1848O	36	1,300.00	16,000.00
1849	654	385.00	3,600.00
1849O	24	2,150.00	24,000.00
1850	291	385.00	4,250.00

	Mintage (in thousands)	Ex. Fine	Unc.
1850O	58	750.00	16,500.00
1851	176	430.00	5,650.00
1851O	263	425.00	5,750.00
1852	263	385.00	4,500.00

	Mintage (in thousands)	Ex. Fine	Unc.	Proof
1852O	18	1,100.00	25,000.00	—
1853	201	400.00	3,850.00	—
1853O	51	425.00	14,000.00	—
1854	54	450.00	6,500.00	—
1854O	53	725.00	11,500.00	—
1854S	124	385.00	12,750.00	—
1855	122	385.00	3,800.00	—
1855O	18	1,350.00	22,500.00	—
1855S	9	2,400.00	31,500.00	—
1856	60	385.00	3,800.00	—
1856O	15	1,600.00	17,500.00	—
1856S	68	525.00	9,750.00	—
1857	17	875.00	13,500.00	—
1857O	6	1,850.00	20,000.00	—
1857S	26	825.00	11,000.00	—
1858	3	6,850.00	35,000.00	—
1858O	20	775.00	9,250.00	—
1858S	12	3,000.00	31,000.00	—
1859	16	775.00	11,000.00	—
1859O	2	7,850.00	50,000.00	—
1859S	7	4,850.00	45,000.00	—
1860	15	775.00	8,500.00	—
1860O	11	1,300.00	14,250.00	—
1860S	5	5,000.00	45,000.00	—
1861	113	385.00	3,100.00	—
1861S	16	3,100.00	36,000.00	—
1862	11	1,050.00	14,750.00	—
1862S	13	3,600.00	38,000.00	—
1863	1	8,500.00	52,500.00	—
1863S	10	3,300.00	26,500.00	—
1864	4	3,900.00	16,500.00	—
1864S	3	13,000.00	55,000.00	—
1865	4	3,750.00	34,000.00	—
1865S	17	9,850.00	47,500.00	—
1866S No Motto	9	3,350.00	46,500.00	—

$10.00 LIBERTY HEAD WITH MOTTO

	Mintage (in thousands)	Ex. Fine	Unc.	Proof
1866 With Motto	4	1,750.00	16,750.00	32,500.00
1866S	12	3,650.00	25,000.00	—
1867	3	2,600.00	28,500.00	32,500.00
1867S	9	6,100.00	45,000.00	—
1868	11	750.00	13,750.00	32,500.00
1868S	14	2,150.00	25,000.00	—
1869	2	2,850.00	35,000.00	31,000.00
1869S	6	2,650.00	25,000.00	—
1870	4	1,200.00	17,500.00	32,500.00
1870CC	6	26,500.00	95,000.00	—
1870S	8	2,400.00	35,000.00	—
1871	2	2,700.00	18,500.00	35,000.00
1871CC	7	5,000.00	57,500.00	—
1871S	17	1,650.00	28,000.00	—
1872	2	3,350.00	19,000.00	32,500.00
1872CC	6	8,000.00	60,000.00	—
1872S	17	950.00	24,000.00	—
1873	1	10,500.00	47,500.00	32,500.00
1873CC	5	9,750.00	60,000.00	—
1873S	12	1,700.00	29,000.00	—
1874	53	210.00	1,950.00	35,000.00
1874CC	17	2,450.00	45,000.00	—
1874S	10	2,850.00	45,000.00	—
1875 (Very rare)	120 Pieces	65,000.00	—	100,000.00
1875CC	8	8,750.00	65,000.00	—
1876	1	7,000.00	55,000.00	31,000.00
1876CC	5	7,250.00	52,500.00	—
1876S	5	1,850.00	40,000.00	—
1877	1	5,000.00	31,000.00	31,000.00
1877CC	3	5,650.00	47,500.00	—
1877S	17	750.00	24,000.00	—
1878	74	205.00	900.00	31,000.00
1878CC	3	8,500.00	50,000.00	—
1878S	26	550.00	21,000.00	—
1879	385	205.00	575.00	25,000.00
1879CC	2	12,000.00	67,500.00	—

	Mintage (in thousands)	Ex. Fine	Unc.	Proof
1879O	2	4,250.00	32,500.00	—
1879S	224	205.00	1,075.00	—
1880	1,645	205.00	285.00	22,500.00
1880CC	11	775.00	13,500.00	—
1880O	9	675.00	8,000.00	—
1880S	506	205.00	365.00	—
1881	3,877	205.00	240.00	22,000.00
1881CC	24	600.00	5,650.00	—
1881O	8	825.00	7,000.00	—
1881S	970	205.00	240.00	—
1882	2,324	205.00	240.00	21,000.00
1882CC	17	1,150.00	14,250.00	—
1882O	11	500.00	5,750.00	—
1882S	132	225.00	425.00	—
1883	209	205.00	240.00	21,000.00
1883CC	12	700.00	13,750.00	—
1883O	1	6,850.00	35,000.00	—
1883S	38	205.00	900.00	—
1884	77	205.00	700.00	21,000.00
1884CC	10	900.00	11,500.00	—
1884S	124	205.00	460.00	—
1885	254	205.00	350.00	17,000.00
1885S	228	205.00	350.00	—
1886	236	210.00	350.00	17,000.00
1886S	826	205.00	315.00	—
1887	54	245.00	775.00	16,000.00
1887S	817	205.00	285.00	—
1888	133	225.00	550.00	16,000.00
1888O	21	205.00	525.00	—
1888S	649	205.00	315.00	—
1889	4	500.00	2,400.00	17,000.00
1889S	425	205.00	315.00	—
1890	58	205.00	675.00	15,000.00
1890CC	18	425.00	1,850.00	—
1891	92	205.00	315.00	14,500.00
1891CC	104	425.00	750.00	—
1892	798	205.00	240.00	15,000.00
1892CC	40	450.00	3,000.00	—
1892O	29	205.00	350.00	—
1892S	116	205.00	425.00	—
1893	1,841	205.00	240.00	15,000.00
1893CC	14	675.00	6,750.00	—
1893O	17	300.00	625.00	—
1893S	141	205.00	335.00	—
1894	2,471	205.00	240.00	15,500.00
1894O	108	235.00	900.00	—

	Mintage (in thousands)	Ex. Fine	Unc.	Proof
1894S	25	385.00	3,750.00	—
1895	568	205.00	240.00	13,000.00
1895O	98	205.00	475.00	—
1895S	49	235.00	2,350.00	—
1896	76	245.00	325.00	13,000.00
1896S	124	225.00	2,600.00	—
1897	1,000	205.00	240.00	12,500.00
1897O	43	250.00	675.00	—
1897S	235	220.00	825.00	—
1898	812	205.00	240.00	13,000.00
1898S	474	205.00	350.00	—
1899	1,262	205.00	240.00	13,000.00
1899O	37	275.00	550.00	—
1899S	841	205.00	320.00	—
1900	294	205.00	310.00	13,000.00
1900S	81	265.00	875.00	—
1901	1,719	205.00	240.00	13,000.00
1901O	72	230.00	350.00	—
1901S	2,813	205.00	240.00	—
1902	83	215.00	300.00	13,000.00
1902S	470	205.00	240.00	—
1903	126	225.00	350.00	13,000.00
1903O	113	225.00	375.00	—
1903S	538	205.00	275.00	—
1904	162	205.00	260.00	13,000.00
1904O	109	225.00	360.00	—
1905	201	205.00	240.00	13,000.00
1905S	369	205.00	1,100.00	—
1906	165	205.00	240.00	13,000.00
1906D	981	205.00	240.00	—
1906O	87	225.00	385.00	—
1906S	457	225.00	475.00	—
1907	1,204	205.00	240.00	13,000.00
1907D	1,030	205.00	240.00	—
1907S	211	210.00	550.00	—

INDIAN HEAD TYPE

$10.00 INDIAN HEAD, NO MOTTO

	Mintage (in thousands)	Ex. Fine	Unc.	Proof
1907 Wire Edge, Periods before and after Legends	500 Pieces	8,500.00	13,750.00	—
1907 Rolled Edge, Periods before and after Legends (Rare)	42 Pieces	21,500.00	29,500.00	—
1907 No Periods before and after Legends	239	330.00	525.00	—
1908 No Motto	34	350.00	850.00	—
1908D No Motto	210	335.00	725.00	—

$10.00 INDIAN HEAD WITH MOTTO

	Mintage	Ex. Fine	Unc.	Proof
1908 With Motto	341	310.00	500.00	15,000.00
1908D With Motto	837	310.00	750.00	—
1908S	60	335.00	1,675.00	—
1909	185	310.00	500.00	17,000.00
1909D	122	310.00	585.00	—
1909S	292	315.00	625.00	—
1910	319	315.00	450.00	17,000.00
1910D	2,357	310.00	450.00	—
1910S	811	310.00	675.00	—
1911	506	300.00	475.00	16,000.00
1911D	30	675.00	3,850.00	—
1911S	51	525.00	1,150.00	—
1912	405	300.00	450.00	16,000.00
1912S	300	310.00	750.00	—
1913	442	300.00	465.00	16,000.00
1913S	66	650.00	3,850.00	—

	Mintage (in thousands)	Ex. Fine	Unc.	Proof
1914	151	310.00	550.00	16,000.00
1914D	344	310.00	565.00	—
1914S	208	310.00	750.00	—
1915	351	310.00	550.00	19,000.00
1915S	59	650.00	3,250.00	—
1916S	139	320.00	775.00	—
1920S (Rare)	127	7,250.00	21,500.00	—
1926	1,014	300.00	375.00	—
1930S	96	7,000.00	9,500.00	—
1932	4,463	300.00	375.00	—
1933 (Rare)	313	—	67,500.00	—

54
DOUBLE EAGLES: 1850–1932

($20.00 GOLD PIECES)
CORONET TYPE

1850 $20.00 LIBERTY HEAD, TYPE I

	Mintage (in thousands)	Ex. Fine	Unc.
1849 Unique—U.S. Mint Collection	—	—	—
1850	1,170	1,000.00	5,850.00
1850O	141	1,300.00	32,000.00
1851	2,087	650.00	3,000.00
1851O	315	750.00	16,500.00
1852	2,053	650.00	3,250.00
1852O	190	750.00	16,000.00
1853	1,261	650.00	5,000.00
1853O	71	1,000.00	26,000.00
1854	758	650.00	5,500.00
1854O (Rare)	3	55,000.00	—

	Mintage (in thousands)	Ex. Fine	Unc.
1854S	141	750.00	3,500.00
1855	365	650.00	8,500.00
1855O	8	6,000.00	85,000.00
1855S	880	625.00	6,350.00
1856	330	650.00	8,500.00
1856O (Rare)	2	70,000.00	—
1856S	1,190	650.00	3,850.00
1857	439	625.00	3,950.00
1857O	30	1,650.00	25,000.00
1857S	971	625.00	3,450.00
1858	212	850.00	4,500.00
1858O	35	1,950.00	25,000.00
1858S	847	650.00	8,000.00
1859	44	1,900.00	32,000.00
1859O	9	6,500.00	77,500.00
1859S	636	625.00	4,850.00
1860	578	625.00	3,950.00
1860O	7	5,650.00	82,500.00
1860S	545	625.00	5,850.00
1861	2,976	625.00	2,400.00
1861O	18	3,100.00	45,000.00
1861S	768	650.00	8,750.00
1862	92	1,325.00	15,000.00
1862S	854	675.00	13,000.00
1863	143	725.00	16,000.00
1863S	967	700.00	6,750.00
1864	204	825.00	14,000.00
1864S	794	625.00	6,750.00
1865	351	650.00	6,250.00
1865S	1,043	650.00	3,750.00
1866S No Motto	—	3,000.00	27,500.00

1871 $20.00 LIBERTY HEAD, TYPE II

1866 With Motto	699	700.00	5,500.00
1866S	842	625.00	16,500.00

	Mintage (in thousands)	Ex. Fine	Unc.
1867	251	575.00	2,150.00
1867S	921	675.00	14,750.00
1868	99	975.00	8,750.00
1868S	838	675.00	8,000.00
1869	175	760.00	5,250.00
1869S	687	560.00	4,750.00
1870	155	775.00	8,000.00
1870CC (Very rare)	4	95,000.00	225,000.00
1870S	982	585.00	4,750.00
1871	80	800.00	3,500.00
1871CC	17	5,250.00	38,500.00
1871S	928	575.00	3,450.00
1872	252	600.00	2,650.00
1872CC	30	1,875.00	24,000.00
1872S	780	475.00	2,850.00
1873	1,710	425.00	825.00
1873CC	22	2,100.00	24,000.00
1873S	1,041	425.00	1,650.00
1874	367	425.00	1,050.00
1874CC	115	1,100.00	7,750.00
1874S	1,241	450.00	1,500.00
1875	296	450.00	800.00
1875CC	111	975.00	2,400.00
1875S	1,230	425.00	825.00
1876	584	425.00	800.00
1876CC	138	975.00	3,600.00
1876S	1,597	425.00	800.00

1900 $20.00 LIBERTY HEAD, TYPE III

	Mintage (in thousands)	Ex. Fine	Unc.
1877	398	400.00	575.00
1877CC	43	1,200.00	16,000.00
1877S	1,735	400.00	575.00
1878	544	400.00	575.00
1878CC	13	2,000.00	18,750.00
1878S	1,739	400.00	750.00

	Mintage (in thousands)	Ex. Fine	Unc.
1879	208	400.00	1,000.00
1879CC	11	2,350.00	27,500.00
1879O	2	7,000.00	40,000.00
1879S	1,224	400.00	1,250.00
1880	51	400.00	2,700.00
1880S	836	400.00	925.00
1881	2	6,500.00	42,000.00
1881S	727	400.00	925.00
1882	1	14,000.00	57,500.00
1882CC	39	1,050.00	6,350.00
1882S	1,125	400.00	525.00
1883 (Rare)	92 Pieces	—	—
1883CC	60	975.00	4,000.00
1883S	1,189	400.00	485.00
1884 (Rare)	71 Pieces	—	—
1884CC	81	975.00	2,600.00
1884S	916	400.00	485.00
1885	1	7,600.00	31,500.00
1885CC	9	2,350.00	11,500.00
1885S	684	400.00	485.00
1886	1	10,500.00	37,500.00
1887 (Rare)	121 Pieces	—	—
1887S	283	425.00	525.00
1888	226	390.00	485.00
1888S	860	390.00	485.00
1889	44	400.00	675.00
1889CC	31	1,150.00	3,500.00
1889S	775	390.00	485.00
1890	76	390.00	485.00
1890CC	91	975.00	2,400.00
1890S	803	390.00	515.00
1891	1	4,600.00	28,500.00
1891CC	5	4,000.00	14,500.00
1891S	1,288	390.00	425.00
1892	5	1,475.00	5,500.00
1892CC	27	1,050.00	3,250.00
1892S	930	390.00	425.00
1893	344	390.00	425.00
1893CC	18	1,200.00	2,400.00
1893S	996	390.00	425.00
1894	1,369	390.00	425.00
1894S	1,049	390.00	425.00
1895	1,115	390.00	425.00
1895S	1,144	390.00	425.00
1896	793	390.00	425.00
1896S	1,404	390.00	425.00

	Mintage (in thousands)	Ex. Fine	Unc.
1897	1,383	390.00	425.00
1897S	1,470	390.00	425.00
1898	170	400.00	470.00
1898S	2,575	390.00	425.00
1899	1,669	390.00	425.00
1899S	2,010	390.00	425.00
1900	1,875	390.00	425.00
1900S	2,460	390.00	435.00
1901	112	390.00	425.00
1901S	1,596	400.00	475.00
1902	31	390.00	825.00
1902S	1,754	390.00	425.00
1903	287	390.00	425.00
1903S	954	390.00	425.00
1904	6,257	390.00	425.00
1904S	5,134	390.00	425.00
1905	59	400.00	950.00
1905S	1,813	400.00	525.00
1906	70	400.00	550.00
1906D	620	390.00	425.00
1906S	2,066	390.00	425.00
1907	1,452	390.00	425.00
1907D	842	390.00	425.00
1907S	2,166	390.00	425.00

ST. GAUDENS TYPE

1907 $20.00 HIGH RELIEF ROMAN NUMERAL

	Mintage	Ex. Fine	Unc.
1907 High Relief Roman Numerals (MCMVII) Wire Rim	11	3,850.00	8,500.00
1907 High Relief Roman Numerals (MCMVII) Flat Rim	(included above)	3,850.00	8,500.00

$20.00 St. Gaudens, no motto

$20.00 St. Gaudens, with motto

	Mintage (in thousands)	Ex. Fine	Unc.
1907 Arabic Numerals, No Motto	362	400.00	550.00
1908	4,272	390.00	425.00
1908D	664	400.00	525.00
1908 With Motto	156	390.00	500.00
1908D	350	390.00	475.00
1908S	22	1,100.00	4,750.00
1909 over 8, All Kinds	161	600.00	1,350.00
1909, All Kinds	—	550.00	750.00
1909D	53	650.00	1,350.00
1909S	2,775	390.00	460.00
1910	482	390.00	425.00
1910D	429	390.00	425.00
1910S	2,128	390.00	475.00
1911	197	390.00	525.00
1911D	847	390.00	425.00
1911S	776	390.00	435.00
1912	150	390.00	525.00
1913	169	390.00	525.00
1913D	394	390.00	435.00
1913S	34	700.00	1,400.00

	Mintage (in thousands)	Ex. Fine	Unc.
1914	95	485.00	575.00
1914D	453	390.00	425.00
1914S	1,498	390.00	425.00
1915	152	425.00	675.00
1915S	568	390.00	425.00
1916S	796	400.00	535.00
1920	228	390.00	450.00
1920S	558	8,600.00	32,500.00
1921	530	17,000.00	43,500.00
1922	1,376	390.00	425.00
1922S	2,658	625.00	875.00
1923	566	390.00	425.00
1923D	1,702	390.00	435.00
1924	4,324	390.00	425.00
1924D	3,050	1,000.00	2,150.00
1924S	2,928	950.00	2,700.00
1925	2,832	390.00	425.00
1925D	2,939	1,600.00	3,650.00
1925S	3,777	1,300.00	6,250.00
1926	817	390.00	425.00
1926D	481	2,650.00	10,000.00
1926S	2,042	1,050.00	1,950.00
1927	2,947	390.00	425.00
1927D (Rare)	180	—	—
1927S	3,107	3,900.00	15,000.00
1928	8,816	390.00	425.00
1929	1,780	6,600.00	10,000.00
1930S	74	8,000.00	25,000.00
1931	2,938	7,650.00	20,000.00
1931D	107	7,250.00	17,000.00
1932	1,102	10,000.00	20,000.00
1933	446	Not Released for Circulation	

(Note: Nearly all Philadelphia Mint double eagle dates exist as *proof;* all are very rare with values typically ranging from $17,500.00 to $32,500.00 for *choice* examples.)

55
PRIVATE AND TERRITORIAL GOLD COINS

GEORGIA

	V. Good	Ex. Fine
1830 $2.50 TEMPLETON REID (Very rare)	—	55,000.00
1830 $5.00 TEMPLETON REID (Very rare)	—	135,000.00

	V. Good	Ex. Fine
1830 $10.00 TEMPLETON REID (Very rare) ...	135,000.00	—
NO DATE $10.00 TEMPLETON REID (Very rare)	95,000.00	—

NORTH CAROLINA

	Fine	Unc.
$1.00 AUGUST BECHTLER	950.00	4,250.00
$5.00 AUGUST BECHTLER	3,750.00	20,000.00
$1.00 CHRISTOPHER BECHTLER	1,200.00	5,250.00
$2.50 CHRISTOPHER BECHTLER	3,500.00	18,000.00
$5.00 CHRISTOPHER BECHTLER	4,000.00	17,500.00

CALIFORNIA

1849 $5.00 NORRIS, GREGG AND NORRIS

NORRIS, GREGG AND NORRIS

1849 $5.00	3,250.00	23,500.00

1850 $5.00 MOFFAT & CO.

MOFFAT & CO.

	V. Fine	Ex. Fine
1849 $10.00	4,000.00	9,000.00
1849 $5.00	1,700.00	3,500.00
1850 $5.00	1,800.00	3,600.00
1852 $10.00	4,250.00	7,750.00

1853 $20.00 U.S. ASSAY OFFICE

	V. Fine	Ex. Fine
1851 $50.00 880 THOUS. "Target" Reverse	8,500.00	13,500.00
1851 $50.00 887 THOUS. "Target" Reverse	8,500.00	13,500.00
1852 $50.00 887 THOUS. "Target" Reverse	9,000.00	14,000.00
1852 $50.00 900 THOUS. "Target" Reverse	9,000.00	14,000.00
1851 $50.00 50 DC Several Varieties: AUGUSTUS HUMBERT UNITED STATES ASSAYER OF GOLD CALIFORNIA 1851	12,500.00	18,000.00
1852 $20.00 1852 over 1	6,250.00	10,000.00
1853 $20.00 884 THOUS.	8,000.00	12,000.00
1853 $20.00 900 THOUS.	2,450.00	3,650.00
1852 $10.00 1852 over 1	2,800.00	4,850.00
1852 $10.00 884 THOUS.	2,000.00	3,250.00
1853 $10.00 884 THOUS. (Rare)	7,750.00	13,500.00
1853 $10.00 900 THOUS.	3,850.00	6,500.00

BALDWIN & COMPANY

	V. Fine	Unc.
1850 $10.00	36,000.00	—
1851 $20.00 (Rare)	—	—
1851 $10.00	11,000.00	—
1850 $5.00	7,500.00	27,000.00

SCHULTZ & COMPANY

1851 $5.00	35,000.00	65,000.00

DUNBAR & COMPANY

1851 $5.00 (Rare)	70,000.00	—

J. H. BOWIE

1849 $5.00 (3 known)	—	175,000.00

CINCINNATI MINING & TRADING CO.

1849 $5.00 (unique)	—	—
1849 $10.00	175,000.00	

MASSACHUSETTS AND CALIFORNIA COMPANY

1849 $5.00	70,000.00	—

MINERS' BANK

(1849) $10.00	8,250.00	45,000.00

DUBOSQ & COMPANY

	V. Fine	Unc.
1850 $10.00	57,500.00	—
1850 $5.00	52,500.00	

WASS, MOLITOR & COMPANY

	Fine	Ex. Fine
1855 $50.00	17,000.00	32,000.00
1855 $20.00, Small Head	8,000.00	26,500.00
1855 $20.00, Large Head (Rare)	—	90,000.00
1852 $10.00, Small Head	4,250.00	13,500.00
1852 $10.00, Large Head	2,000.00	5,500.00
1855 $10.00	10,000.00	23,000.00
1852 $5.00, Small Head	2,650.00	10,500.00
1852 $5.00, Large Head	2,650.00	10,000.00

KELLOGG & COMPANY

1854 $5.00 KELLOGG & CO.

1855 $50.00 (Rare)	—	—
1854 $20.00	1,750.00	3,850.00
1855 $20.00	1,750.00	3,950.00

CALIFORNIA FRACTIONAL GOLD

Note: Between 1852 and 1882, round and octagonal one-dollar, fifty-cent, and twenty-five-cent gold pieces were also privately minted in California. After an act of 1864 made private coinage illegal, their makers were anonymous; their initials, however, can be found on some coins.

There are many copies of these small coins, some made to be worn as charms. Genuine pieces all show their denomination—"1/2 Dol.," or "1/2 Dollar," or "half dollar," etc.

These coins are valued as follows:

CALIFORNIA HALF DOLLAR INDIAN HEAD

CALIFORNIA $1.00 LIBERTY HEAD

	V. Fine	Unc.
25¢ Round Indian or Liberty Heads	100.00	250.00
25¢ Octagonal Indian or Liberty Heads	100.00	225.00
50¢ Round Indian or Liberty Heads	115.00	275.00
50¢ Octagonal Indian or Liberty Heads	120.00	275.00
$1.00 Round Indian Heads	750.00	2,750.00
$1.00 Octagonal Indian or Liberty Heads	275.00	1,000.00
$1.00 Round Liberty Heads	650.00	2,250.00

(Washington Heads bring about 50 percent more.)

OREGON
OREGON EXCHANGE COMPANY

	Fine	Ex. Fine
1849 $10.00 (Rare)	28,500.00	62,500.00
1849 $5.00	12,000.00	28,500.00

UTAH
MORMON GOLD

	Fine	V. Fine
1849 $20.00 (Rare)	32,500.00	57,500.00
1849 $10.00 (Rare)	95,000.00	130,000.00
1849 $5.00	6,500.00	14,000.00
1849 $2.50	6,750.00	15,000.00
1850 $5.00	7,000.00	15,000.00
1860 $5.00	9,500.00	25,000.00

CLARK, GRUBER & CO. $10.00

COLORADO
CLARK, GRUBER & COMPANY

1860 $20.00 (Rare)	30,000.00	70,000.00
1860 $10.00	3,750.00	9,500.00
1860 $5.00	1,350.00	3,000.00
1860 $2.50	1,150.00	2,800.00

	Fine	Ex. Fine
1861 $20.00	5,500.00	21,500.00
1861 $10.00	1,750.00	5,250.00
1861 $5.00	1,500.00	3,500.00
1861 $2.50	1,350.00	3,000.00
JOHN PARSONS & COMPANY		
(1861) Undated 21/2D (Rare)	65,000.00	—
(1861) Undated FIVE D (Rare)	85,000.00	—
J. J. CONWAY & COMPANY		
(1861) 2-1/2 DOLL'S (Rare)	47,500.00	—
(1861) $5.00 (Rare)	65,000.00	—
1861 $10.00 (Very rare)	—	—

56
HARD TIMES TOKENS

These are tokens, usually satirically political in nature, that were privately struck and issued in the period of 1832–1844. The tokens are normally struck in copper or brass and are predominantly the same size as the large one-cent piece of the period. Descriptions of the major types follow. (Tradesman's or advertising tokens of the same approximate period encompass hundreds of varieties, which are outside the scope of this listing. The value of the more common of the commercial varieties are: *Good* $10.00; *Fine* $15.00; *Ex. Fine* $40.00; *Unc.* $150.00.)

HARD TIMES TOKENS

Type	Good	Fine	Ex. Fine	Unc.
1. Jackson Head Right/Legend in Wreath	3,000.00	4,500.00	9,000.00	—
2. Jackson Bust Right/Legend	85.00	175.00	600.00	—
3. Jackson Bust Facing/Eagle	175.00	250.00	700.00	—
4. Van Buren Bust Facing/Chest	—	2,500.00	4,000.00	10,000.00
5. Van Buren Bust Right/Eagle	—	300.00	700.00	1,650.00
6. Van Buren Bust Left/Safe	—	75.00	175.00	450.00
7. Seward Bust Left/Eagle	65.00	175.00	300.00	750.00
8. Verplanck Bust Left/Eagle	50.00	125.00	275.00	575.00
9. Ship Left/Victorious Whigs of New York	125.00	300.00	725.00	—
10. Liberty Cap/Ship	750.00	1,750.00	3,250.00	—
11. Cow Right/Ship	50.00	100.00	375.00	1,000.00
12. Kneeling Woman/Legend	50.00	85.00	225.00	600.00
13. Liberty Head Left/Legend "Mint Drop"	15.00	30.00	75.00	275.00
14. Man Standing Left/Jackass	10.00	15.00	65.00	225.00
15. Man in Chest/Jackass	10.00	15.00	40.00	175.00
16. Pig Running Left/Bust Over Legend	10.00	20.00	55.00	200.00
17. Turtle Right/Jackass	10.00	15.00	40.00	175.00
18. Liberty Head Left/Legend "Not One Cent"	10.00	15.00	50.00	175.00
19. Liberty Head Left/Legend "May Tenth"	10.00	15.00	60.00	185.00
20. Phoenix/Legend	10.00	15.00	40.00	185.00
21. Ship/Shipwreck	10.00	15.00	40.00	175.00
22. Shipwreck/Man in Chest	10.00	15.00	40.00	175.00
23. Ship/Legend	10.00	15.00	40.00	175.00
24. Ship/Liberty Head	25.00	65.00	150.00	375.00
25. Half-Cent	30.00	50.00	150.00	450.00

57
CIVIL WAR TOKENS

These tokens, usually struck in either copper or brass, were privately minted during the years 1860–1866. Their purpose was, ostensibly, to help alleviate the shortage of Federal cents caused by hoarding. Although they were approximately the size of an Indian Head cent, many were underweight. As they were sold to merchants by their manufacturers at a discount from face value, this underweight condition is to be expected. War profiteers existed then as now. Several hundred varieties of the patriotic kind exist, and prices are listed for the major types. Many thousands of varieties exist for the merchants' or advertising types, and they fall beyond our scope. (Values for common advertising Civil War tokens are: *Good* $5.00; *Fine* $8.00; *Ex. Fine* $13.00; *Unc.* $35.00.)

Type	Good	Fine	Ex. Fine	Unc.
1. Liberty Head Left	7.00	10.00	15.00	40.00
2. Liberty Head Right	8.00	11.00	17.00	45.00
3. Indian Head Left	5.00	8.00	13.00	35.00
4. Washington Head Left	25.00	40.00	65.00	150.00
5. Washington Head Right	10.00	15.00	30.00	60.00
6. Lincoln Head Left	15.00	25.00	40.00	100.00
7. Lincoln Head Right	15.00	28.00	50.00	125.00
8. McClellan Head Left	7.00	15.00	20.00	65.00
9. McClellan Head Right	7.00	15.00	20.00	60.00
10. Franklin Head Left	20.00	55.00	80.00	250.00
11. Franklin Head Right	15.00	30.00	65.00	200.00
12. Flying Eagle Right	35.00	65.00	125.00	500.00
13. Flying Eagle Left	40.00	75.00	150.00	450.00
14. Upright Eagle	25.00	55.00	80.00	250.00
15. Eagle on Shield	8.00	10.00	15.00	35.00
16. Cannon	11.00	15.00	20.00	60.00
17. Man on Horseback	11.00	15.00	20.00	60.00
18. Flag	5.00	8.00	13.00	35.00
19. Ship	11.00	18.00	35.00	75.00
20. Walking Man	11.00	18.00	35.00	75.00
21. Scroll	30.00	75.00	175.00	700.00
22. Wreath	5.00	8.00	13.00	35.00

58
COINS OF HAWAII

There was an issue of dimes, quarters, half dollars, and dollars struck by King Kalakaua I in 1883. These were manufactured at the San Francisco Mint, although no mint mark appears on the pieces. There was also an issue of cents in 1847, bearing the bust of Kamehameha III and the legend "Apuni Hawaii, Hapa Haneri." (Beware of Spurious Specimens, which have an unnatural golden appearance.) We should also note that rare ⅛ dollar (12½-cent pieces) also were struck as patterns in 1883, and unofficial five-cent pieces were coined in 1881.

	Good	Fine	Ex. Fine	Unc.	Proof
1847 Cent	100.00	225.00	500.00	1,500.00	—
1883 Dime	25.00	60.00	225.00	1,500.00	8,000.00
1883 Quarter	25.00	45.00	100.00	275.00	9,000.00
1883 Half Dollar	35.00	75.00	250.00	1,650.00	11,000.00
1883 Dollar	125.00	250.00	650.00	4,750.00	15,000.00

PART FOUR

Resources and Further Reading

59
NUMISMATIC REFERENCE BOOKS

EARLY BOOKS ON NUMISMATICS

The references included in the following list have laid much of the groundwork for the texts used today. They remain a very important part of our numismatic heritage.

Edgar H. Adams and William H. Woodin. *United States Pattern, Trial, and Experimental Pieces.*
M. L. Beistle. *A Register of Half Dollar Die Varieties and Sub-Varieties.*
M. H. Bolender. *The United States Early Silver Dollars from 1794 to 1803.*
Sylvester Crosby. *The Early Coins of America.*
Ebenezer Gilbert. *United States Half Cents.*
J. Hewitt Judd. *United States Pattern, Experimental, and Trial Pieces.*
Kenneth W. Lee. *California Gold Dollars, Half Dollars, Quarter Dollars.*
Howard R. Newcomb. *United States Copper Cents, 1816–1857.*
William H. Sheldon. *Penny Whimsy.*
Don Taxay. *The United States Mint and Coinage.*
D. W. Valentine. *The United States Half Dimes.*
John Willem. *The United States Trade Dollar.*

MORE RECENT REFERENCES

The books listed below are of particular significance to any collector desiring to form a well-rounded numismatic library. These texts currently represent some of the most up-to-date, thorough, user-friendly information.

David W. Akers. *United States Gold Coins—An Analysis of Auction Records.*
David Alexander. *Comprehensive Catalogue and Encyclopedia of United States Coins.*
American Numismatic Association. *Counterfeit Detection—Volume I.*
American Numismatic Association. *Counterfeit Detection—Volume II.*
Al Blythe. *The Complete Guide to Liberty Seated Half Dimes.*

Q. David Bowers. *Silver Dollars and Trade Dollars of the United States: A Complete Encyclopedia.*

Walter Breen. *Walter Breen's Encyclopedia of United States Half Cents.*

Walter Breen. *Walter Breen's Complete Encyclopedia of U.S. and Colonial Coins.*

Walter Breen. *Walter Breen's Encyclopedia of Early United States Cents, 1793–1814.*

Walter Breen. *Walter Breen's Encyclopedia of U.S. and Colonial Proof Coins.*

Walter Breen and Ronald Gillio. *California Pioneer Fractional Gold.*

Larry Briggs. *The Comprehensive Encyclopedia of United States Liberty Seated Quarters.*

A. W. Browning updated by Walter Breen. *The Early Quarters of the United States, 1796–1838.*

Bill Bugert and Randy Wiley. *The Complete Guide to Liberty Seated Half Dollars.*

Tony Carlotto. *The Copper Coins of Vermont and Those Bearing the Vermont Name.*

J. H. Cline. *Standing Liberty Quarters.*

Roger S. Cohen. *American Half Cents: the "Little Half Sisters."*

David J. Davis, et al. *Early United States Dimes, 1796–1837.*

Jeff Garrett and John Dannreuther. *United States Gold Coinage: Significant Auction Records.*

Jeff Garrett and John Dannreuther. *United States Half Cents, Large Cents, Commems, Colonials, Territorials, Confederate, Cal. Gold, Patterns, Errors, Misc.: Significant Auction Records.*

Jeff Garrett and John Dannreuther. *United States Small Cents to Silver Dollars: Significant Auction Records.*

Brian Greer. *The Complete Guide to Liberty Seated Dimes.*

J. R. Grellman and Jules Reiver. *Attribution Guide for U.S. Large Cents, 1840–1857.*

Louis Jordan. *John Hull, the Mint and the Economics of Massachusetts Coinage.*

Donald Kagin. *Private Gold Coins and Patterns of the United States.*

Alan Kessler. *The Fugio Cents.*

Russell J. Logan and John W. McCloskey. *Federal Half Dimes, 1792–1837.*

Edward Maris. *The Coins of New Jersey.*

Henry Miller. *The State Coinage of Connecticut.*

Robert W. Miller. *United States Half Eagle Gold Coins, 1795–1834.*

Philip Mossman. *Money of the American Colonies and Confederation.*

Eric P. Newman. *Coinage for Colonial Virginia.*

Eric P. Newman. *Studies on Money in Early America.*

248

Sydney P. Noe. *The Silver Coinage of Massachusetts.*
William C. Noyes. *United States Large Cents, 1793–1814.*
William C. Noyes. *United States Large Cents, 1816–1839.*
Al C. Overton. *Early Half Dollar Die Varieties, 1794–1836.*
Andrew W. Pollack. *United States Patterns and Related Issues.*
Jules Reiver. *The United States Early Silver Dollars, 1794–1803.*
Russell Rulau. *Standard Catalog of United States Tokens, 1866–1889.*
Hillyer Ryder. *The Colonial Coins of Vermont and Vermont Cents.*
Hillyer Ryder. *The Copper Coins of Massachusetts.*
Anthony Swiatek. *The Walking Liberty Half Dollar.*
Anthony Swiatek and Walter Breen. *The Encyclopedia of U.S. Silver and Gold Commemorative Coins, 1892–1989.*
Anthony J. Taraszka. *United States Ten Dollar Gold Eagles, 1795–1804.*
Sol Taylor. *The Standard Guide to the Lincoln Cent.*
Leroy C. Van Allen and George A. Mallis. *Comprehensive Catalog and Encyclopedia of Morgan and Peace Dollars.*
Weimar White. *The Liberty Seated Dollar, 1840–1873.*
Douglas Winter. *Gold Coins of the Charlotte Mint.*
Douglas Winter. *Gold Coins of the Carson City Mint, 1870–1893.*
Douglas Winter. *Gold Coins of the Dahlonega Mint.*
Douglas Winter. *New Orleans Mint Gold Coins: 1839–1909.*
R. S. Yeoman. *A Guidebook of United States Coins.*

60
PERIODICALS AND OTHER PUBLICATIONS

Besides the texts listed in the previous section, there are a number of periodicals and additional publications that can be of tremendous use to a collector. These further resources will aid both beginner and advanced collectors not only with respect to buying, selling, and evaluating the material in their cabinets, but they will also educate numismatists in the history and importance of each aspect of coin collecting.

The Certified Coin Dealer Newsletter. Torrance, CA.
COINage. Ventura, CA.
The Coin Dealer Newsletter. Torrance, CA.

Coin Prices. Krause Publications. Iola, WI.

Coins. Krause Publications. Iola, WI.

Coin World. Amos Press. Sidney, OH.

Numismatic News. Krause Publications. Iola, WI.

World Coin News. Krause Publications. Iola, WI.

61
COLLECTOR CLUBS AND ASSOCIATIONS

The following national and major regional associations are of primary importance in the U.S. numismatic marketplace. Individual collectors and local coin clubs will find the support of these organizations to be quite valuable.

The American Numismatic Association, Colorado Springs, CO.

The American Numismatic Society, New York, NY.

Blue Ridge Numismatic Association, East Bend, NC.

California State Numismatic Association, Fresno, CA.

Central States Numismatic Society, Milwaukee, WI.

Combined Organization of Numismatic Error Collectors of America, Fort Worth, TX.

Early American Coppers, Cincinnati, OH.

Florida United Numismatists, Lake Mary, FL.

Garden State Numismatic Association, Somerset, NJ.

Hawaii State Numismatic Association, Honolulu, HI.

Illinois Numismatic Association, Bloomington, IL.

Industry Council for Tangible Assets, Severna Park, MD.

John Reich Collectors Society, Harrison, OH.

Liberty Seated Collectors Club, Wellington, OH.

Michigan State Numismatic Society, Lansing, MI.

Mississippi Numismatic Association, Biloxi, MS.

Missouri Numismatic Society, St. Peters, MO.

North Carolina Numismatic Association, Chapel Hill, NC.

Numismatic Association of Southern California, Panorama City, CA.

Numismatic Bibliomania Society, Ocala, FL.

Pacific Northwest Numismatic Association, Federal Way, WA.

Professional Numismatists Guild, Fallbrook, CA.
Society for U.S. Commemorative Coins, Thousand Oaks, CA.
South Carolina State Numismatic Association, Greenville, SC.
Tennessee State Numismatic Association, Memphis, TN.
Texas Numismatic Association, Seymour, TX.
Women in Numismatics, Irvine, CA.

62
AUCTION HOUSES

There are well over one hundred numismatic auction companies in the United States, ranging from world-class auction houses with huge market share, to small country and local auction establishments. Some of the largest are listed below:

Auctions by Bowers and Merena, Wolfeboro, NH.
Centennial Auctions, Effingham, NH.
Coin Galleries, New York, NY.
Early American History Auctions, La Jolla, CA.
Heritage Numismatic Auctions, Dallas, TX.
Ira and Larry Goldberg Coins & Collectibles, Beverly Hills, CA.
R. M. Smythe & Company, New York, NY.
Sotheby's, New York, NY.
Stack's, New York, NY.
Superior Galleries, Beverly Hills, CA.

63
MAJOR COIN DEALERS IN THE UNITED STATES

From vest pocket coin dealers to world and nationally recognized dealers with impressive galleries and/or showrooms, there are literally thousands of businesses across the country that buy and sell rare coins. Some of the largest of these dealers with particular specialty in U.S. coins are listed below:

Bowers and Merena Galleries, Wolfeboro, NH.
David Hall Rare Coins, Newport Beach, CA.
Delaware Valley Rare Coin Co., Broomall, PA.
Heritage Rare Coin Galleries, Dallas, TX.
Ira and Larry Goldberg Coins and Collectibles, Beverly Hills, CA.
Kagin's, Tiburon, CA.
National Gold Exchange, Tampa, FL.
Rare Coin Company of America, Willowbrook, IL.
Ronald J. Gillio, Inc., Santa Barbara, CA.
Silver Towne, Winchester, IN.
Spectrum Numismatics International, Irvine, CA.
Stack's/Coin Galleries, New York, NY.
Superior Galleries, Beverly Hills, CA.
Tangible Investments of America, Laguna Beach, CA.

64
ONLINE RESOURCES

MAJOR AUCTION HOUSES AND NUMISMATIC DEALERS

A-Mark Precious Metals	www.amark.com
Auctions by Bowers and Merena	www.bowersandmerena.com
Collector's Universe	www.collectorsuniverse.com
Early American History Auctions	www.earlyamerican.com
Greg Manning Auctions	www.gregmanning.com
Heritage Numismatic Auctions	www.heritagecoin.com
Ira and Larry Goldberg Coins & Collectibles	www.goldbergcoins.com
Jay Parrino's The Mint, LLC	www.jp-themint.com
National Gold Exchange	www.ngegold.com
Northeast Numismatics	www.northeastcoin.com
R.M. Smythe & Company	www.rm-smythe.com
Silver Towne	www.silvertowne.com
Sotheby's	www.sothebys.com
Spink & Son, Ltd.	www.spink-online.com

Stack's	www.stacks.com
Superior Galleries	www.superiorgalleries.com
Teletrade Auctions	www.teletrade.com

NUMISMATIC ORGANIZATIONS AND OTHER WEBSITES OF INTEREST

American Numismatic Association	www.money.org
American Numismatic Society	www.amnumsoc.org
ANACS	www.anacs.com
Blue Ridge Numismatic Association	www.brna.com
California State Numismatic Association	www.coinmall.com/csna
Capital Collectors Plastics	www.capitalplastics.com/nnn
Central States Numismatic Society	www.money.org/club_csns.html
Coin Facts	www.coinfacts.com
Combined Organization of Numismatic Error Collectors of America	www.conecaonline.org
Early American Coppers	www.eacs.org
Florida United Numismatists	www.funtopics.com
Garden State Numismatic Association	www.money.org/clubs/gsna.html
Hawaii State Numismatic Association	www.hawaiicollectibles.org
Illinois Numismatic Association	http://ilna.davesworld.net
Independent Coin Grading Company	www.icgcoin.com
Industry Council for Tangible Assets	www.ictaonline.org
John Reich Collectors Society	www.logan.com/jrcs
Kitco	www.kitco.com
Krause Publications	www.krause.com
Liberty Seated Collectors Club	www.numsmalink.com/lscc.html
Long Beach Coin & Collectibles Expo	www.longbeachshow.com
Maryland State Numismatic Association	www.money.org/clubs/mdtams/ mdtams.html
Michigan State Numismatic Society	www.workingnet.com/msns
National Numismatic Collection	www.americanhistory.si.edu/ csr/cadnnc.htm
North Carolina Numismatic Association	www.ncnaonline.org
Numismatic Association of Southern California	www.nasc.net
Numismatic Bibliomania Society	www.coinbooks.org
Numismatic Guaranty Corporation	www.ngccoin.com

Pacific Coast Numismatic Society	www.pcns.org
Pacific Northwest Numismatic Association	www.pnna.org
PCI Coin Grading Services	www.chattanooga.net/pci
Professional Coin Grading Service	www.pcgs.com
Professional Numismatists Guild	www.pngdealers.com
Smithsonian Institution	www.si.edu
Society for U.S. Commemorative Coins	www.money.org/clubs/sussc.html
Society of U.S. Pattern Collectors	www.uspatterns.com
Sovereign Entities Grading Service	www.segsgrading.com
Tennessee State Numismatic Society	www.tsns.org
Texas Numismatic Association	www.tna.org
The United States Mint	www.usmint.gov
Women in Numismatics	www.money.org/sum-baber.html
Young Numismatists of America	www.ynaclub.org and http://members.aol.com/TheYNA/